Singing Out

MUSIC AND SOCIAL JUSTICE

Series Editors: William Cheng and Andrew Dell'Antonio

From Plato to Public Enemy, people have debated the relationship between music and justice—rarely arriving at much consensus over the art form's ethics and aesthetics, uses and abuses, virtues and vices. So what roles can music and musicians play in agendas of justice? And what should musicians and music scholars do if—during moments of upheaval, complacency, ennui—music ends up seemingly drained of its beauty, power, and even relevance?

Created by editors William Cheng and Andrew Dell'Antonio, this endeavor welcomes projects that shine new light on familiar subjects such as protest songs, humanitarian artists, war and peace, community formation, cultural diplomacy, globalization, and political resistance. Simultaneously, the series invites authors to critique and expand on what qualifies as justice—or, for that matter, music—in the first place.

Singing Out

GALA Choruses and Social Change

Heather MacLachlan

University of Michigan Press • Ann Arbor

Published in the United States of America by the
University of Michigan Press
Manufactured in the United States of America
Printed on acid-free paper

First published December 2020

A CIP catalog record for this book is available from the British Library.

ISBN 978-0-472-13218-8 (hardcover : alk. paper)
ISBN 978-0-472-12724-5 (ebook)
Library of Congress Control Number: 2020944269

Contents

Digital materials related to this title can be found on the Fulcrum platform via the following citable URL: https://doi.org/10.3998/mpub.11579619

Acknowledgments

This book was made possible by the support and encouragement of many individuals and organizations. I am deeply grateful to all of them. I thank them for their wisdom and counsel; any errors in this text are mine alone.

First, I thank the people of GALA Choruses. It was a joy to hear them sing at venues across North America. I am especially grateful to those individuals who granted me interviews. Most of the interviews lasted about ninety minutes. My interlocutors were patient with my questions and generous with their responses. I thank two men in particular: Jason Schuler was the very first GALA Choruses participant I met; in 2010 he invited me to the Dayton Gay Men's Chorus Christmas concert, which he conducted. Meeting Jason and hearing his chorus perform spurred my interest in this project. Charlie Beale is a scholar and a musician of great breadth, although in this book only his work with the New York City Gay Men's Chorus is mentioned. He made time to meet with me, corresponded with me, and even wrote a letter of recommendation for me. I am deeply grateful for his support.

Second, I thank my colleagues and friends at the University of Dayton. The university's Human Rights Center provided funding in support of my research and honored me with the title of Research Fellow. I appreciate the center's faith in my work. Thanks also go to the university's Institutional Review Board, which reviewed and approved the ethnographic and empirical research that undergird the book. I extend special thanks to Stefanie Acevedo, who provided tremendous help with the statistical analysis described in chapter 8. I also thank Samuel Dorf and Sharon Davis Gratto of the Department of Music for their kind suggestions and their continual confidence in my ability to complete this project. I am grateful to the members of my UD writing group, who met with me bimonthly during all the years I conducted research for and wrote this manuscript; their faithful attendance at the group helped me stay accountable to myself. Gloria Dodd is one of the longest-participating members of the group; I thank her for praying for me and for being a role model of scholarly productivity. Finally, my heartfelt thanks to my weekly prayer partner, Ryu-Kyung Kim, who prayed unwaveringly for me as I worked (and worked, and worked) on this book.

Third, I thank scholars from across the academic world. Many of them listened attentively to my conference presentations, during which I laid out lines of thinking and arguments that eventually became central to this book. I want to make special mention of ethnomusicologists Lawrence Witzleben, Ricardo Trimillos, Adriana Helbig, Sean Williams, and Amber Clifford-Napoleone, all of whom made insightful comments about the project as it progressed. I am also grateful to the faculty and students of the Parami Institute of Liberal Arts and Sciences in Yangon, Myanmar, which provided me an academic home from January to June 2018. I especially thank Dr. Kyaw Moe Tun, the founder of Parami, for hiring me as a visiting professor and for gently urging me to continue working on this project while I lived in Yangon. In September 2018, the Cornell University Department of Music invited me to present some of my ongoing research to their assembled graduate students and faculty members; it was a privilege to receive their feedback on this project. I will forever be grateful to Catherine Appert, Judith Peraino, and Benjamin Piekut for their words of encouragement when I most needed to be encouraged. Finally, I thank the members of the Society for Ethnomusicology's Gender and Sexualities Task Force, which elected me Chair in 2017; I was honored to hold the position for two years while completing this book.

The *Journal of American Culture* published an article I wrote about GALA Choruses in 2015. I thank Daniel Margolies for inviting me to write that article, and the journal's publisher, Wiley, for permission to reuse material from the article in chapter 5 of this book. I also thank the two scholars who reviewed this book manuscript, and the editors and staff members at University of Michigan Press for their help in preparing it for publication.

Finally, and most fervently, I thank my family. My husband, Christopher St. Amand, and my son, Riel St. Amand, are the two people I most cherish, and I am so very honored to share my life with them. I am deeply grateful for their unending patience with the demands of my career (which often involves travel and time away from home), and for their quiet faith that I can and will succeed as a scholar. May I uplift them both as they have uplifted me.

Introduction

Singing Out: GALA Choruses and Social Change is a mixed methods study of LGBT-identified community choirs in the United States and Canada.[1] This book investigates how amateur singers participate in a particular form of music making as a way of advancing both their artistic and their political goals. The book analyzes the findings from eight years of research conducted among the people of the Gay and Lesbian Association of Choruses (GALA Choruses), a parent organization for more than two hundred such choirs. GALA Choruses' member groups include so-called men's choruses (in which the large majority of singers are gay men), women's choruses (in which about half of the singers are lesbian women), and mixed choruses (which include both men and women, and in which transgender singers are most likely to participate). GALA choirs are located in big cities and small towns across the continent and collectively include tens of thousands of singers. The largest of the choirs include hundreds of choristers, employ full-time artistic directors with doctorates in music, and successfully solicit millions of dollars in individual and corporate donations. They perform for large audiences in important venues, including, for example, at the inauguration of President Barack Obama. All told, the member choirs of GALA Choruses sing for tens of thousands of listeners every year. They do this because—as GALA's leaders and choristers reiterate frequently—they are committed to "changing our world through song."

Why is this book important? Pundits often wax eloquent about the power of music, asserting that it can, in some positive way, change the world. Indeed, the mission statement of the Department of Music at the University of Dayton, where I work, refers to "the transformative power of music" and the goal of training students to deploy music to "change the world" (University of Dayton 2014). Such statements often rest on an unexamined claim that music can and does foster social change. The series to which this book belongs, Music and Social Justice, is dedicated to investigating this widespread notion and to tackling the premise underlying such rhetoric. *Singing Out: GALA Choruses and Social Change* contributes to the series by analyzing a salient case study, that of groups of amateur singers who are explicitly committed to an agenda of social justice. Ultimately this book asks and answers two important questions: Does public concertizing by LGBT community choirs cause a decrease in homophobic attitudes and, thereby, foster a more inclusive society? And by extension, does music making actually change the world?

The central argument of the book is that GALA Choruses' affiliated groups are best understood as belonging simultaneously to the US and Canadian community choir scene, and to the LGBT rights movement. GALA choruses sing in service of their mission—"changing our world through song"—and their commitment to this mission shapes norms of practice and understanding that constitute a unique choral singing culture. GALA's unique culture is described and analyzed throughout the book. One aspect of that culture that bears mentioning here is GALA groups' preference for the word *chorus*—rather than *choir*—to describe their constellations of singers. Both words usually refer to a group of people who sing together. However, historically, founders of GALA groups preferred *chorus* because *choir* is the word always used to describe singers in Christian churches. As I explain in chapter 4, many GALA choristers grew up singing in church choirs and experienced deep hurt and rejection by those same choirs. They therefore wanted to reserve the word *chorus* for their own groups, groups that affirmed rather than rejected LGBT singers.[2] Although this practice is not universal—in Canada it is much more likely that a GALA group will call itself a choir—I found it useful in writing about GALA groups, especially when distinguishing them from other constellations of singers. Throughout the rest of this book, I thus refer to GALA-affiliated groups as *choruses* and to all other community-based groups as *choirs*.

GALA Choruses: A Brief History

Gay and lesbian choruses first formed in the United States during the 1970s, and they spread across the world during the ensuing decades. What GALA choristers sometimes refer to as "our movement" began in the mid-1970s with the advent of lesbian feminist choruses; the GALA Choruses website marks the founding of the Philadelphia-based ANNA Crusis Women's

Choir in 1975 as the official beginning of this movement (GALA Choruses n.d.b.). However, the origin moment that GALA insiders often point to is the founding of the San Francisco Gay Men's Chorus in 1978. This chorus emerged from a group of men who gathered to sing hymns at a vigil for Harvey Milk, a gay activist and politician, in the wake of Milk's murder. The GALA Choruses organization was officially founded in 1982, and the "movement" grew quickly through the 1980s and 1990s with the establishment of men's choruses, women's choruses, and mixed choruses across the United States and Canada. Starting around 2016, some choruses began classifying themselves by voice part; today insiders sometimes say—or write— TTBB (tenor-tenor-baritone-bass) instead of men's chorus, SSAA (soprano-soprano-alto-alto) instead of women's chorus, or SATB (soprano-alto-tenor-bass) instead of mixed chorus. (See chapter 3 for more discussion of the associations between gender and voice parts). However, at the time of the publication of this book, the older nomenclature was still most frequently used; in this book I specify the three main types of GALA choruses as men's choruses, women's choruses, and mixed choruses, following the pervasive use of these terms in GALA circles.

Although GALA choruses are evolving in many important ways, including in how they name themselves, they remain true to the mission they articulated for themselves at the advent of their movement. GALA choristers continue to believe, and to act on the belief, that their concertizing contributes to progressive social change. As Diane Benjamin, an accompanist to the Calliope Women's Chorus of Saint Paul, Minnesota, and a former GALA Choruses board member, said, "It's easy now to forget how really revolutionary this was, just to stand up and sing as gay and lesbian people" (interview, February 10, 2012). Indeed, it was revolutionary; and to identify oneself, or one's chorus, as LGBT still marks one as a somewhat marginal participant in the US and Canadian choral singing tradition. As this book shows, GALA choristers continue to uphold the values of that tradition, while at the same time they are expanding its boundaries and redefining its purpose.

Today, LGBT-identified choruses are most numerous in the United States and Canada, but they exist in many European countries and other English-speaking countries where choral music has been an important tradition among middle-class White people. China saw the debut of its first LGBT-identified community choirs in 2008, and in early 2018, an as-yet-unnamed LGBT choir made its debut in Yangon, Myanmar.[3] Importantly, not all LGBT-identified choirs count themselves members of GALA Choruses; for example, the two conductors of the Yangon-based choir told me that neither of them had any experience singing with any GALA chorus, and they were fascinated to learn of the organization's existence.[4] LGBT choral singing, then, extends beyond the borders of GALA Choruses. This book focuses on GALA groups because the GALA organization still represents a majority of the world's LGBT choruses and is an appropriate frame through which to understand LGBT choral singing.

Methodology

Singing Out: GALA Choruses and Social Change is the result of a mixed methods investigation. I am an ethnomusicologist by training and profession, and therefore I pursue all of my scholarly projects using ethnographic research methods—that is, by conducting observations, participant observations, and interviews. These methods underlie most of the data reported in this book; chapter 8 also reports the results of a quantitative experiment of the type usually pursued by social scientists. I engaged all these research methods because a mixed methods approach ultimately proved best suited to understanding a large musical phenomenon that, as its leaders claim, is changing the world through song. Part of this book is devoted to analyzing the songs and performance practices of GALA choruses. In addition, I seek throughout the book to understand those songs—and their singers—in context. I ask: Why do these musicians choose to sing these songs at the times and places in which they sing them? And how does their singing change the world?

During my investigation, I pursued answers to these questions by attending rehearsals, concerts, workshops, and business meetings held by GALA choruses in both the United States and Canada. I also carried out an experiment in measuring levels of homophobia (recorded before and after attending a GALA chorus concert) with students from my own university; their anonymized responses to a survey appear near the end of this book. In addition, I conducted interviews with ninety-seven GALA insiders, including singers, artistic directors, board members, accompanists, composers, guest conductors, and other supporters. All the people I interviewed are identified by their real names in this book, with two exceptions. They all signed a consent form that offered them the option of being quoted anonymously; in a handful of instances, I exercised that option on their behalf because their quoted remarks refer to sensitive information. One person (referred to in the book as Katie Eadie) asked to be identified by a pseudonym. Additionally, I include all the interviewees' titles, meaning that I cite the role they play in their GALA chorus, such as "singer in X chorus, located in Y city." Their title

reflects the position they held in GALA Choruses during the time I conducted my research, during the second decade of the twenty-first century.
After I interviewed them, a number of my interlocutors moved on from the
GALA chorus that they sang in, conducted, or otherwise supported (and
sadly, one man, Allen Kimbrough, died).

Singing Out: GALA Choruses and Social Change is largely focused on
men's choruses and on the cisgender White men who sing in and lead these
choruses. As we have already seen, the GALA Choruses organization represents many diverse individuals and groups, and this diversity encompasses
both ethnic identification and gender. However, men's choruses predomi-
nate in GALA Choruses; most of the large and well-funded GALA choruses
are men's choruses, and the artistic directors of those choruses (who are,
again, mostly cisgender White men) are thought leaders in GALA circles.
This reality shaped my research: the majority of the performances I was able
to observe were presented by men's choruses, and the majority of the people
I was able to interview were cisgender White men. The result is that this
book is often oriented toward men and toward men's choruses; my analysis is
largely based on the sung and spoken statements of the cisgender White men
who constitute GALA's dominant population and who provided the majority of my data. As my research progressed, I made a special attempt to interview people of color, and eventually they became somewhat overrepresented
in my interview sample. But in general, the GALA insiders I interviewed and
observed represented the demographics of the organization as a whole;
therefore, the voices of cisgender White men are the most frequently featured in this book, although I seek to give pride of place to the perspectives
of women, people of color, and transgender singers as well.

Scholarly Context and Contributions

Scholars have only recently developed a broad interest in GALA choruses.
Through the 1990s and early 2000s, academics and practitioners contributed a handful of articles, book chapters, and dissertations to the literature.
During the second decade of the millennium, while I conducted the
research for this book, two more dissertations and more articles were written, and presentations at academic conferences about LGBT choruses and
"the queer voice" became commonplace. In 2017, the first full-length mono-
graph about GALA choruses appeared (Balén 2017). Singing Out: GALA
Choruses and Social Change contributes to this small but growing body of
work and, in so doing, speaks to a number of academic fields: choral music

studies, social movement studies, and gay and lesbian anthropology. Further, it utilizes an intersectional approach to make these contributions.

First, this book expands our understanding of choral music and thereby speaks to the larger field of musicology. Choral singing is a widespread community activity; numerous studies have shown that it is "the most popular public arts activity" in the United States and that more than twenty million adults engage in choral singing weekly (Bell 2004, 39). Writing about choral singing is dominated by practitioners, especially music educators sharing their own best practices with their colleagues. The few ethnographic investigations of community choral singing include insightful dissertations (Kinney 2010; Redman 2016; Rensink-Hoff 2009; Vincent 1997; Wilson 2011), monographs (Averill 2003; Duchan 2012), and edited collections (Ahlquist 2006a), all of which inform this book. Paul Attinello (1994, 325), in an important early book chapter about GALA choruses, recounted the results of the questionnaires he distributed to singers in five large GALA men's choruses, but he noted that many fascinating aspects of such choruses remained to be studied and that his own written survey method produced insights that "pale in comparison with live conversations that can be heard in the groups studied." In this book I recount live conversations I overheard at GALA rehearsals and workshops—see for example in chapter 1—and, most importantly, quote widely from the interviews I conducted with ninety-seven individuals associated with GALA choruses. In their conversations with each other and with me, GALA insiders revealed profound truths about the nature of their music making and the dissonances within it.

Second, this book addresses and responds to academic studies of social movements. Social movement studies is a rich field of inquiry, and social movement scholars often take the broadest of perspectives to analyze large-scale movements. As James Jasper (1997, 98, 172) argues, these scholars therefore sometimes neglect "cultural and biographical factors," the kinds of factors that are illuminated by ethnographic research methods. While conducting research for this book, I paid great attention to such factors, asking all interviewees about their early musical training, their initial involvement in a GALA chorus, and so on. As Jasper points out, this kind of focus reveals the emotions that motivate participants in social movements, and so it does in my study. My study also reveals that singers in GALA choruses understand themselves to be agents in the gay rights movement, and therefore this book constitutes a contribution to the study of the gay rights movement writ large (Bernstein 1997; Rayside 2008; Rimmerman 2002; Vaid 1995). I devote a significant section of the book to examining the position GALA choruses occupy in the wider gay rights movement, and the ways in which they do (or do not) advance the goals of factions within that movement. In so doing, I avoid easy claims that GALA choruses are engaging in "resistance," a term that became fashionable, and then entirely overused, in academic circles in the late twentieth and early twenty-first centuries (Rosenthal and Flacks 2012, 192). As Ellen Lewin points out, academics often "romanticized" resistance, assuming that gay and lesbian people by their very existence somehow resisted and even subverted social norms (1996c, 108; also 1996a, 7); later, this easy resort to resistance was applied to self-identified queer people (Green 2002, 531; Taylor 2012, 198). Not one of the ninety-seven people I interviewed for this book ever used the word *resistance*, as either a noun or a verb, although they spoke in nuanced ways about how exactly their concertizing aimed to fulfill certain social goals, including the goal of celebrating same-sex love.

Third, this book is part of the growing field of gay and lesbian anthropology. Like GALA choruses, this field of scholarly inquiry emerged in the wake of the Stonewall riots; in recent years we have seen detailed studies of various American LGBT communities, including youth in the American Bible Belt (Gray 2009; Barton 2012), cross-dressers in New York City (Valentine 2007), lesbians in a college town (Brown-Saracino 2011), and same-sex couples in suburbia (Carrington 1999). Such specific studies are extremely valuable because, as John Hollister (1999, 64) argues, there is no singular gay community and no all-encompassing LGBT scene. "The literature. . . . may analyze 'gay, lesbian and bisexual' identities in general, and occasionally observe how they may interact with race, gender and even class, but it does little to account for how jarring the contrasts among their meanings in different settings can get. The 'gay' of the lesbian and gay social movement organization, the 'gay' of a cruising area, and the 'gay' of a gay bar are distinct entities. . . . What it means to be gay is site-specific" (1999, 69; see also White 1991, 279). This book traces what it means to be a gay, or lesbian, or transgender choral singer in the United States or in Canada, providing detailed accounts of rehearsals, performances, and sites such as the quadrennial GALA Festival, during which thousands of GALA choristers meet for one week. Throughout the book, I maintain an anthropological focus on the people who participate in GALA choruses because I agree with Lewin (2009, 100): "We are obliged, as anthropologists, to elucidate the meanings that real people bring to their social and cultural lives. Such obligations are matters of scholarly rigor but they are also elements of an ethical mandate—to represent people in ways that elucidate their own understandings of themselves and that enhance the clarity of their voices." GALA singers project their own voices in a wide variety of performance venues; however, a deeper understanding of the meanings they attach to their singing was revealed in the many interviews I conducted for this book, and I quote, summarize, and analyze these to the best of my ability throughout. It seemed to me important to do so in part because people in my own community or site—that is, schools and departments of music located in the universities of the Western world—are largely ignorant of LGBT choruses and the important contributions such choruses are making to local music scenes and to broader political efforts. Indeed, some are openly dismissive of GALA choruses, as I explain in chapter 1.

In claiming a place for this book in gay and lesbian anthropology, I distinguish such anthropology from queer theory. Following other scholars in these two fields, I understand them both as deeply valuable (Warner 2012) but ultimately separate endeavors (Duggan 1995). Queer theory emerged from analyses of canonical English-language texts (Turner 2000, 146), and it continues to prioritize "queer readings" of classic and mainstream literary and musical texts (Jarman-Ivens 2011; Peraino 2006). Anthropologists have rightly, in my view, critiqued queer theory for its lack of "connection to the empirical world and the sociohistorical forces that shape sexual practice and identity" (Green 2002, 533; see also Lewin and Leap 2002, 11; Leap and Lewin 2009a, 7). My book insists on connecting to the empirical world by relaying, at length, my observations derived from my attendance at events and questioning of insiders. At the same time, I agree with Lisa Duggan (1995, 205) that "it is a terrible mistake to dismiss work in queer theory as jargon-ridden, elitist claptrap, as some do." Chapter 5 of this book in fact owes a debt to queer theory; that chapter is in essence an application of the ideas of an important queer theorist, José Esteban Muñoz. Furthermore, in that chapter I depend on other prominent queer theorists to understand how canonical choral songs "become gay," and how GALA's songs expand the scholarly understanding of gay culture.

Anthropology insists that researchers divulge their own positionality in relation to the people among whom they conduct their research (see an excellent example in E. Hayes 2010, 10). This action is especially important in gay and lesbian anthropology because, as Lewin and William Leap point out (2002, 12), "conducting lesbian/gay research is tantamount to coming out—whether one is actually lesbian/gay or not." I myself am a straight (heterosexual), cisgender woman, married to a straight, cisgender man. Prefacing other important themes in this book, I make clear here that I also identify as Canadian, White, middle class, and Christian. While I am a supporter of GALA choristers' ideals—for example, the idea that human beings of all sexual orientations and gender identifications are fundamentally equal and ought to be treated as such—I am not an activist on LGBT issues. Specifically, I am not aiming in this book to make a contribution to gay or queer activism, unlike some other scholars of gay and queer studies (Bronski 1984; Butler 1999, xvii; Cohen 2001, 202; D'Emilio 1992, xix). Most importantly, I have never sung in a GALA chorus, although I have sung in and conducted other school and community choirs. For my GALA interlocutors, therefore, I was fundamentally an outsider to their experience. It is a measure of their tremendous graciousness that they so freely shared with me their thoughts and expertise.

This project depends on an intersectional mode of analysis. Given that cisgender White men constitute the dominant majority of the population in GALA choruses, characterizing the book as an intersectional study requires an explanation. Intersectionality is an analytical frame that emerged from Black feminism and was codified through sociological methodology; its central insight is that subjects are often multiply marginalized, and that they experience distinct forms of oppression at the intersections of their identities. Black women, for example, are discriminated against on the basis of their gender (as women) *and* on the basis of their racial identification (as African Americans). Therefore scholarly studies, legal briefs, or activist agendas that focus only on gender discrimination, or only on racism, fail to address the full range of marginalization experienced by women of color. Scholars in a wide variety of fields have found intersectionality to be "a productive concept" because it continually exposes the paucity of "single-axis thinking." Today intersectionality is defined as "a gathering place for open-ended investigations of the overlapping and conflicting dynamics of race, gender, class, sexuality, nationality and other inequalities" (Cho, Crenshaw, and McCall 2013, 787–88).

With the tremendous growth in the number of intersectional studies, writers have, perhaps predictably, queried the nature of the field. Some have worried that as "'intersectionality' has become a scholarly buzzword" (Nash 2008, 3), the field has narrowed, or has been misconstrued, to focus only on subjects who can be reliably portrayed as marginalized. In particular, that literature has neglected the study of White men, overlooking the fact that they—like all people everywhere—may experience multiple forms of dominance and subordination not only on the basis of their race and gender, but also on the basis of their social class, their nationality, their sexual orientation, and other nodes of inequality (Nash 2008, 10). As intersectionality has matured, scholars have clarified that its inquiry is directed not toward identity—or toward particular identities—but rather toward power (Cho, Crenshaw, and McCall 2013, 797). Kimberlé Williams Crenshaw—who coined the term *intersectionality*—and her coauthors sum it up thusly: "If intersectionality is an analytic disposition, a way of thinking about and conducting analyses, then what makes an analysis intersectional is not its use of the term 'intersectionality,' nor its being situated in a familiar genealogy, nor its drawing on lists of standard citations. Rather, what makes an analysis intersectional—whatever terms it deploys, whatever its iteration, whatever its field or discipline—is its adoption of an intersectional way of thinking about the problem of sameness and difference and its relation to power" (2013, 795).

This book examines the people who sing in, conduct, and administrate GALA choruses, with a focus on how their subject positions influence their relationships to mainstream society in Canada and the United States. GALA singers overwhelmingly identify as LGBT (mostly as gay or lesbian), and they have experienced stigmatization and discrimination on that basis (see chapter 1). As chapter 2 explains, one reason for the vitality of GALA choruses is that those who participate in them view them as their families; as LGBT persons they have a tremendous appreciation for "family" because so many of them have been rejected by their families of origin and by their faith communities. At the same time, most GALA choristers are White and middle class. This positionality gives them a considerable degree of privilege; one marker of that privilege, of course, is that they have the income and leisure time to participate in a community choir. Most importantly, their racial and class positions go a long way toward explaining why the GALA organization—so consistently committed to progressive social change—uses an integrationist rather than a liberationist approach. Its members, White middle-class people pursuing activism, focus on the few institutions closed to them by virtue of their status as sexual and gender minorities (marriage and the military) and on a diffuse notion of "changing hearts and minds" (see chapter 6). The GALA organization is marked by internal divisions that are often glossed as identity politics but that are better understood as differential relationships to power; for example, the amount of money and attention received by men's choruses far outweighs that received by choruses that include women (i.e., mixed choruses and women's choruses; see chapter 2). Moreover, as groups populated overwhelmingly by cisgender people who love the gender-binary-confirming Western choral music tradition, GALA choruses have struggled to welcome transgender singers (see chapter 3). Throughout this book, as the reader will discover, I attend to all these dynamics of gender, race, and social class.

A Further Word about a Word

The word *queer* appears in this book infrequently, usually only when I am referencing the proper name of a group or quoting another scholar. The reason for this scarcity is that I endeavor throughout to faithfully reflect the words of my GALA interlocutors. The middle-aged, middle-class White people who constitute the majority of the singers in GALA choruses and who dominated my interview sample almost never use the word *queer* to describe themselves, their choruses, or their music. (From my total interview sample of ninety-seven people, only four singers and one artistic director described themselves as queer when asked about their sexual orientation). It is true, as Julia Balén (2017, 180) reports, that queer is increasingly coming into common usage among LGBT people; indeed, this uptick is one of Balén's justifications for using the term in the title and throughout the text of her own book about GALA Choruses. However, the word has a long and varied history. In the early twentieth century in New York City, middle-class gay men used it to describe themselves and to distinguish their own experience of homosexuality from that of the working-class effeminate "fairies" whom they largely disliked (Chauncey 1994, 106). At the same time, mainstream English speakers began using the word to insultingly refer to all homosexual men, and queer became a form of hate speech. In the early 1970s, gay activists reappropriated the word as a name for their protest movements, and it remained associated with radical liberationists through the early twenty-first century (Faderman 2015, 528). A small minority of queer activists publicly supported what is now referred to as pedophilia (White 1991, 308–10; Bawer 1993, 157), and that stance, more than any other, has made gay integrationists decline to use the word queer. They understand queer to be an insult deployed by homophobes (Jagose 1996, 103; Leap 1996, 106). To the extent that queer is now "a catch-all term" to refer to LGBT people (Taylor 2012, 14), GALA insiders do recognize it and—infrequently—use it. But they are aware that queer is also "a term of resistance" that "opposes hegemonic identificatory and behavioral norms, including liberal lesbian and gay identity politics" (Taylor 2012, 14), and therefore, they generally agree with the founder of two different GALA choruses who said to me, "I'm offended by the word queer!"[5]

Chapter Outlines

Chapter 1, "GALA Choruses as Community Choirs," begins with an ethnographic description of a representative GALA chorus rehearsal. The central argument of the chapter is that GALA choruses are part of the community choral music scene, and they both resemble and differ from other community choirs in significant ways. After exploring other scholars' defi-

nitions of community choirs, I delineate commonalities that GALA choruses share with other community choirs: commitment to fundraising,
choristers' previous musical experience, and valorization of a particular
understanding of artistic excellence. GALA choruses, however, are remarkably successful at their fundraising when compared to other community
choirs, and they are also criticized by choral music gatekeepers as musically
inferior. The discussion of excellence leads to an explanation of GALA's
relationship to the American Choral Directors Association (ACDA), a
leading professional music society and gatekeeping organization that has
had a contentious relationship with GALA choruses in the past. GALA's
marginalization within the ACDA is but one example of the discrimination various choruses have experienced as a result of identifying as LGBT.
GALA choruses' experience with (and continuing fear of) discrimination
is an important way in which they differ from other community choirs.
Chapter 1 concludes with an extended analysis of the quadrennial GALA
Festival. Again, like other community choirs, GALA choruses prioritize
attendance at choral festivals, but their own festival is unique, and it is
uniquely important to GALA choristers. It is at this festival that GALA
choristers learn that they are participants in a movement. Moments of Dur-
kheimian effervescence foster in the choristers a deeply emotional conviction that together they are changing the world through song.

Chapter 2, "'Community' and Its Significance to GALA Choristers,"
argues that local GALA choruses are of overriding importance to the choristers who sing in them because they are communities of friendship, which are
immensely valuable to LGBT people and which are increasingly rare in US
and Canadian society at large. However, the GALA organization, understood as one overarching community, displays significant divisions along
gender lines. I begin by explaining choristers' varying motivations to join
their local choruses, noting that desire to find a supportive community is by
far their most common motivation. Correspondingly, GALA choruses are
marked by a strong commitment to the ideal of "community." Following Kay
Kaufman Shelemay's (2011) analysis of three types of musical communities
and the processes that lead to their formations, I show that various GALA
choristers and leaders exemplify all three; however, most GALA insiders see
their choruses as communities of descent—that is, groups that come together
on the basis of a shared identity. And it is this shared LGBT identity—and
the life experience it implies—that explains why GALA choruses are so
deeply important to their members. Participation in voluntary face-to-face
communities has plummeted in recent decades in the United States and
Canada; LGBT persons are especially in need of such communities because

they are often excluded from their families of origin and from their churches. The chapter continues by exploring divisions within the GALA Choruses organization, arguing that men's (TTBB) choruses are much more prominent, and seemingly more valued, in GALA circles than are mixed (SATB) choruses or women's (SSAA) choruses. GALA insiders often discuss the gender division within their organization by pointing to differences in chorus governance, claiming that men prefer hierarchy and women prefer consensus. I argue that the overwhelming majority of GALA choruses do not adhere to the purest form of either of these modes of governance; rather, power is shared between choristers and their leaders in a variety of ways.

Chapter 3, "Diversity and Its Discontents," pursues one of the central arguments of the book, that GALA's commitment to promoting broad-based support for various dimensions of diversity is tested in its own backyard. I begin with an ethnographic description of a performance by a GALA chorus, a performance that sought to promote diversity. The chapter explores the lack of ethnic diversity among GALA choruses, which are overwhelmingly White organizations. GALA Choruses and its various member choruses are not exceptional in this way; Whiteness predominates in the Canadian and American choral music scenes. I offer four possible reasons why GALA choruses include so few singers (and even fewer artistic directors) of color. Chief among these reasons—as numerous other scholars have argued—is that LGBT identities are often understood to be incompatible with various ethnic identities. GALA's leaders have spearheaded various diversity initiatives during the four decades of the organization's existence, both at the international and local levels. Beginning in 2016, they focused on greater inclusion and visibility for transgender singers. However, as I argue, transgender singers' greatest desires cannot always be accommodated by GALA choruses, which have a continuing commitment to the norms of the Western choral music tradition, a tradition that prizes homogeneity of sound and appearance.

Chapter 4, "Homonormativity: GALA Choruses as Middle-Class Organizations," argues that GALA choruses are homonormative organizations—that is, they are marked by a cisgender, White, middle-class, US/Canadian ethos. Having explored the dominance of Whiteness and of traditional gender norms in GALA in the previous chapter, here I turn to socioeconomic class as a powerful determinant of GALA insiders' preferences and values, as revealed by their offstage behavior and their onstage performances. GALA's homonormative ethos is most tellingly revealed in its valorization of monogamy and same-sex marriage, a cause for which its choruses have composed and performed a number of songs. (I note that during the GALA Festival, a quadrennial event at which thousands of GALA choristers assemble, hooking up is common, or is perceived as common. However, GALA insiders insist that their choruses are not venues for hooking up, and "dating" is sometimes explicitly forbidden in chorus bylaws.) GALA choristers frequently talk about and even sing about how their choruses are *not* like gay bars—that is, places where "excessive appetites" (Lynch 1992) may be indulged, and where people are ruthlessly judged according to their "erotic capital" (Green 2011). GALA artistic directors more frequently compare their choruses to churches, venues that (supposedly) welcome all kinds of people, and that are also dedicated to proclaiming a persuasive message. The discussion of the church analogy leads to GALA choruses' complicated relationship with the performance of sacred music, or songs that reference Christian beliefs. I explain that GALA's artistic directors pursue four different strategies when programming sacred music. One increasingly common choice is to program songs that affirm both Christian dogma and same-sex love.

Chapter 5, "Disidentifying: The Music and Performance Practices of GALA Choruses," argues that what GALA choruses do with their performances—as evident in both the songs they sing and the ways they present those songs—is disidentifying, a concept first advanced by scholar José Esteban Muñoz (1999). GALA singers and artistic directors disidentify with the Western choral music tradition by upholding its heteronormative values while simultaneously proclaiming their own narrative within it. GALA choristers disidentify in two primary ways: by singing so-called gay songs, and by developing innovative performance practices. The chapter begins by analyzing a number of gay songs. Some of GALA's gay songs are unabashedly campy, but others are deeply serious and are presented with sincerity. Because of this multiplicity, I argue that scholars of LGBT life, who have focused largely on camp, should expand their understanding of gay culture. I then turn to an analysis of GALA's performance practices; I explain that GALA performances exist on a spectrum marked by two poles (the choral recital and the show). Following detailed descriptions of a variety of chorus performances, I claim that most fall somewhere along the middle of the spectrum. Importantly, the large majority of GALA performances demonstrate some form of innovation, transcending the norms of the traditional choral recital. As other scholars have argued, artistic innovation—especially in the area of stage performance—is something of a gay male specialization, and is linked to early life experiences that are common to members of sexual and gender minorities who grow up in heteronormative society. Returning to Muñoz, I affirm his claim that the kinds of disidentifications that GALA choruses engage in have political implications. In the following chapters, I explore those political implications, which GALA insiders most often gloss as "our mission."

Chapter 6, "GALA Choruses on a Mission," argues that GALA choruses are mission-driven groups. The choruses' mission is to foster a particular kind of social change through their singing—that is, "to change hearts and minds." Importantly, the change they seek is in the attitudes of their (potentially homophobic) listeners, and not usually in the laws or institutions that structure mainstream society. Chapter 6 illuminates the ways in which the choruses' commitment to their social change mission drives both shared norms and disagreements across the GALA organization. I begin by analyzing GALA choruses' various mission statements, showing that most emphasize both musicking and social change. Artistic directors work hard to foster a sense of commitment to the mission, and my interviews with dozens of choristers show that they do identify strongly with the mission. However, both leaders and singers from across GALA disagree about whether choruses should be characterized as doing political work. This disagreement is linked, I argue, to diverging opinions on how choruses ought to pursue their mission. Most commonly, insiders link their social change work to concertizing, claiming that by conveying a transformational message they can persuade listeners to respect LGBT people. Therefore, programming decisions are of utmost importance to GALA singers. In addition, GALA choristers believe that by identifying as LGBT people onstage and in public, they embody their mission. The stakes surrounding that identification are correspondingly high, and GALA insiders have debated for decades what exactly their choruses ought to be named. I conclude by citing some of GALA's most influential thought leaders, who openly speculate whether hearing an LGBT-identified chorus sing can, in fact, change the hearts and minds of listeners. This central question—does GALA choruses' pursuit of their mission actually lead to social change?—animates the last two chapters of the book.

Chapter 7, "GALA Choruses as Part of the Gay Rights Movement," examines GALA choruses' musicking through the lens of social movement theory. I begin by outlining social movement theorists' definitions of social movements, explaining how GALA choruses can be thus characterized as belonging to the gay rights movement. One of the most important findings from studies of social movements is that all of them are marked by an internal divide, and the gay rights movement is no exception. I delineate the arguments of the liberationist and integrationist wings of the gay rights movement and argue that GALA choruses are best understood as belonging to the integrationist wing. The integrationist ethos of GALA is revealed both in many statements that interviewees made to me (emphasizing their desire to present themselves as "normal") and in directives issued by GALA leaders. Most tellingly, however, GALA choruses' integrationist commitment is evident in their choice of tactic, the choral concert. Following Don Handelman's (1998) theory of public events, I analyze a number of performances by GALA choruses as "events-that-re-present" and as "events-that-model," arguing that these performances are indeed intended to "act upon and change the ordering of" the social world.

Finally, chapter 8, "Social Change: Assessing GALA Choruses' Central Claim," begins by acknowledging what social movement scholars have long claimed, that it is very difficult to gauge the success of a social movement. I explain that GALA choristers have a widespread belief that their efforts are leading to the social change they pursue—to the changing of hearts and minds—and they provide anecdotal evidence for their belief, both in interviews and in their organization's public statements. Scholars have long engaged with the question of how such social change is effected, conducting decades of research on the contact hypothesis, which investigates how contact with members of minority groups affects the way that majority group members think. I describe in detail an empirical experiment I conducted with students from my own university, using Gregory Herek's (1994) ATLG questionnaire to assess their reported levels of homophobia before and after a GALA men's chorus concert. After the concert, the students generally demonstrated no change in their attitudes toward gay men, although intriguingly, they more profoundly disagreed with a negative statement about gay men. I point out that GALA's artistic directors and singers could rightly choose to interpret this study as buttressing their claim that their concertizing changes hearts and minds. Much previous scholarship has shown that coming out is a powerful way to foster increased tolerance of LGBT people. I therefore argue that GALA choruses' best claim to advancing a social change agenda rests on the fact that they have provided a way for thousands of choristers to come out as LGBT. GALA performances allow listeners to experience positive interpersonal experiences with groups of people (not just scattered individuals) who self-identify as LGBT; as previous social science research has shown, such experiences are central to reducing the stigma attached to LGBT people.

1 • GALA Choruses as Community Choirs

Fall 2010: the Dayton Gay Men's Chorus is rehearsing for its annual holiday concert, always presented on the first Saturday in December. Through the fall the choristers meet weekly in a church basement in downtown Dayton, Ohio, a bare bones space containing folding chairs and a spinet piano. The artistic director, Jason Schuler, and the piano accompanist, Raymonde Rougier, have been leading the chorus for years. Schuler's affectionate relationship with the choristers is clear: he hugs arriving singers, and they in turn congratulate him on his recent marriage. A total of twenty-six singers are attending rehearsals this season; all of them are White men. Most wear button-down shirts and jeans to rehearsal. To greet one another, some of the older men exchange hugs, and some of the younger men punch each other in the shoulder. The men are grouped into four voice parts, or sections: Tenor I, Tenor II, Baritone, and Bass. Each of these sections sit together, and all singers in each section are expected to sing the same note at the same time.

Through the two-hour rehearsal, all present work hard, drilling difficult rhythms and pitches; at one point they spend ten minutes practicing a challenging cutoff in "Jingle Bells."[1] The conductor gives the singers a number of friendly reminders about posture, vocal technique, and the chorus's rule that all music must be performed from memory. The chorus's American Sign Language (ASL) interpreter, seated beside the singers, is using music notation as she rehearses her signing; eventually she too will perform the entire concert program from memory. The conductor asks the singers questions ("Do you want to sing this part again?") and listens to their answers. The choristers, for their part, make a number of funny and sexually suggestive comments. For example, when the chorus reconvenes after dividing briefly to rehearse in sections, the conductor asks, "Where are the tenors?"; a singer in the second row retorts, "They aren't allowed within two hundred yards of a school!"[2]

Most of the time, though, is spent on perfecting the singing, and the choristers seem deeply engaged in this endeavor. Some of them record the rehearsal so they can review it later. Others pose specific questions and request that particular moments in songs be repeated; for example, "I Saw Daddy Kissing Santa Claus" provokes the question, "Is it pronounced 'kissing' or 'kissin'?"[3] The announcements, given before a brief break, include a reminder of this month's social gathering and a plea for choristers to sell advertising space in the December concert program.

Readers who have spent time participating in amateur choirs will recognize a number of elements in the above description—and find that other aspects of this account are unusual. For example, choristers from all types of community choirs understand that choirs are divided into sections, and that rehearsal time is principally devoted to musical learning (cutoffs and the like). Community choirs are usually "grassroots and relatively communal" (Balén 2009, 36–37), and therefore it is understood among them that singers will be asked to help with fundraising. However, most community choirs do not include ASL interpreters, and men openly hugging other men is not common in the heteronormative space of a community choir. Perhaps the most notable aspect of the Dayton Gay Men's Chorus, and of the dozens of other gay men's choruses that belong to the GALA organization, is that all the singers are men. The problem of the "missing males" in choral singing has been remarked on (Cusick 1999, 33; Engelhardt 2015, 8) and lamented by scholars who have examined the situation in the United States (Freer 2012, 13; Harrison, Welch, and Adler 2012a, 3–4), in Canada (Adler 2012, 54), in Australia (Harrison 2012, 68), and in the United Kingdom (Davies 2012, 335). If men are increasingly absent from community choirs in general, they are present in full force in GALA choruses, helping create a "successful and well sustaining male choral community" (Adler 2012, 59).

In this chapter, I put GALA choruses in context, in order to understand them as they understand themselves, as part of the choral singing scene in the United States and Canada. I argue that GALA choruses resemble other community choirs but also differ from them in significant ways. Or, as Miguel Felipe, former artistic director of the Maine Gay Men's Chorus, put it: "GALA Choruses are pretty much plain old community choruses, except when they're not" (interview July 31, 2013).

Defining a Community Choir

To begin, it is important to note that "there is no consensus on what, exactly, is meant by a community chorus" (Bell 2008, 231). Caroline Bithell (2014,

222) points out that in the United Kingdom, a community choir is understood to be distinct from an amateur and/or professional choir: a community choir generally does not expect its singers to be able to sight-read Western staff notation, while amateur and professional choirs do. According to Bithell, lesbian and gay choirs fall under the rubric of community choirs because they are open to singers of all backgrounds, including those with no prior experience in choral singing. In this book I use *community choir* as a gloss for groups of singers who meet regularly to rehearse and perform, and who are not paid for this volunteer activity. Contrary to some other writers (see Bell 2008, 231), I do *not* exclude church choirs, barbershop quartets, children's choirs, school-based choirs, and the like from this categorization. My main reason for conceiving of community choirs in such broad terms is that my interlocutors who sing in GALA choruses had previous experience singing in other choirs like those listed, choirs that differed in terms of audition requirements and affiliation, but that were identical in that they did not pay their singers. GALA insiders often compare and contrast their experiences in those other community choirs with their GALA chorus experiences—which is exactly what I will do in this chapter.

One further caveat: I do not distinguish between GALA choruses and community choirs on the basis of the sexual orientation of the singers involved. GALA choruses include both LGBT and straight singers. Self-identified LGBT people constitute the demographic majority of most GALA groups, but straight women and men also participate in GALA's men's, women's, and mixed choruses, including youth choruses.[4] And LGBT singers, for their part, can be found in all kinds of community choirs (Durrant 2012, 119; Mook 2007, 469). As Miguel Felipe once commented, "Let's face it, most church choirs are gay men's choruses!" (interview, July 31, 2013). Charlie Beale, artistic director of the New York City Gay Men's Chorus, put it bluntly: "There's no such thing as a straight choir" (interview, August 16, 2011). Both straight and LGBT singers sing in both GALA choruses and in other community choirs. The difference is that GALA choruses self-identify as groups of LGBT and allied singers, whereas other community choirs do not.

GALA Choruses as Community Choirs

GALA choruses are part of the international community choral music scene and resemble other community choirs in several important ways. For instance, GALA choruses are set up as nonprofit organizations; they apply for government grants, and they accept donations from private individuals and corporate donors. And like other community choirs (and like other

ity," one way to burnish their image and ultimately to market their prod-

amateur arts organizations), GALA choruses must focus continually on raising money to support their activities; "the money issues facing community choirs are daunting" (Avery, Hayes, and Bell 2013, 253). Indeed, scholar and former GALA chorus artistic director Casey J. Hayes (2007, 66) claims that funding is the primary nonartistic concern of LGBT choirs. My own observations of meetings of GALA artistic directors and board members suggest that Hayes is correct; much of the discussion at such meetings is devoted to funding-related topics including how to sell the maximum numbers of tickets, how to use social media to effectively promote concerts, and how to approach potential donors.[5] GALA conferences also feature workshops to train chorus leaders on how to raise money and build audiences for their choruses.[6] Charlie Beale pointed out that the New York City Gay Men's Chorus—one of GALA's oldest and largest choruses—had a $600,000 annual budget as of 2011, "and in order to break even, we are *constantly* fundraising" (interview, August 16, 2011). Beale explained that much of his daily experience as an artistic director is related in some way to money, and that many of his programming decisions are strongly influenced by financial considerations. "I have to think about, will this [proposed] show be profitable? Where is the cheapest rehearsal space? Which guest artist will sell the most tickets?"

One advantage that GALA choruses have over other community choirs is that corporate donors are increasingly interested in funding "diversity." The funding of diversity is part of modern corporations' "quest for legitimacy," one way to burnish their image and ultimately to market their products (Chasin 2000, 204). Arts groups that are LGBT identified, like GALA choruses, are a clear fit for philanthropic budgets focused on supporting diversity in the local area.[7] As one GALA singer who works as a bank consultant phrased it, "Sometimes corporate partners want to be *seen* to be supportive" (Bryan Fetty, interview, October 9, 2014). GALA's men's choruses, in particular, benefit from this type of support (see chapter 2 for further discussion on the inequities between men's and women's choruses). Charlie Beale shared that most "big" donations to the New York City Gay Men's Chorus come from wealthy individuals and from the diversity budgets of businesses (interview, August 16, 2011). A much smaller GALA chorus, the Dayton Gay Men's Chorus, has a similar funding model. As of 2009, its annual budget was $30,000, and most of that money came from corporate sponsors, according to the group's artistic director (Jason Schuler, interview, September 16, 2010). The 2017 concert program of the Dayton Gay Men's Chorus revealed much of its funding structure for the 2016–17 year: its concertizing was "made possible by generous grants from the Dayton Foundation, the Miriam Rosenthal Foundation for the Arts and the Ohio Arts Council." Sponsors were also listed in the program; that year, the two most generous donors (who gave $5,000 or more) were individuals, but Lexis-Nexis, one of the largest employers in the Dayton area, was next on the list (having donated between $1,000 and $2,500). Further, the Elizabeth Diamond Company purchased a full-page advertisement on the back cover of the program, with the caption, "Helping to educate about diversity is of tremendous value. We always enjoy your performances."

Though some GALA choruses have ceased operations in recent years, the LGBT choral movement is vibrantly healthy, and the GALA organization continues to grow, representing more and more local community choruses. Most of these, especially the men's choruses, are on solid financial footing; indeed, they could serve as models to other arts organizations. The Gay Men's Chorus of Charlotte, North Carolina, for example, commissions more new compositions than do all the city's other musical ensembles combined; it is able to do so because it not only raises money but also receives some matching funds from the GALA organization (John Quillin, interview, March 29, 2011). The Gay Men's Chorus of Washington, DC, regularly presents ambitious programs featuring paid soloists; in 2016, for example, it performed Carl Orff's *Carmina Burana*, which included not only professional soloists but also instrumentalists and costumed dancers. Frank Albinder, the artistic director of the all-male Washington Men's Camerata, pointed out that Washington is "a choral town" and therefore the city's choral music fans are somewhat spoiled for choice (interview, January 30, 2012). In this competitive environment, the Gay Men's Chorus of Washington, DC, sells out four shows each December, for a total of ten thousand tickets—a feat that Albinder somewhat wistfully compared to the Camerata's ability to sell about eight hundred tickets during the same season. He pointed out that the Camerata "doesn't have tons of volunteers or a big budget" like the Gay Men's Chorus of Washington, DC. If developing financial resources is a challenge—and virtually all GALA insiders agree that it is—then GALA's men's choruses are rising to meet this challenge in admirable fashion.

In-Group Banter

As we have already seen, a GALA chorus rehearsal is intelligible to anyone who has participated in any other community choir rehearsal because the organization of the group and the norms of practicing together are largely the same. One distinguishing feature of GALA rehearsals—found espe-

cially but not exclusively in men's choruses—is the sexually suggestive banter between singers, and even sometimes between singers and their artistic
directors. Research on the behavior of choristers during choir rehearsals is
limited, but a study of a men's chorus in Iceland revealed that the "lighthearted banter" in that (non-gay-identified) group was competitive rather
than sexually suggestive (Faulkner and Davidson 2006, 225–26), and the
lead researcher found specifically that the "jokes tend not to be sexually
explicit" (Faulkner 2012, 226). In an ethnographic study of barbershop
quartets, Richard Mook (2007, 470–72) found that the men sometimes
engaged in homoerotic behavior (such as kissing another man on the cheek)
during rehearsals. However, the barbershoppers did so mockingly, in order
to emphasize their commitment to heterosexuality and traditional masculine identity.[8] In gay men's chorus rehearsals, conversely, raw sexual humor
is par for the course.

I also heard this kind of banter at GALA conferences and workshops for
artistic directors and board members, and between people attending the
GALA Festival—in other words, at events where significant numbers of
women were in attendance. Sexualized banter can be fairly said to be part of
the GALA ethos. However, this sort of sexually suggestive joking is usually
not part of GALA concert performances; it is generally an offstage practice.
Here are a few examples, all of which provoked loud laughter among the
groups that heard them: At a Calgary Men's Chorus rehearsal, the conductor
began by announcing which songs the chorus would rehearse; he mentioned,
"We won't do 'Go Down Moses.'" A chorister called out, "That's a damn
shame!"[9] At a gathering of artistic directors held in Palm Springs, California,
someone asked the facilitator, "What is permitted onstage at the [upcom-
ing] Festival?" A man near the front of the room yelled, "Full frontal!"[10] At
another meeting the next day, in reference to copyright permissions for the
upcoming GALA Festival, Robin Godfrey, GALA's executive director, was
asked, "Are you going to require that everything be legal?" Before she could
answer, someone else asked, "Wait . . . are you talking about the music?"
When Godfrey replied "No"—meaning that the GALA organization did
not plan to check the scores of the six thousand singers at the Festival to
ensure that all the music notation was legally obtained—one man sitting
behind me said to another, "Hey, you can do that fifteen-year-old."[11] During
the same conference, during a discussion of the use of social media to accept
donations, one chorus director pointed out that this practice might not work
at concerts: audience members, he said, use their iPhones for other purposes
during performances, and the Grindr site gets overloaded.[12]

Ethnographers of gay and lesbian life have noted repeatedly that humor, especially humor focused on sexuality, is common among groups of gay men and lesbians (Jacobs 1996, 62). Psychologists find that humor serves many different social functions and that "a vast amount of humor" functions "to solidify the group" (Martineau 1972, 116). The sexually suggestive humor found in GALA circles, I argue, functions in exactly this way. The jokes at rehearsals and meetings reinforce group cohesion, highlighting the participants' shared sensibility. These humorous remarks are also part of what distinguishes GALA groups from other community choirs. As Frances Bird of the mixed chorus the Glammaphones (of Wellington, New Zealand) explained, "If anyone walked into a [Glammaphones] rehearsal, they would pick up that this is a group of queer people, by listening to the jokes" (interview, March 8, 2014). She recalled that most of the jokes contained some kind of sexual innuendo; examples included jokes about blow jobs and rimming. She noted, "It's not just men making these jokes, definitely women do it too . . . and I have to admit, I'm guilty of a lot of it!" Ciaran Krueger, artistic director of the Buffalo Gay Men's Chorus and other community choirs, told me that all choristers make jokes but that the banter is "different" in the Buffalo Gay Men's Chorus: "Some nights, I know they're waiting for me, because they know I'm straight. They're waiting to make a joke out of what I say" (interview, January 28, 2012). Krueger explained that when he began engaging in the sexually suggestive banter of the choristers, he experienced a more profound sense of acceptance from them. Krueger called one particular chorister a "bitch" after this man was jokingly referred to as such by other singers. "I think some [of the singers] didn't really trust me until then," he said. "In fact, after that rehearsal, a few of the guys told me, 'I couldn't really relax with you until you started joking with us.'"

Previous Musical Experience

GALA singers strongly resemble singers in other community choirs in that the majority of GALA singers have some other kind of musical experience before they join their GALA chorus. Cindy L. Bell's (2004, 44) review article, for example, which compiles the results of studies of choral singers conducted throughout the last three decades of the twentieth century, explains that large majorities of community choir singers (from 59 to 82 percent) sang in their high school choir. In my sample of fifty-seven GALA singers, thirty-three people (58 percent) claimed previous experience in a school choir, and twenty-eight (49 percent) said they sang previously in a church or synagogue choir. Twenty-two (39 percent) said they played a musical instrument while growing up, mostly brass instruments (trombone, French horn, trumpet) and piano. Again, this kind of instrumental music background is common to community singers across the United States (Bell 2004, 45). Of course, many GALA choristers have a variety of earlier musical experiences, reporting that they both sang *and* played instruments in other ensembles before coming to GALA. To give just one example: Donald Butchko, a baritone in the North Coast Men's Chorus of Cleveland, Ohio, sang in community, school, and church choirs as a youth, participated in a barbershop quartet during his high school years, and took piano lessons (interview, September 25, 2014). Others in my sample reported that they had earned university degrees in music, without specifying whether they had participated in school ensembles prior to their university study—although this is the logical assumption. My own conclusions, expressed as percentages, are suggestive rather than definitive. One finding leaps out, however: of the fifty-seven GALA singers I interviewed, only three (5 percent) said that they had never sung in a choir or played in an instrumental group prior to joining their GALA chorus. Clearly, previous musical experience is overwhelmingly common to GALA singers. In other words, they arrive at their GALA choruses with years of training in the Western art music tradition.

Because GALA singers have long experience with and appreciation for Western art music, they hire chorus directors who have extensive training in this tradition. Of the twenty-five GALA artistic directors I interviewed, seventeen (68 percent) had master's or doctoral degrees in some area of music, usually choral conducting. Four others (16 percent) had bachelor's degrees in music, bringing the total number of university-trained music specialists to 84 percent. Of the remaining four GALA artistic directors in this study, one held a PhD in a different field of study, one was working on (and has since completed) a music degree, and the other two had many years of experience in church music prior to picking up their GALA batons. To summarize: GALA choristers deeply value traditional choral music expertise, as they demonstrate in their hiring patterns. It is this kind of professional preparation that they prioritize, rather than the sexual orientation of the artistic director.[13]

Artistic Excellence

GALA choruses share another important trait with other community choirs: the singers and artistic directors of GALA choruses are committed to choral excellence. I heard this focus on excellence articulated in different ways by many different people. For example, Derek Smith, a baritone in the Gay Men's Chorus of Washington, DC, said that the musical excellence of this chorus is one of the main reasons he participates in it: "I'm very proud of it! The musicality and the talent in this chorus is mind-blowing—and I get to be part of that. It's one of the best choruses in the world" (interview, September 2, 2016). Catherine Roma, founder of MUSE, Cincinnati's Women's Choir, explained that MUSE first belonged to an umbrella organization called Sister Singers Network, which represents feminist choruses. MUSE was glad to claim membership in GALA Choruses as well, Roma said, because "GALA encouraged us in our focus on musical excellence" (interview, January 19, 2012).[14] At a meeting of GALA artistic directors in 2011, a participant raised the idea of GALA choruses performing with Lesbian and Gay Band Association (LGBA) bands in their respective cities; the consensus was that such performances are rare because LGBA groups "usually aren't up to the musical standard."[15] And Eve Campbell, an influential leader in GALA circles, argued that the pursuit of musical excellence must be central to GALA choruses' endeavors: "Artistic quality is what will allow GALA choruses to survive [in the future]; we can't survive on being gay and proud anymore" (interview, January 17, 2011).

Generally, GALA insiders understand choral excellence in two ways: first, as collective sound; and second, as songs, often called repertoire. When they spoke about their choruses' efforts to inculcate excellence, singers generally focused on the first of these understandings, describing how their choruses insisted that individuals sing the right note, at the right time, in the right way. Brandon Dowdy, for example, said that the chorus in which he sings, the Turtle Creek Chorale (of Dallas, Texas), has "an almost professional level of expectation" for its choral sound (interview, August 11, 2012). The Turtle Creek Chorale established the Turtle Academy, a series of musicianship classes designed for chorale singers, in 2013.[16] Veronica Crowe-Carpenter explained that the policy of her chorus, Windsong, Cleveland's Feminist Chorus, is that if a singer misses two or more rehearsals prior to a concert, she must "audition" to sing in that concert. Furthermore, the chorus sometimes calls extra required rehearsals for sections of the group, in order to ensure that these sections learn their music thoroughly. Crowe-Carpenter had mixed emotions about Windsong's commitment to an excellent sound. On the one hand, some singers had left the group because they "couldn't keep up" with the requirements, but on the other hand, she pointed out, the group's excellence is noted and celebrated: "Some audience members said [after a recent performance], 'I can't believe you're a non-auditioned chorus!'" (interview, November 2, 2014). Aditya Adiredja explained that his chorus, the Reveille Men's Chorus (of Tucson, Arizona), has a similar approach to fostering excellent sound. Reveille accepts all singers who wish to join, but the chorus has a "quality control mechanism" called CPR (for Choral Performance Review). Singers who have missed more than five rehearsals must undergo CPR—prove that they can sing their own parts independently—before being allowed to participate in the performance. Adiredja said that the process has real consequences: he personally knows some Reveille singers who "failed CPR" and were therefore not allowed to perform (interview, December 20, 2016).

Having heard many GALA choruses perform, I concur with the interlocutors who claimed that the choral sound of GALA choruses is generally excellent. An excellent choral sound is a subjective idea, but there is a consensus about what it entails among practitioners and scholars of Western art music (Ahlquist 2006b, 9). Among the GALA groups I have heard, the overwhelming majority sing the notes written on their scores; they sing these notes in tune (according to the Western diatonic scale) and with a full, clear, sound, such that each note is clearly audible. Moreover they sing these notes at the time notated on the score, meaning that their rhythmic control is tight. This timing is no easy feat, given that most of their songs include at least four voice parts, and each part is independent—that is, each part has its own notes and rhythms. GALA singers vary the volume at which they sing (from quiet to loud) and emphasize the pronunciation of the words in order to convey the meaning of the text. They work to include every voice; generally, no individual singer is audible above the others, unless that individual sings a solo. The technical terms for the sound events I have just described are tuning, timbre, ensemble, dynamics, diction, and blend. Across all these dimensions, so valued by choral singers and listeners, GALA choruses consistently perform excellently. As scholar and choral music director Adam Adler said, "GALA choruses have a real tradition of excellence and polish. I'm also impressed by the amount of music they learn, memorize, and perform in a given year. It's an exceptionally high amount compared to other community choirs" (interview, July 11, 2014). Adler also pointed out that GALA choruses increasingly attract "top-notch, well-trained conductors" with their excellent sound. Choir directors' reputations rise and fall based on the perceived sound of their choirs, and—as explained above—the opportunity to conduct a GALA chorus is increasingly of interest to people holding advanced degrees in choral conducting.

When composers and artistic directors discussed GALA's relative excellence, they more often focused on the repertoire the choruses sing and, especially, the quality of the many songs GALA groups have commissioned (that is, have paid composers to write). Quality of songs, or repertoire, is an even more amorphous idea than quality of choral sound, and I struggled to understand what my interlocutors meant by this notion, in part because they themselves were reluctant to be openly critical. However, it did become clear that there is a sense among *some* GALA insiders and outsiders that the repertoire of GALA choirs is less interesting—read: compelling or excellent—than that of other community choirs. David Mcintyre, former artistic director of Prairie Pride in Regina, Saskatchewan, said that when he arrived at Prairie Pride, "I realized, oh, their music is so dismal! They were singing a lot of corny lyrics. The music itself was badly written, and the texts were quite trite. Our music should be more meaningful than that!" (interview, July 31, 2012). To his credit, Mcintyre set about composing new music for the group in order to rectify this problem. Miguel Felipe, who holds a doctorate in choral conducting, said that his "academic colors shine" when he thinks about GALA repertoire and especially GALA commissions: "Some of it is so vapid and soooo cheesy; most GALA commissions are just not interesting" (interview, July 31, 2013). David Hodgkins, artistic director of Coro Allegro in Boston, Massachusetts, said gently that many GALA commissions "are not a good fit for Coro Allegro; they're just not challenging or interesting to sing" (interview, April 9, 2014). Vance George, artistic director emeritus of the San Francisco Symphony Chorus and guest conductor of some GALA choruses, underlined that "gay choruses are absolutely committed to artistic excellence" (interview, April 18, 2014). With that said, George admitted that while he has coached some GALA commissions that have premiered at the GALA Festival, he has never considered programming that music for the other community choirs with which he works. "I don't know that anyone would be interested," he said. Frank Albinder is an outsider to GALA. As a gay man, he is sympathetic to the mission of GALA choruses, but he has a strong critique of GALA repertoire: "GALA groups don't sing enough high-quality repertoire to meet my taste; their music doesn't appeal to me as a singer, as a conductor or as a listener. [GALA choruses'] mission statements put music at the top, but it's really not" (interview, January 30, 2012). Emphasizing that he is "a total musical snob," Albinder asserted that he too would not program any GALA commissions: "They're just not that good or interesting."

People who have composed commissioned works for GALA choruses include participants such as accompanists who have written a small amount of music (and only for their own GALA ensemble), full-time composers who hold academic positions, and some of the most celebrated composers in recent choral music history. David P. DeVenny's (1999) magisterial survey of American choral literature highlights dozens of composers who have written what are, in DeVenny's view, important and enduring works for choirs. DeVenny's book is valuable because it reflects the consensus opinion of many choral music lovers. At least ten composers celebrated by DeVenny have composed works on commission for various GALA choruses, among them Gwyneth Walker, Ned Rorem, Conrad Susa, David Diamond, Gian Carlo Menotti, Daniel Pinkham, David Conte, and Roger Bourland. Libby Larsen, who composed a piece for the first-ever GALA Festival in 1983, is described by DeVenny as "heiress to the compositional mantle" of Aaron Copland and other storied American composers (260). John Corigliano, who composed for GALA in 2016, is "one of today's reigning composers" (252) according to DeVenny. Most followers of choral music would agree with these assessments. It is hard to imagine that these composers, whose other compositions are so widely appreciated, wrote uninteresting or low-quality works when they were commissioned by GALA choruses. Where then does this idea originate that all of GALA's compositions are uninteresting? DeVenny labels the composers listed above as "traditionalists" rather than "experimentalists," and it is true that their works for GALA choruses have generally not pushed the musical boundaries of the Western art music tradition. It is possible also that these works are less challenging to perform than the works these composers wrote for professional musicians.

The full-time composers I interviewed for this book—Roger Bourland, Mark Carlson, and David Conte—have impressive careers creating music for a variety of musical organizations and individuals, and each was insistent that they were honored to write for GALA Choruses. "I am very grateful to the San Francisco Gay Men's Chorus and other groups for making some of my works possible," said Conte (interview, April 21, 2014). However, these composers also acknowledged that GALA choruses are community choruses, and because they were aiming for successful performances, they kept the amateur status of the singers in mind while writing. Bourland pointed out that "there are probably only three or four GALA choruses who actively say, 'We want to do difficult music.' When I wrote for GALA, I kept in mind that the singers come from all walks of life. So I tried to write in a variety of styles. Some of the pieces were more pop sounding than classical, and they were very melodically driven" (interview, December 10, 2012). Carlson explained that at the time he wrote his first GALA commission, in the early 1990s, he was not especially familiar with the GALA organization. "I would never compose such a technically challenging piece for them again," he said (interview, July 30, 2013).

Some other GALA insiders, who declined to go on the record with their negative opinions about the quality of GALA's commissioned repertoire, used terms like "two-dimensional," and "schlocky." Overall, we can say that GALA choruses, in contrast with other community choirs, corporately commission a large number of songs and multimovement works. Furthermore, they commission music from a variety of composers, some of whom have less experience, formal training, and confidence than others.[17] Within this large body of recently created music, some songs stand out for their beauty and impact, while others—to my ear at least—do not merit the time and attention of GALA's dedicated volunteer performers. I agree with Joe Buches, artistic director of the Philadelphia Gay Men's Chorus, who said, "There's lots of great music in GALA! And a lot of it does sound similar . . . some composers have cranked things out that aren't very good. But that happens in the classical world too!" (interview, March 27, 2012).

It is important to examine how choral excellence is understood inside and outside GALA circles because there is a persistent—although hopefully dying—impression among some choral music leaders in the United States and Canada that GALA choruses are not excellent, either in their sound or by virtue of the repertoire they perform.[18] Again, conductors and others who expressed this view to me were generally unwilling to go on the record. However evidence of this stigma is clear from the experiences of GALA insiders. David Hodgkins recalled vividly that when he considered becoming a GALA chorus conductor, "There was a bit of an uproar. My mentor said, "Be careful, David, this could label you" (interview, April 9, 2014). More recently, a doctoral student, who shall remain anonymous here, proposed to write her dissertation about one of America's largest and best-known men's choruses. Her graduate school advisor refused for an entire year to approve her proposal, "because he believed that gay choirs were not a worthy subject of study. He said to me, 'What could we possibly learn about choral music from a gay men's chorus?'" (interview, July 4, 2016). Tim Seelig, a longtime GALA leader, served on the Chorus America board for a number of years. He became convinced that his fellow board members' continual criticisms stemmed from jealousy. "They were threatened by the rising success of GALA. They believed that gays were leaving symphony choruses and other choirs for GALA, so their reaction was to say that GALA groups don't make good music," Seelig reported (interview, September 15, 2011).

The reality is that GALA Choruses is a large and growing organization, currently representing more than two hundred member choruses. Some perform on a level playing field with professional ensembles in the large cultural centers where they are located. Other smaller choruses present shorter, simpler programs—and at times, they even sing out of tune. But they universally strive for choral excellence, and generally, they achieve it. Joe Nadeau, the artistic director of the Gay Men's Chorus of Los Angeles, has attended the GALA Festival five times. He averred that he has seen "a sharp increase in artistic quality" among GALA choruses during this time (interview, July 8, 2012). Ben Riggs, artistic director of the Twin Cities Gay Men's Chorus (of Minneapolis, Minnesota) echoed Nadeau—and indeed, many of my interviewees—saying that he too has noticed a tangible increase in choral excellence during his years working with GALA groups. "But there ought to be room for *all* choirs in GALA," he stated (interview, August 15, 2013). Composer Mark Carlson was blunt: "People who turn up their nose at GALA probably haven't heard many groups recently" (interview, July 30, 2013).

GALA insiders acknowledge that their commitment to choral excellence exists in tension with other values they hold dear. Specifically, choruses struggle to maintain the principle of inclusivity—including all singers who wish to participate—while simultaneously building an excellent sound and learning difficult music. Choral singing is a learned skill, and some singers are more skillful than others. "It's a fine line we walk," said Eric Unhold of the North Coast Men's Chorus, "creating top-quality music while also fostering a brotherhood" (interview, October 13, 2014). Cory Barrett, leader of the Mosaic Youth Chorus in Denver, Colorado, said, "My greatest desire is that we would sing the highest quality of music possible, but . . . seeing young people find a sense of comfort by being their authentic selves outweighed that. There is a tension between musical excellence and providing a safe space" (interview, December 12, 2016). Jody Malone, artistic director of Singing OUT in Toronto, Canada, resolves this tension in favor of upholding inclusivity: "I won't ever kick the monotone angels out of my choir, so I accept that this means that the highest quality singing is not always possible" (interview, October 13, 2011). Vic Hooper, former artistic director of the Rainbow Harmony Project in Winnipeg, Manitoba, expressed concern that the excellent sound of the group might in fact be a barrier to inclusivity: "Accepting all singers can work against the musical excellence focus in RHP's mission statement," he agreed. "But now the music level [of the Rainbow Harmony Project] is so high, I worry that people may be afraid to audition" (interview, September 9, 2011).

This tension is pervasive. Some interviewees argued that GALA choruses should define themselves as upholding one or the other principle; that is, a GALA chorus should state forthrightly either that it is committed to pursuing choral excellence above all else or that it values inclusivity more highly than excellence.[19] But others—including some of the most influential leaders in GALA Choruses—insisted that the drives to sound excellent and to be broadly inclusive are complementary rather than mutually exclusive. Dennis Coleman, artistic director emeritus of the Seattle Men's Chorus and the Seattle Women's Chorus, understands why these two priorities might seem to conflict; he points out that the artistic directors who are now being attracted to GALA choruses are products of the US and Canadian higher education system and have absorbed that system's values. "In academia, the idea is to perform 'great works,' and there's no training in social activism" (interview, September 1, 2011). "But *because* I believe so strongly in the mission, I feel compelled to make the finest art possible" (interview, September 24, 2011). Stan Hill, retired artistic director of the Twin Cities Gay Men's Chorus, elucidated the idea that his chorus ought to give gay men a voice: "Singing is super important for my [chorus] members. I give them a tool to tell their story" (interview, September 24, 2011). At the same time, he acknowledged, "The chorus should sound good. I believe I best serve my singers by training them to excellence." Rich Cook, artistic director emeritus of MenAlive, the Orange County Gay Men's Chorus, said that music and message are intricately linked: "If the artistic standards decline, the social aspect will also decline, because then the drive and purpose is gone. We have a mission to reach into the community at large, and to do that, you have to be worth listening to" (interview, May 14, 2012).

Ultimately, the large majority of my interlocutors robustly defended their GALA choruses as being musically excellent, or of high quality, or some other synonym, while agreeing that excellence can be difficult to define. Some pointed out that excellence is routinely assessed by others, such as leaders of professional ensembles and judges at musical competitions. They argued that many GALA choruses have been deemed excellent by such outsiders, and that receiving their imprimatur was confirmation of the choruses' excellence. Drew Kotchan of the Calgary Men's Chorus pointed out that this group has twice been invited to perform with the Calgary Philharmonic Orchestra, "so our sound must be, well, not amateur" (interview, July 27, 2013). Vic Hooper rejoiced that the Rainbow Harmony Project had twice won prestigious prizes at the Winnipeg Music Festival, and was engaged to perform with the Winnipeg Symphony Orchestra (interview, September 9, 2011). Bryan Fetty explained that the North Coast Men's Chorus has been invited to perform with the Cleveland Pops Orchestra and for the Cleveland Foundation, and has even opened for Joan Rivers: "If we were shoddy, they wouldn't have invited us" (interview, October 9, 2014). However, most of the US-based GALA insiders I interviewed pointed to one particular organization as that which provides the most important stamp of approval: the

American Choral Directors Association (ACDA). David Conte outlined the situation explicitly; speaking of "really good choirs," he said, "I mean that they have attained a degree of excellence that would result in being invited to an ACDA convention—as some of the GALA choruses have been" (interview, April 21, 2014).

GALA Choruses and the ACDA

Established in 1959, the ACDA is a professional music society to which most university-based choral conductors belong; it also represents thousands of other choir directors across the United States, including conductors of school, community, and professional choirs. Its mission is "to inspire excellence in choral music." The ACDA offers many resources to its members, including a webpage showing advertisements for jobs in choral performance and administration. ACDA members especially value the organization's annual conferences, which are held at the state, regional, and national level. Many activities take place at these conferences, such as workshops and reading sessions, but most importantly for our consideration—and most importantly for GALA singers and directors—the conferences always include performances by selected choirs. Because the ACDA is a widely recognized arbiter of choral excellence, an invitation to sing at an ACDA conference is an imprimatur of quality. Singers and conductors across America are honored to be selected to perform at an ACDA venue, and this honor is reflected in the way they speak about this opportunity. To give just one example: in an article in the Rutgers University student newspaper celebrating the selection of the Rutgers University Glee Club to sing at the 2017 national ACDA conference, the author characterizes the glee club as "esteemed," points out that "only ensembles singing at the highest level" are considered for performance at an ACDA conference, and calls the conference "the premiere choral event of the season" (Peterson 2017). GALA insiders also quietly brag about their performances at ACDA events, both during interviews and on their choruses' websites.[20] For GALA choruses, being selected to sing at an ACDA conference is especially meaningful because of the ACDA's history of discriminating against gay-identified choirs. In other words, to be selected by the ACDA is not only to be evaluated as excellent, it is also to be recognized as an equal member of the choral music community. Longtime GALA participants vividly recall an era when such recognition was unfairly denied.

To understand how the ACDA has discriminated against GALA choruses, we must first understand how the ACDA leadership selects the choirs that will perform at its conferences. Elected and appointed leaders of the ACDA—including conductors whose choirs have previously been selected to perform at an ACDA conference—hold so-called blind auditions, during which they listen to submitted recordings without knowing the name of either the choir or the conductor. Ben Riggs, who has participated in these ACDA blind auditions, says that the process has integrity, and that as a member of the audition committee he did not know the identifying information of the choirs to whom he listened (interview, August 15, 2013). The audition committee members are supposed to issue invitations "based solely on the quality of the musical performances as demonstrated in the audition recordings" (American Choral Directors Association 2016).

Gary Miller, the founding artistic director of the New York City Gay Men's Chorus, recounted to me the history that follows.[21] The residual anger in Miller's voice in 2014, when we spoke about what had occurred thirty years earlier, was significant. In 1984, just four years after it was founded, the New York City Gay Men's Chorus submitted an audition tape to the ACDA, seeking to perform at the upcoming Eastern Division conference. The ACDA accepted the chorus's submission due to the quality of the men's singing on the tape, only belatedly realizing that it had issued an invitation to a gay men's chorus. ACDA representatives then said that the group would only be allowed to perform if it agreed to be billed as a "Men's Chorus"—rather than as a "Gay Men's Chorus." Miller recalled that a number of choir directors rallied to the support of the New York City Gay Men's Chorus, and it did ultimately perform at the Eastern Division conference (interview, June 27, 2014). But he also pointed out that the official program from that conference did not list the chorus's true name, and that this official record has never been corrected. Ultimately, the New York City Gay Men's Chorus took the ACDA to court over this issue and won. Two years later, similar events transpired in California: the Gay Men's Chorus of Los Angeles won a blind audition to perform at the ACDA's Western Division conference in 1986. However, the organizers of the conference denied the chorus the right to print its full name in the conference program; they insisted that identifying the chorus as "gay" would be too controversial. The Gay Men's Chorus of Los Angeles enlisted the help of the American Civil Liberties Union in filing a lawsuit against the ACDA. Here again, the gay men's chorus ultimately prevailed in court.

Current GALA participants still remember and resent the treatment that these influential gay men's choruses received from the ACDA in the 1980s. GALA chorus websites explain the importance of performing at ACDA conferences using their full names. For example, the website of the Windy

City Gay Chorus of Chicago says, "WCGC was greeted by a standing ovation on April 5, 1986, at the ACDA Central Regional Conference in Indianapolis after winning the fight to sing using its full name, instead of being barred because the word 'Gay' was part of the chorus' moniker. WCGC benefited from earlier litigation brought, and won out of court, by the Gay Men's Chorus of Los Angeles" (Windy City Sings n.d.b.). Similarly, the Wikipedia page of the Twin Cities Gay Men's Chorus recounts, "In November 2006, TCGMC became the first gay men's chorus with the word 'gay' in its name to perform for the American Choral Directors Association at an ACDA convention since 1986, when the Los Angeles Gay Men's Chorus successfully sued for inclusion" (Wikipedia n.d.). Indeed, being in some way "the first" GALA chorus at a particular ACDA event has become a point of pride in itself. Singer John Whalen told me that his chorus, One Voice Mixed Chorus in Saint Paul, Minnesota, had been "one of the first [GALA choruses] to sing at ACDA" (interview, January 3, 2013). Jane Ramseyer-Miller, the artistic director of this chorus, told me that because One Voice does not have a gay name, she "made it very clear from the stage and from telling our story. I identified who we were at ACDA" (interview, November 1, 2011).

In the wake of the legal battles between the ACDA and GALA choruses, in April 1990, the ACDA published an article by Eric A. Gordon titled "GALA: The Lesbian and Gay Community of Song" in its professional magazine, the *Choral Journal*. One of the earliest publications about GALA choruses, this article laid out a great amount of factual information and dipped into some of the questions explored in this book, including why singers join GALA choruses, and whether the choruses are "any good" (29). The reaction to this article was swift and strong. In a subsequent issue, three letters to the editor objected to the publication of the article. The authors of these letters, all of whom identified themselves as church music ministers, said they were "utterly disgusted," "greatly disturbed," and "physically sick" on seeing the article in an ACDA publication, and they threatened to withdraw their memberships from the ACDA (*Choral Journal* 31, no. 1, 5–6). They claimed to be speaking on behalf of "a good percentage of ACDA members" who held church-related positions. (One other letter, which lauded the publication of the Gordon article, also appeared; it was much shorter). Importantly, none of these letters addressed any substantive claims of the Gordon article; rather, the writers objected to the ACDA giving any kind of positive recognition whatsoever to practicers of "sexual perversion." The objections continued in the next issue of the journal, but the editors also included rebuttals from GALA's Dennis Coleman and Gary Miller. Finally, in the October 1990 issue of the journal (31, no. 3), the balance tipped. The editors included one letter representing the objecting faction but printed three other letters—again from church music ministers—condemning the prejudice articulated in the first letters. At this point, the journal editor felt compelled to add this note: "I have received many more communications concerning the GALA article and subsequent responses to it. . . . No further letters on the GALA subject will be published" (*Choral Journal* 31, no. 3, 8).

This correspondence, aired in the pages of a widely circulated ACDA publication, further demonstrated the homophobic attitudes of some substantial faction of the ACDA membership, attitudes that had first come to light during litigation. Longtime GALA artistic directors remember it distinctly and cite it as proof that GALA choruses, through their first decade of existence at least, were not welcome in the ACDA. They also recall more subtle forms of discrimination by ACDA members, ways in which ACDA conference attendees endeavored to show their disapproval of GALA choruses and of homosexuality more generally. Gary Miller remembered manning a booth at the 1985 ACDA national conference in Salt Lake City; "it was funny to see how some ACDA members avoided even walking by," he said (interview, June 27, 2014). Tim Seelig recalled that ACDA members threatened to boycott a performance by the Turtle Creek Chorale (interview, September 15, 2011), and Ben Riggs confirmed that he saw numerous people walk out of the Turtle Creek Chorale's ACDA performance in 2004 (interview, August 15, 2013). Memories of this kind of behavior inspire angry comments from GALA insiders. Gary Holt, former artistic director of the San Diego Gay Men's Chorus, for example, said that "GALA has been treated like an illegitimate stepchild by the ACDA for years."[22] The overt hostility toward LGBT people in ACDA circles was apparent to, and acknowledged by, GALA outsiders as well. For example, Frank Albinder, a former ACDA national chair for repertoire and standards, said he was convinced that the reason that Chanticleer, a Grammy Award–winning professional men's ensemble from San Francisco, was not invited to the ACDA's national conferences for several years was that "people suspected they were gay" (interview, January 30, 2012).

Reflecting on the history of discrimination against gay-identified choruses by the ACDA, Ben Riggs argued that the appropriate response is for GALA choruses and their artistic directors to continue to push for recognition and inclusion by the ACDA. "GALA directors must join the ACDA. We must break down that wall! It comes from a lot of pain. But the more involvement with the ACDA, the better" (interview, August 15, 2013). It seems that many of GALA's current artistic directors agree with Riggs. For example, at a meeting of forty-four GALA artistic directors in 2011, seven raised their hand when asked, "Who plans to attend the ACDA national convention in Chicago?"[23] Now that a critical mass of GALA conductors attend ACDA events, they hold informal GALA only meetings at ACDA conferences (David Hodgkins, interview, April 9, 2014). Furthermore, some GALA artistic directors make ACDA conference presentations. Joe Buches presented on GALA repertoire at the February 2012 ACDA Eastern Division conference. His presentation was introduced by the ACDA president (the most senior person in the ACDA), and Buches's impression was that the approximately thirty people in the audience "loved it" (interview, March 27, 2012). Finally, three of the twenty-five GALA artistic directors I interviewed took on leadership roles in the ACDA, sitting on state or national committees, organizing conferences, and the like.[24]

By the time I conducted the research for this book, GALA choruses seemed to be welcome in the ACDA. In fact, the "Men's/TTBB Choirs" page of the ACDA's website now links to the GALA website, encouraging ACDA members to see GALA as a "resource" (American Choral Directors Association n.d.). Still, as we have seen, acts of discrimination perpetrated by the ACDA loom large in GALA's collective memory. And it is this facet of their experience—being subject to discrimination as LGBT-identified choirs—that sharply distinguishes GALA choruses from other community choirs.

Discrimination against LGBT Individuals and GALA Choruses

Scholars acknowledge that experiencing discrimination based on one's sexual identity—or fearing this kind of discrimination—is normative for LGBT people. Frank Browning (1993, 166) asserts that groups of gay men are always marked by a "fear of loss and obliteration" due to the history of persecution of gay men by straight societies. In fact, he says, it is almost impossible to grow up suspecting that one is gay and *not* fear marginalization and death. In an ethnographic study of gay and lesbian people, Kath Weston (1991, 62) found that one-third of her interviewees were rejected by their families when they came out—that is, revealed their sexual orientation to their families— and that the "vast majority" of them feared being either rejected or disowned (see also Gray 2009, 133–34). While conducting research among GALA insiders, I encountered two stories of horrific, sexually-based discrimination: one singer incurred life-threatening injuries when he was violently attacked outside a gay bar by White supremacists who were determined to assault a "faggot" (Patrick Holcomb, interview, September 14, 2014); another was viciously and repeatedly harassed at his workplace (David Greene, interview, October 10, 2014). In GALA circles, however, it is more common to fear or anticipate discrimination, although both individuals and choruses have experienced unmistakable episodes of discrimination stemming from their identification as LGBT people or groups.

This fear of sexually-based discrimination is the cause of some GALA norms that are unknown in other community choirs. For example, artistic directors and choristers understand that some singers may decline to participate in specific concerts because these concerts have a larger-than-usual audience or may mark the chorus as "gay" more strongly than usual. Singers have therefore bowed out of concerts that were televised, or concerts performed as part of Pride month.[25] And in the past, artistic directors of GALA choruses sometimes declined to list their GALA conducting experience on their résumés in order to avoid a negative impression at being identified with an LGBT group. Willi Zwozdesky, the longtime artistic director of the Vancouver Men's Chorus, remembers that when he first contemplated assuming this position, colleagues told him that he would "commit professional suicide" if he conducted a gay chorus (interview, September 5, 2011). Dennis Coleman independently used the same expression; in the 1980s, he said, "taking a GALA job as your first [choral conducting] job would have been professional suicide, because no church or university would hire you with a gay chorus on your résumé" (interview, September 24, 2011). This stigma explains why, in past decades, artistic directors like Regina Carlow did not actually claim their work on their professional documents. Carlow, the former director of the Lesbian and Gay Chorus of Washington, DC, reported that she began including that experience on her résumé only in 2004—years after she actually served in the position—because she "feared it would hinder [her] chance of being hired" for future jobs (interview, September 15, 2012).

Rank-and-file singers, too, have resisted being identified in printed materials associated with their choruses. Choristers have asked to be removed from their own chorus's mailing list because the chorus had its name printed on its envelopes (Amy Moore, interview, February 16, 2012). In addition, choristers have requested that their names not be printed in concert programs. Chorus administrators have dealt with this request in different ways: by leaving out certain names entirely, or by listing choristers as "anonymous," or by printing choristers' first names only.[26] Although this concern among singers seems to have abated over time, as of the second decade of the twenty-first century, some GALA choruses still ask each singer to sign a release form allowing for their name to be printed in concert programs, and for their image to be included in chorus photos.[27] Jean-Louis Bleau, former artistic director of the Calgary Men's Chorus, remembered a specific concert in 2007 because it was the first time all of the singers' names were printed in the program, a milestone for which he was grateful (interview, June 24, 2016).

Other GALA choruses are still working toward this milestone. It is important to note that choristers' fear of being identified in print materials that are intended for circulation has a rational, historical basis. In the United States, during the 1950s, departments of the federal government worked to identify and then prosecute homosexuals. The US Postal Service identified homosexual men by placing tracers on physique magazines (that is, magazines that were appreciated by gay men), and then by tracking the mail of those with whom the suspected homosexuals corresponded. The US Postal Service reported these names to the Federal Bureau of Investigation; as a result, people lost their jobs (D'Emilio 1983, 47). Indeed, this fear of being identified in print material that could be mailed was so pervasive that, through the 1990s, "nearly all gay and lesbian rights organizations [did] not mail newsletters or mailings in envelopes that identify them as gay or lesbian [organizations]" (Vaid 1995, 29).

What specific forms of discrimination do GALA participants fear? The most common response to this question was that they feared losing their jobs once they were identified as LGBT, as Regina Carlow explained above.[28] Again, that fear of job loss is based not on speculation but on the historical experiences of individuals, including individuals who are very well known in GALA circles and who were fired from religiously-affiliated institutions.[29] Dennis Coleman and Joe Nadeau both lost their jobs (as an ordained Southern Baptist music minister, and as a music teacher at a Catholic school, respectively) when they revealed that they were gay (Coleman, interview, September 1, 2011; Nadeau, interview, February 20, 2011). Eve Campbell, one of GALA's 411 advisors (serving as a consultant for member choruses), worked for twenty years as a nurse at Presbyterian Women's Clinic in Dallas, Texas; after she appeared in a photo accompanying a news story about her GALA chorus, the clinic never called again to offer her work (interview, January 7, 2011). While I conducted research for this book, another of my interlocutors suffered the same discrimination: Al Fischer, the former artistic director of the Gateway Men's Chorus in St. Louis, Missouri, was fired from both of his jobs—at a Catholic school and at a Catholic church—when he married his longtime male partner (Leland 2012).

Individual GALA participants' experiences with discrimination—and their legitimate fear of discrimination based on the personal stories they have heard from their GALA colleagues—are echoed by the discrimination they have suffered corporately as choruses. In the past, GALA choruses have been threatened with, or even subjected to, physical violence. Sue Fink, founding artistic director of the Los Angeles Women's Community Chorus, recalled that during the 1980s, when the chorus performed in Mississippi, the Ku Klux Klan burned a cross in front of the performance venue (interview, March 12, 2012). In the same time period, while the Vancouver Men's Chorus was rehearsing in downtown Vancouver, a group of people banged on the door yelling "Faggot!" Willi Zwozdesky was dismissive of this incident when he told me about it, but then acknowledged that choristers were concerned enough at the time that they began asking nonsinging members of the group to serve as security guards (interview, September 5, 2011). On March 10, 2001, while the Vancouver Lesbian and Gay Choir was onstage performing, it was attacked with bear spray, which, as their artistic director pointed out, is ten times stronger than pepper spray (Carol Sirianni, interview, October 9, 2011).

More commonly, GALA choruses have been marginalized and slighted. Insiders vividly recall incidents during which audience members made their disapproval clear by walking out of GALA chorus performances after the performances began, such as what Ben Riggs observed at the 2004 ACDA conference. The same thing occurred when the Heartland Men's Chorus of Kansas City, Missouri, performed at a large retirement community (Eric Aufdengarten, interview, October 25, 2011). And when One Voice was invited to perform at a local school, parents of the students not only declined to send their children to school that day but also wrote letters to the principal demanding that the music teacher—who had invited One Voice—be fired (Jane Ramseyer-Miller, interview, November 1, 2011). Other instances of singling out GALA choruses for unfair treatment abound. For years in Dayton, Ohio, the local CBS affiliate (WHIO-TV) refused to include the Dayton Gay Men's Chorus concerts in its announcements of community events.[30] The Rainbow Harmony Project once reserved a local Bible camp for a choir retreat; when the camp leaders realized that the Rainbow Harmony Project consists mostly of gay- and lesbian-identified people, they canceled the reservation (Vic Hooper, interview, September 9, 2011). In 1996, the First Baptist Church of Dallas, Texas, canceled an ACDA event that it had previously agreed to host, when it discovered that the concert was to include the Turtle Creek Chorale and the Dallas Women's Chorus.[31]

Discriminatory incidents like the ones just listed—in which institutions or individuals refused to offer the same services (or even the same basic respect) to a GALA chorus that they would offer to any other community choir—provide historical context for contemporary incidents and influence how more recent events are interpreted. For example, in May 2016, the San Diego Gay Men's Chorus agreed to sing the US national anthem at a San

Diego Padres baseball game (Moran 2016). When the time came to sing, instead of the sound of the choir, the audience heard a recording of a solo woman singing the anthem. The Padres organization later blamed a control room error. However, as the official statement from the San Diego Gay Men's Chorus pointed out, the error could have been easily corrected in real time. Instead, the recording played for the entire duration of the song, forcing the group of men to stand on the field in silence, while being represented—and possibly mocked—by a female voice. The singers found this event to be an embarrassing "nightmare"; the chorus immediately called on the Padres to conduct an investigation into whether a hate crime had occurred. Ultimately, the San Diego Gay Men's Chorus agreed with the findings of the investigation, which were that the incident resulted from human error rather than from homophobic intent (Kenney and Serna 2016). However, given the long history of discrimination leveled against LGBT individuals and against GALA choruses, choristers had a rational basis for suspecting they had been publicly discriminated against, and for demanding an investigation into this possibility.

GALA Festival

As we have seen, GALA choruses resemble other community choirs in important ways, including their singers' level of previous musical experience, their focus on fundraising, and their commitment to artistic excellence as defined by the gatekeepers of the choral music scene (although they have not always been given credit for the last). They also differ from other community choirs in other ways, including how singers behave during rehearsals and their experiences with significant discrimination by outside organizations. In the balance of this chapter, I outline another aspect of GALA choruses' work and life together: their participation in the quadrennial GALA Festival. Here again, with this regularly scheduled international choral event, we see that GALA choruses bear both a resemblance to and a distinction from other community choirs. Many choirs attend local and international choral festivals, and their singers often spend months raising money in order to travel to these events. Choral festivals are therefore significant to community choirs in general. The GALA Festival, however, is distinct: it is a momentous event that functions to foster in GALA singers, artistic directors, composers, and board members the sense that they are participants in a movement. Every four years, the GALA Festival reinforces to GALA insiders that they are working for a cause bigger than themselves, "changing our world through song" as their GALA mission statement says. Indeed, attending the Festival is so important to the GALA experience of many singers and artistic directors that, during interviews with me, they recounted their history with the organization by listing all the Festivals they had attended. In fact, they often conflated GALA with the Festival in statements like: *I went to my first GALA in 1996 in Tampa*. It became abundantly clear that the GALA Festival is the crowning event in the lives of choruses and individuals.

GALA Choruses began hosting the Festival in 1983, and the organization has continued to host the Festival every three or four years since then (GALA Choruses n.d.b.). During the Festival, member choruses come together in a designated city to perform for each other and for audiences in that city. Most attendees therefore participate as singers for a brief part of their Festival time, and as listeners for the bulk of the remaining time. The main focus of the Festival is choral performances, which go on from morning to night for roughly one week. All attending singers also have the opportunity to participate in other events, including so-called Festival choruses, which are ad hoc groups that convene during the Festival week for two or three rehearsals and then perform a short concert together. (The 2016 GALA Festival, for example, included both a People of Color chorus and a Transgender Singers chorus.) In addition, the convening of thousands of GALA choristers affords the opportunity for other kinds of events, such as professional development workshops, sing-alongs, and parties hosted by specific choruses.

Although I speak about the GALA Festival in rather general terms in what follows, focusing on the Festival's consistent patterns, the GALA organization continues to evolve, and changes are most apparent at the Festivals. Therefore each Festival is a unique event, although each also belongs to a longer history in which certain norms are perpetuated. I attended the GALA Festival in 2012 and again in 2016, both times in Denver, Colorado. One consistent pattern I observed was the common, although not constant, appearance of ASL interpreters, who performed with various choruses (Balén 2009, 33). GALA choruses have no significant audience within the Deaf community, and during all the time I spent researching this book, I never heard any discussion of possible outreach to Deaf people. The ASL interpreters were simply symbols of GALA choruses' commitment to their mission of greater inclusion for diverse groups of people (Attinello 1994, 320). Although they are greatly valued by many GALA groups—indeed, some ASL interpreters are listed as staff members on choruses' websites—the regular featuring of ASL interpretation for Festival audiences who have no understanding of ASL is an unmistakable instance of tokenism. Other perfunctory gestures symbolizing concern for people outside of GALA are made during the Festival: for example, at the 2012 Festival, one of the local Denver-area choruses dedicated their performance to those who had suffered because of recent wildfires in Colorado.[32] In 2016, many choruses dedicated their singing to victims of the mass shooting at the Pulse Nightclub in Orlando, Florida. With that said, most of what happens at the Festival is not empty virtue-signaling, but rather sincere efforts to demonstrate choruses' musical and political commitments.

At the 2016 Festival, the organizers made a serious attempt to acknowledge diversity in the GALA ranks and to promote inclusivity, launching some new initiatives at that Festival (as I describe in chapter 3). Perhaps the most significant change I observed between 2012 and 2016 was in the demographic makeup of Festival delegates (as GALA calls all those who pay for a Festival pass). In 2012 I noted that the large majority of people at the Festival site were cisgender White men who appeared to be between the ages of twenty-five and sixty-five.[33] In 2016 I saw more young people who seemed to be flouting gender conventions in their choice of clothing or facial grooming, although the dominant majority of Festival delegates still appeared to be White, cisgender men.[34] If this trend holds, it will be tangible proof that GALA's efforts to support youth choruses and to celebrate gender diversity more openly are paying off.

Most of what I saw in 2012, however, was repeated in 2016. My sense of knowing what to expect in 2016 was no doubt reinforced by the fact that both years' events were held in downtown Denver. Both years, Denver's international airport displayed a large banner welcoming GALA delegates, and more banners were hung on lampposts around the Festival site. "The Mile High City Welcomes GALA," they proclaimed, demonstrating the common tendency to conflate the entire GALA organization with the quadrennial Festival.[35] The Festival program book contained an official welcome letter from the mayor of Denver, and all indications were that city officials were genuinely glad to host more than six thousand delegates and their families. No doubt they appreciated the financial boon the middle-class GALA delegates brought to their city for a week in high summer. The Festival site—a number of adjacent concert performance spaces—was further marked as a GALA space by the inclusion of a GALA store, which sold T-shirts and other clothing bearing the Festival logo. In 2012, one popular T-shirt read, "What happens at GALA . . . is life changing!" Vendors set up booths around the site; businesses represented included Kimpton Hotels (a chain of LGBT-friendly hotels), Yelton Rhodes (a music publisher that specializes in choral music by and for LGBT people),[36] and the San Francisco Gay Men's Chorus and other large GALA choruses, which sold their own recordings.

Celebrating Each Other at the Festival

The famed friendliness of the GALA Festival became evident to me the minute I boarded the airport shuttle in 2012: a fellow passenger immediately engaged me in conversation, asking, "Are you going to GALA?" Our dialogue quickly expanded to include all of the people on the shuttle, all of whom were also "going to GALA." This pattern continued throughout both my Festival experiences; every time I sat down beside a stranger, either at a local restaurant or at a Festival venue, they immediately began a friendly conversation with me. In fact, many interviews referenced in this book stem from an initial encounter at a Festival event. Notably, during all the time I spent at the Festival both years, I was never asked about my sexual orientation. As a straight woman, I had wondered whether I might feel something of an outsider at the Festival; I discovered that, while the Festival location is definitely an LGBT-friendly and LGBT-majority space, it includes absolutely no instances of mockery or disparagement of heterosexual people. Even as the streets of downtown Denver were mobbed with thousands of people wearing T-shirts identifying their local chorus, and a few of these people engaged in same-sex physical affection (holding hands, hugging, and kissing), there was no sense in which straight people were excluded.

During a workshop for artistic directors in 2011, the participants were reminded that the GALA Festival is all about "celebration and reunification."[37] Importantly, the GALA Festival, unlike many other choral festivals, is not a competition. GALA choruses do not compete for prizes at their Festival; they are not assigned rankings or given comments by judges. Prior to the 2012 Festival, there was some discussion among GALA artistic directors about organizing adjudicators (judges) who could offer optional assessments to choruses after their performances, but there were no adjudicators in evidence at the Festival itself, and for a chorus to have been subjected to scrutiny would have seemed bizarre in that context.[38] GALA singers and artistic directors gather together at the Festival not to assess one another's musical skills, but rather to appreciate one another and to revel in the knowledge that their musicianship is also equally appreciated.

Festival delegates show their appreciation for one another most consistently in their responses to performances. As GALA insiders often say, "Everyone at the Festival gets a standing O" (that is, a standing ovation). And indeed, in observing audience responses to dozens of Festival performances in 2012 and 2016, I found that almost every chorus received a standing ovation from its fellow GALA choristers. The sound of the applause was noticeably enthusiastic, often including feet stamping and wolf whistles. Some choruses received multiple standing ovations, with listeners rising to their feet to applaud repeatedly during a single performance. Some choruses even received standing ovations before they began to sing; examples included the combined Denver area choruses in 2012, the Beijing Queer Chorus in 2016, and youth choruses at both years' events. That the applause for all choruses, no matter how large or small, how experienced or how new, is so reliably enthusiastic, is a point of pride for GALA insiders. "I adore that everyone gets a standing O at Festival" said Darryl Hollister, accompanist for Coro Allegro (interview, June 30, 2014). Eric Unhold said of the Festival audience, "It is the most overwhelmingly supportive audience we have, because we're all in the same boat. It's a big happy lovefest!" (interview, October 13, 2014). Artistic directors no doubt appreciate the enthusiastic applause too, but they must take a pragmatic approach to this aspect of the Festival experience. As artistic directors were told during the previously mentioned 2011 GALA workshop, Festival stage managers hold choruses strictly to their time limits. Conductors must take the applause into account when calculating how long choruses can sing while onstage. GALA audiences are "very energetic and expressive," and therefore Festival ovations take longer than do ovations in other contexts.[39]

With that said, Festival delegates do display different levels of enthusiasm for their colleagues' Festival performances; we might say that they vote with both their hands and their feet. Over the course of the two years' events, I kept track of the very few choruses who did not—against expectations—receive standing ovations. Each of those were choruses whose sound impressed me as somewhat less than excellent—that is, as noticeably lower in quality than the high standard maintained across the GALA organization. Because this pattern was consistent, I deduced that for all the sincere friendliness and support that suffuses the GALA Festival, GALA insiders do exercise some artistic discrimination. They have a common understanding of what constitutes fine singing, and while they are willing to applaud singers who sing less well, they are not willing to affirm their performances as equal to the others (and therefore, not willing to grant them a standing ovation).

The Purpose of the GALA Festival

Festival delegates often speak about the Festival using superlatives, including "amazing" (Mike Killen, interview, September 23, 2016; Fred Poland, interview, June 16, 2011), "enlightening" (Manny Agon, interview, January 17, 2013), and "life-changing" (Brent Simmons, field notes, July 5, 2016). Stan Hill said about the Festival that "it's the most important, edifying, rich thing we do" (interview, September 24, 2011). For Katie Eadie, attending the 2016 Festival was deeply significant because it gave her the courage to begin telling others that she is a lesbian: "For me GALA [i.e., the Festival] was absolutely life-changing. Seeing people live authentically like that, and seeing the positive side of that, and believing that I could have that for myself. Before that, I had a lot of fear of coming out, but afterwards . . . it was like going from fear to hope" (interview, August 10, 2016). Those on the periphery of GALA, too, find that attending the Festival is an impactful experience because it clearly reveals not only what makes GALA choruses distinct, but also how emotionally salient that distinction is. Mark Carlson had little exposure to GALA groups when he attended the 1996 Festival. "It completely transformed the way that I thought about writing for GALA choruses," he said. It was at that Festival that Carlson realized that "[the] focus of these groups is primarily social, even those that are the most technically adept. [I realized that the singers were] gay men or lesbians who wanted the support of being together. It was a transformational experience for me because the energy was so high, musically and emotionally. . . . I heard groups from rural areas. I just sat there crying the whole time because of how brave they were" (interview, July 30, 2013). Donald Nally, an eminent choral conductor who was invited to guest conduct at the 2000 Festival, said that "it was a huge growing experience for me, and I'm very glad someone made me do that. I noticed that the setting was quite different from what I'm used to [at other competitive choral Festivals]. There are so many people chatting in the hall, and there's not much [rehearsal] time onstage before the performance, and so on. In the professional music scene [where I work] there are lots of gay people, and being out isn't a big deal. But at the GALA Festival I saw singers who weren't even out at their workplaces, standing onstage and proclaiming themselves as artists and gay people. And I saw that the audience would just go *nuts*, even for some very questionable performances. It was so moving, oh my God! It was eye-opening to me" (interview, September 10, 2012).

When pressed, Festival delegates sometimes have a hard time articulating the emotional impact of Festival participation, but they affirm that it is powerful: "The feeling inside, when you sit and listen to other choruses, and the tears, and the laughter. . . ." said Tom Fortuna, who trailed off when describing the importance of his having attended the GALA Festival three times (interview, October 16, 2014). It seems that for most GALA insiders, their most memorable activity during the Festival is not performing with their own chorus but rather listening to other choruses sing—an activity that sometimes causes them to weep. David Hodgkins, for example, has attended every Festival since Coro Allegro was founded in 1992. "It's a very powerful experience for the singers and the audience. And it reminds me that in certain parts of the country, it takes tremendous courage [for LGBT people] just to get together. It's very moving. There's an extra gear there, an extra sense of purpose: being proud of being out, and being proud of musical accomplishments. There's something else fueling that performance. It's just amazing" (interview, April 9, 2014).

The Festival is commonly known to be emotionally riveting, and the Festival space welcomes open displays of emotion, especially in response to choral performances. It is unremarkable for audience members to weep while listening to other choruses sing; I observed this occurrence, for example, in response to a 2012 Festival performance of Bobby Scott and Bob Russell's "He Ain't Heavy, He's My Brother."[40] I also saw singers in tears as they exited their performance venues to applauding listeners, who lined up outside the doors to continue to show appreciation, in another display of emotion. These red-carpet moments—as I thought of them, since they resembled the scenes at movie premieres—are common at the Festival. Listeners tend to line up to applaud at the end of a concert block, after four or more choirs have concluded their performances, and they appear in great numbers to support the largest choruses, especially men's choruses. In 2012, when the Kansas City Women's Chorus (of Missouri) exited its Festival venue and encountered red-carpet supporters, I counted five singers who were visibly crying. I told this story to Lisa Brotz, who is a singer in Harmony: A Colorado Chorale (of Denver) and a Festival veteran, and who had observed and experienced such red-carpet moments in the past. To her it made perfect sense that a show of support would move GALA singers to tears: "A lot of us have not had many opportunities to be applauded and cheered" (interview, July 10, 2012).

Why is Festival participation so consistently emotionally powerful? The answer to this question is tied to participants' sense of being motivated by that "extra gear" and "extra sense of purpose," as David Hodgkins put it. At the GALA Festival, all participating choruses are celebrated for their performances with enthusiastic applause, if not standing ovations, and—even more importantly—GALA insiders listen to and watch each other express their commonly held values. Ultimately, the GALA Festival serves to emphasize to GALA participants that they are part of something bigger than themselves, and it provokes emotions that motivate people to bind themselves to this overarching endeavor. Indeed, the Festival teaches delegates that they are participating in a "movement," as so many of them told me during interviews (see chapters 7 and 8 for more on GALA as a social movement). Congregating together during the Festival to sing to one another, Festival delegates take part in an event that they rightly compare to a religious experience.

This sense that Festival attendance is akin to participation in a religious activity was most potently demonstrated in an impromptu street performance following the final concert of the 2012 Festival. The last event of the concert consisted of a sing-along song that Jane Ramseyer-Miller, GALA's artistic director in residence, taught to the audience by rote. The song's lyrics are: "We are the ones / We are the change we've been waiting for / And we are dawning / We are the rising sun." Audience members joined hands, swaying together as they sang. After Ramseyer-Miller exited the stage, the audience continued to sing this song. I was seated on the upper balcony of the venue, and it took me nearly ten minutes to descend to the street; the song continued all that time. We headed out to the streets of downtown Denver, still singing. That week, city management had placed upright pianos on each block of the main street traversing the downtown area. When a group of singers arrived at one of these pianos, a man sat down and began to accompany the singers. The singers then began improvising their parts, in the style of an African American church choir. A large crowd gathered around, and several people filmed the event.

Standing beside that piano, singing the song over and over during that spontaneous performance, I experienced what Émile Durkheim ([1915] 1965, 241) called *effervescence*, which he believed was at the heart of religious rituals and the source of religious belief. "In the midst of an assembly animated by a common passion," Durkheim argued more than a century ago, "we become susceptible of [*sic*] acts and sentiments of which we are incapable when reduced to our own forces" (240). Durkheim explained that when an individual hears their own ideas echoed back to them by those around them—for example in the lyrics of a song being sung by the group—that individual's sentiments are "enlarged and amplified" (241). The "strengthening influence of society" causes individuals to feel their emotions more intensely (241), and the "collective force" that they experience is often identified using religious terms (240). The 2012 spontaneous event aroused in me a passionate conviction—something resembling a religious belief—that GALA choruses are a tangible and powerful force for good in the world. I felt joy in knowing that I was, for a few moments at least, a part of that "collective force." A man beside me referred to the effervescence of this moment by referencing religious experience directly. "This is better than a gospel camp meeting!" he said.[41]

Because hundreds of people continued to sing the same simple song for at least twenty minutes—and because at least three participants found this event to be important enough to film and archive on YouTube—I am confident that others also experienced a sense of effervescence. Some claimed to have experienced powerful emotions: Rick Aiello, who posted footage of the event on YouTube, commented that he found the experience to be "truly magical," and differencz, another poster, wrote, "It was a very moving experience." Lysander910 left a comment saying, "This still gives me goosebumps!"[42] There were other times when I witnessed festival delegates identify the emotions they were feeling by using religious analogies. For example, at the opening concert of the 2012 Festival, when all in attendance sang in call-and-response fashion with a soloist, someone behind me said, "Wow, it feels like church!"[43] So strongly did these and other Festival experiences resemble church services, as audiences sang in unison with choirs, and as audience members held hands and wept, that I found myself writing the word *congregation*—when I meant to write *audience*—in my notes.

Conclusion

The following chapters of this book amplify the themes raised in this chapter. In what follows I explain how GALA singers and artistic directors experience a powerful and motivating sense of community not only during the GALA Festival but also during weekly rehearsals in their local choruses, how they articulate and fulfill their common "mission," and how they pursue progressive social change. A significant amount of the text is devoted to thick description of musical performances; in other words, I prioritize what GALA insiders themselves prioritize. Throughout, I reiterate the idea that GALA choruses are community choirs, and that we must keep this understanding of their activities in mind while analyzing them as social actors doing political work.

2 • "Community" and Its Significance to GALA Choristers

The Gay Men's Chorus of Charlotte, North Carolina, maintained the following schedule during the 2009–10 concert year: two and a half hours of rehearsal per week, twenty-five short, free-of-charge performances, six ticketed concerts, three day-long retreats, three choral workshops, and two employment workshops (a number of choristers were struggling with unemployment during the recession). It also filmed a video that year, which required eight days of collaborative work. The artistic director of the Gay Men's Chorus of Charlotte, John Quillin, has a full-time job in Charlotte; however, he not only conducts all rehearsals and performances, he also takes responsibility for "the administrative and business side" of the chorus. He does all this work as a volunteer, which, as he points out, "keeps [him] in touch with what [he] is asking from the chorus members" (interview, March 29, 2011).

The Gay Men's Chorus of Charlotte is perhaps an exceptionally busy chorus. However, it is generally representative of GALA choruses across the United States and Canada; these choruses are vibrant community choirs that expect their singers to contribute significant amounts of time and effort to the collective. This chapter begins by exploring how and why the middle-aged, middle-class adults who constitute the large majority of the singers and leadership of these community choirs are motivated to join, and then continue to participate in, a voluntary activity that demands so much of their leisure time (and no small amount of money). As I argue in what follows, local GALA choruses are of overriding importance to the choristers who sing in them because they are communities of friendship, which are immensely valuable to LGBT people and which are increasingly rare among adults in the United States and Canada. However, the GALA Choruses organization at large, understood as one overarching community, displays deep divisions along gender lines.

Participating in a GALA Chorus: A Labor of Love

Most GALA choruses rehearse at least once per week for two or three hours. Adding travel time extends this commitment; David Greene, for example, drove 120 miles round trip (from Canton, Ohio, to Cleveland, Ohio) to attend Sunday evening rehearsals of the North Coast Men's Chorus for the first five years he was a member (interview, October 10, 2014), and Tara Napoleone-Clifford spent 65 minutes driving each way to and from Kansas City, Missouri, for Kansas City Women's Chorus rehearsals (interview, June 30, 2011). Most choruses present three full concerts per year (performing at least an hour's worth of songs at each), and many chorus directors require that all the music be memorized. Choristers therefore spend additional time at home singing along with practice recordings and drilling themselves on lyrics. Before each full concert, choruses usually add additional rehearsals, sometimes designating the week before the concert as "tech week," requiring that all singers attend rehearsal every night.

Further, a subset of the choristers participate in what are called "small ensembles," which are groups of fewer than twenty singers who perform additional gigs, often in response to invitations from corporate or community groups. Small ensemble singers therefore devote additional rehearsal, travel, and performance time to the chorus. Other choristers volunteer to take special parts in the full concerts, such as singing solos, dancing, acting, and narrating. Again, these commitments—especially the dancing, which is usually carefully choreographed—require extra rehearsal time. Still other choristers volunteer to do administrative tasks, such as keeping track of song scores (music notation), and others serve as board members, organizing performances, fundraisers, and social events. All these volunteer tasks may consume a fair amount of time. For example, Hugh Gabrielson of Coro Allegro (in Boston, Massachusetts) told me that he spearheaded and then maintained his chorus's website for two years; he spent about four hours every Saturday updating the website. Gabrielson also serves as the tenor section leader in Coro Allegro, a position that—as he pointed out—offers "no salary or any perks. It's entirely honorific. Of course, I drop it into every conversation I can!" (interview, August 22, 2016). Other GALA participants I interviewed were similarly lighthearted in discussing the time and effort they devote to their choruses. The most involved and committed singers were likely overrepresented in my interview sample, given that they were also likely to consent to speak to a researcher. Nevertheless, it is fair to say that the average GALA chorister spends a significant amount of time in an unpaid, voluntary activity.

Most GALA artistic directors are paid for their work, but not enough that they rely on their GALA salary as a full-time income. There are exceptions, such as John Quillin, the volunteer who was described above. By contrast, the biggest men's choruses pay full-time salaries to their artistic directors, and in some cases to other staff people. Because income figures are rather sensitive for most people, I avoided asking artistic directors about this topic. Some information, however, is made public. We know, for example, that in 2010 Dr. Tim Seelig received a salary of $92,000 as artistic director of the San Francisco Gay Men's Chorus, thanks to an article in the *Bay Area Reporter* (Hemmelgarn 2010). A few artistic directors spoke with me about their GALA incomes; the only one who gave me a precise number was Paul Jones, the former artistic director of the Sacramento Gay Men's Chorus, who said that he earned $6,900 per year from 2005 to 2011 (interview, January 8, 2011).

The average income among GALA artistic directors is closer to that of Jones than that of Seelig. GALA choruses, like many community arts organizations, have rather small budgets. According to Robin Godfrey, the executive director of GALA Choruses, 75 percent of GALA groups had annual budgets of US$70,000 or less as of 2011.[1] Jody Malone, artistic director of the mixed chorus Singing OUT (in Toronto) told me that her group has a budget of less than Can$60,000 per year, and therefore she receives what she described as an "honorarium" (interview, October 13, 2011). Jean-Louis Bleau of the Calgary Men's Chorus said that he was grateful that the artistic directorship of that chorus was always a paid position; he has led other community choirs for no salary whatsoever (interview, June 24, 2016). He characterized his leadership of the Calgary Men's Chorus as "a part-time passion of love." Nancy Bell, a soprano singer and board member of The Quire in Iowa City, Iowa, told me that her chorus only began paying a regular salary to its artistic director in 2014; prior to that, the singers took up a collection at each concert and donated the proceeds to the director (interview, November 18, 2016). Typically the donation amounted to between six hundred and seven hundred dollars.

In sum, most GALA conductors must hold other jobs to supplement the income they derive from their GALA work. The singers—who often function as board members and in other volunteer capacities—are not paid, and in fact they usually contribute membership fees of several hundred dollars per year to their choruses. Cory Barrett, who spent many hours working as the director of operations for Mosaic Youth Chorus in Denver, Colorado, is one typical example. Barrett laughingly told me that he was never paid for any of these labors: "Or as I like to say, I paid!"—meaning that he donated his own time and money to Mosaic (interview, December 12, 2016). GALA also includes pianists who play at all weekly rehearsals and concerts, as well as people who compose and arrange musical scores; in most of the cases I was able to identify, these workers are paid rather small amounts or not at all.[2] To put it most broadly: money is not a motivating factor for most GALA participants, including those who devote the largest amounts of time and effort to their respective choruses. It is in light of this fact that I examine how and why singers, artistic directors, and other volunteers become involved in their local GALA choruses.

Deciding to Join a GALA Chorus

GALA singers initially become aware of, and then decide to join, their local chorus in a variety of ways. A significant number are introduced to the idea by hearing a concert performance by a GALA chorus. Sharon Donning, for example, said that she discovered the West Coast Singers of Los Angeles, California, when she heard the chorus perform at a Pride Festival: "I thought, They're pretty good—and I was amazed by the fact that there was a gay and lesbian chorus out there! I thought, I've got to be part of this" (interview, April 24, 2012). Jane Hoffman heard a small ensemble from the Lesbian and Gay Chorus of Washington, DC, sing at a gay and lesbian bookstore in 1995; she recalled speaking to some of the singers and being immediately "intrigued" (interview, March 1, 2012). For some, hearing a GALA chorus sing is a revelatory experience. Fred Fishman vividly remembers seeing the San Francisco Gay Men's Chorus sing at the Kennedy Center during its first tour in 1981: "And it was a life-changing event. I was crying from the moment they came on stage. I had never seen a group of gay men singing out, singing in the Kennedy Center [a prestigious performance venue in Washington, DC], identifying as gay men" (interview, April 25, 2012). It was then that Fishman decided to join the Lesbian and Gay Chorus of Washington, DC. Brian Tombow, now a baritone in the Dayton Gay Men's Chorus, said that when he heard the chorus perform, "It was like a calling. I knew I belonged up there!" (interview, August 17, 2011).

Other GALA singers reported more prosaic initial encounters with their local chorus and/or the notion of singing with a LGBT-identified group. In

2004, Shari Goettl saw an ad in a lesbian newsletter for an open house hosted by Desert Voices (of Tucson, Arizona) (interview, August 14, 2013). Brandon Dowdy heard about the Turtle Creek Chorale (of Dallas, Texas) at Youth First Texas, a Dallas-based LGBT youth support group he attended; the chorale distributed free concert tickets to the youth group members (interview, August 11, 2012). Dorian Osborne joined the Dayton Gay Men's Chorus after bartending one of its fundraising events, while he was working part-time for a friend's catering business (interview, August 16, 2011). Matthew Gillespie of the Calgary Men's Chorus first heard about the chorus in a local gay publication and later heard more about it from players in his gay volleyball league (interview, January 5, 2013). A large majority of my interviewees said that they joined their local chorus after being invited to do so by a friend who was, in most cases, already singing in that chorus. (I discuss this phenomenon further below).

Regardless of how they first became linked with a GALA chorus, GALA singers pointed out, over and over, that two main forces motivate them to stay involved, and to eventually devote serious amounts of time and energy to their choruses: their love for music making, and their desire to be part of a supportive community. Although some interlocutors focused more on the first (emphasizing how much they love to sing, for example) and others focused more on the second (often using words like "camaraderie" and "home"), most referenced both factors repeatedly during their interviews with me. Frances Bird of the Glammaphones (in Wellington, New Zealand) cogently stated, "My motivations are one, the music, and two, the community. If I didn't have both elements, I wouldn't continue" (interview, March 8, 2014). Similarly, Eric Unhold of the North Coast Men's Chorus said that he is motivated by his love of performance and "the musical experience," and equally by his desire to meet and forge bonds with other gay people (interview, October 13, 2014).

Some singers spoke at length about their love for making music, explaining how this love motivated them to participate in their local chorus. Bryan Fetty of the North Coast Men's Chorus, for example, said that he finds a great sense of accomplishment in "creating something that's artistically really good" (interview, October 9, 2014). Similarly, Neka Zimmerman of the Rochester Gay Men's Chorus said that he likes learning new songs and working toward a performance, and that he particularly appreciates the chance to learn music he would never otherwise learn, or even hear (interview, December 19, 2016).[3] Other GALA singers specified that the music-making opportunity afforded by their chorus helped them build their mental and physical strengths, and that they found this aspect motivating. Henry Chau, a tenor in the Philadelphia Gay Men's Chorus who has endured a serious illness in the recent past, said that he appreciates the "challenge" that chorus participation provides. He noted that he has to perform all the songs from memory, find his part amid the multivoice texture, and perform movements coordinated with the singing. Membership in the Philadelphia Gay Men's Chorus therefore helps keep his brain and body active, and because he is "determined to be as healthy as I can," he is motivated to continue (interview, December 13, 2016). Linda Krasienko noted that she cannot read staff notation, and that she is motivated to sing in Windsong, Cleveland's Feminist Chorus, because it gives her the chance to learn about dynamics (changes in the volume of the sound) and "complex music" (interview, November 25, 2014). Bill Sharp likened chorus participation to voice lessons, saying that his range has improved (that is, widened) and that he has "learned a lot about breath control" while singing in the Dayton Gay Men's Chorus: "It really benefits my voice" (interview, July 22, 2011).

Other GALA choristers said that singing serves as a kind of relief from the pressures of everyday life, and that this aspect made participation in their local chorus very motivating.[4] David Greene explained that during the five years he drove sixty miles each way to rehearsal, he was also caring for his aging parents. "Every Sunday night [rehearsal] was my out. I joined as an outlet, I guess you'd say" (interview, October 10, 2014). Scott Meier of the Dayton Gay Men's Chorus said, "DGMC is like therapy. I spent a lot of years depressed. Singing allows me to get emotions out in the music" (interview, August 2, 2011). Dorian Osborne echoed both of these men, characterizing his chorus participation as "therapeutic" and "an outlet" (interview, August 16, 2011). Octavio Partida explained that when he first joined Reveille Men's Chorus in Tucson, Arizona, his mother was dying of cancer and he had to leave university for financial reasons. Therefore, "I was depressed. And singing is a valve, a way to relieve the stress of the week. I enjoy the psychological relief of three hours [in rehearsal] every Monday" (interview, November 7, 2016).

While appreciation of music making is consistent and widespread among GALA singers, their desire to participate in their choruses' communities emerged even more strongly in their explanations of what motivates them to join and stay involved in GALA. Many invoked the term *community* as soon as I raised the question of why they participate in a GALA chorus. For example, Peter Criswell said that when he joined the Seattle Men's Chorus, "It was instant community for me. It was a great haven for me. I made a lot of friends" (interview, January 8, 2013). Derek Smith, a baritone in the Gay Men's Chorus of Washington, DC, described joining the chorus by saying, "It gave me a feeling of belonging" (interview, September 2, 2016). Beth Fox, a soprano in the ANNA Crusis Women's Choir (of Philadelphia), told me that when she joined, "I was looking for a community, and I found that in ANNA. . . . It's a very loving, very supportive community. I probably couldn't have gotten through a lot of hard times in the past nine years without ANNA. . . . There's always a hug waiting if you need it" (interview, August 15, 2012).

Indeed some singers said that the sense of community they experience in their GALA chorus is their primary motivation for participating. Anne Bush, for example, stated that the most important aspect of her involvement in the Seattle Women's Chorus is "community," saying that she values how choristers help each other in times of difficulty and enjoy social events such as dessert socials: "It's such a bright spot in my week. Rehearsals are really fun. I've been in rehearsals [of other choirs] where you can hear a pin drop! But this feels like a real community . . . it feeds me in a way that I don't get elsewhere. There's a lot of laughing and joking. I keep thinking of taking a quarter off, but then they announce the next concert, and I think 'Oh, I want to be a part of that.' I keep thinking I'll take time off, but I just can't" (interview, August 1, 2012). Jim Johnson, a baritone and former board member in the Quarryland Men's Chorus of Bloomington, Indiana, emphasized to me that "community is at the core of our mission statement," and he shared that "I've heard a number of people express that they are proud of our concerts, et cetera, but they especially value the good group of friends that make up the chorus" (interview, June 24, 2012). Johnson then explained how community is manifested in the activities of the group: choristers "hang out" outside of rehearsal, often going to restaurants. At least three people go out for dinner after every weekly rehearsal. Singers attend other musical performances together, and some even travel together to hear the Indianapolis Men's Chorus. "We want to provide a welcoming place for people," Johnson said, "and I believe we accomplish this. We enjoy each other's company a lot."

Many GALA choristers value their chorus communities specifically because their choruses are "safe spaces."[5] As was explained in chapter 1, LGBT people are subject to subtle and overt forms of discrimination, both as individuals and as members of LGBT-identified groups, and therefore they especially value the sense of safety that they experience in choral rehearsals and during chorus social events. Mike Killen, singer and board member of the Rainbow Harmony Project of Winnipeg, Manitoba, explained the sense of safety he experiences in his chorus community: "We create a safe space for people to come and sing. . . . When I sing, I'm free. I've got friends in the choir. When I'm there, I'm surrounded by people who like music as much as I do, and that's all that matters. And I don't have to worry about perceptions, about how the world treats anybody—we sing, we laugh, we joke, we practice. You try to sing one more note correctly this time, and away you go" (interview, September 23, 2016).

GALA artistic directors and board members seek to present their choruses as safe places by making the audition process as welcoming as possible. *Audition* is perhaps an awkward word to use here, in that the large majority of GALA choruses accept all singers who wish to join. Nevertheless, it is the term my interlocutors most often employed to describe a potential chorister's initial encounter with the conductor. In most cases, the conductor does not test the singer's voice against a standard, but rather asks them to sing in order to determine their voice placement—that is, to determine which voice part (soprano, alto, tenor, or bass) their vocal range will most comfortably allow them to sing. In other words, during a GALA audition, the question is not whether the singer will be accepted into the group, but only which section of the group they will join.

The Reveille Men's Chorus has one of the more creative so-called audition processes I have found in GALA circles. The chorus hosts a party at a karaoke bar at the beginning of each season; choristers are encouraged to bring friends. If these friends prove themselves to be promising singers, they are encouraged to attend an "open rehearsal," of which there are three every season. After attending an open rehearsal, an interested singer undergoes a "voice check" with the conductor, again, only to determine voice placement (Aditya Adiredja, interview, December 20, 2016). Cory Barrett summarized GALA's common sentiment about auditions: he said that the leaders of the Mosaic Youth Chorus had undergone "a lot of discussion" about auditions, ultimately deciding that no one would be excluded based on a lack of musical ability. "So we never turned any young people away," he said, "and the audition was more like an interview—in the spirit of creating a safe space" (interview, December 12, 2016).

GALA auditions never include any question or litmus test about sexual orientation; when GALA conductors say that they welcome people of all orientations, they mean it (Willi Zwozdesky, interview, September 5, 2011). Straight singers and artistic directors who participate in GALA choruses made this point to me repeatedly: GALA choruses are truly inclusive communities, they argued, and the proof of this inclusivity is that they attract and retain singers who do not identify as gay or lesbian. Moreover, straight singers have found that they are treated not as exotic or special cases, but as equal participants of their choruses. Although they are sometimes questioned about their sexual orientation by curious fellow singers, they are also "very much included in the friendship of the group" (Jim Johnson, interview,

June 24, 2012).[6] In this sense, GALA communities have evolved; when Paul Attinello (1994, 329) studied five large gay men's choruses in the early 1990s, he found that only 50 percent of the singers expressed a positive view of including straight singers in their groups. In addition, his sample of 172 questionnaire respondents were "very negative" on the idea of hiring a straight conductor. Two decades later, straight artistic directors are commonly found conducting GALA choruses, and the inclusion of straight singers is a point of pride for many GALA insiders, who bragged about this fact during interviews. For example, Jean-Louis Bleau told me happily that the Calgary Men's Chorus has "a number" of straight men in its ranks, including a father and his son: "I think it's a huge accomplishment that we have straight men in the chorus" (interview, May 31, 2016).

Community as a Distinguishing Feature of GALA Choruses

For some, the strong sense of community that pervades GALA choruses is what ultimately distinguishes them from other choral groups. I was particularly interested in hearing this assertion from those who would have reason to know—that is, artistic directors who have extensive experience conducting other community choirs. Ciaran Krueger, for example, is the artistic director of the Buffalo Gay Men's Chorus; he holds a master's degree in choral conducting and has been involved with a variety of church and community choirs since the age of six. A straight man, Krueger said that the Buffalo Gay Men's Chorus is "in some ways very similar to other choirs I conduct" (interview, January 28, 2012). He pointed out, however, that the choristers frequently say, "It's a family," and that in fact, "there's a sense of togetherness that doesn't exist in other choral groups." Jean-Louis Bleau also has an extensive choral conducting résumé. He agrees with Krueger: "Definitely, GALA choirs are distinct. It's the sense of community, of coming together and supporting each other. There's a vibrant queer community and also a vibrant musical community, and [GALA choruses] are a realization of that" (interview, June 24, 2016). Steven Hankle, a straight director of university choirs, spent a year singing with the San Francisco Gay Men's Chorus. He said that he "saw a very strong brotherhood" among the singers, and "I took notes on this!" (interview, July 5, 2018). Hankle shared that the experience inspired him to "make a space in my own choirs where men [of any sexual orientation] can find friends." Rich Cook, the artistic director of MenAlive, the Orange County Gay Men's Chorus of Santa Ana, California, spent thirty years conducting choirs in evangelical churches and television ministries before founding MenAlive. He said, "[MenAlive] has a family side. . . . We know each other; we have more of a social connection than a typical large community chorus. There's something of a support group in a gay men's chorus" (interview, May 14, 2012).

Donald Nally is professor of conducting and ensembles at Northwestern University; he has served as a workshop facilitator and guest conductor for various GALA choruses. When Nally was first invited to conduct at the GALA Festival in San Jose, California, in 2000, he was unsure what to expect. After participating in the festival he realized, "For many people involved in GALA . . . this community was a huge part of why people belonged to it. Which is so different from the world I live in! In my choir, people may be friends and get together, but it's not the reason they're there. There just isn't that social aspect to it [in my choir]. So this was the lesson I learned" (interview, September 10, 2012). Miguel Felipe, the former artistic director of the Maine Gay Men's Chorus and a current faculty member at the University of Hawai'i at Mānoa, reiterated the sentiments of all of those mentioned above. Felipe commended GALA choruses for focusing so strongly on community-making: "This is why even straight people join; it's just a great place to be. I lament the fact that so many of my colleagues get so focused on repertoire and miss the [community aspect] that GALA chorus conductors seem to get" (interview, July 31, 2013).

By creating communities in their local choruses, GALA groups are defying a trend identified by Robert D. Putnam (2000) in his book *Bowling Alone*. As Putnam points out, in the United States, as the twentieth century came to an end, "active involvement in face-to-face organizations . . . plummeted. . . . Active involvement in clubs and other voluntary associations has collapsed at an astonishing rate, more than halving most indexes of participation within barely a few decades" (63). The practice of eating a meal with friends (at a restaurant, at a picnic, or in one's home) "seems on the path to extinction" (100). Ultimately, "our evidence also suggests that over a very wide range of activities, the last several decades have witnessed a striking diminution of regular contacts with our friends and neighbors" (115). Putnam made these arguments based on data collected in the 1980s and 1990s; in a more recent book he summarizes the twenty-first-century evidence of "Americans' disengagement and their retreat to relative social isolation" and finds that these trends have only continued (2015, 211). GALA choruses, however, offer weekly face-to-face interactions with one's peers by way of rehearsals. Just as important, as many of my interlocutors underlined, the choruses encourage "breaking bread with friends" (Putnam 2000, 100) by organizing all manner of potluck suppers, regular outings to restaurants before or after rehearsals, Christmas and Thanksgiving Day parties, and the like. In short, the choruses foster the social connectedness that is so important to all human societies and that has "visibly diminished in the course of a single generation" (Putnam 2000, 100). It is understandable, therefore, why so many GALA insiders emphasized to me the importance of the community they discovered in their GALA chorus: this kind of community has become exceptional in the experience of adults in the United States and Canada.

Describing GALA Communities

Scholars have pondered the notion of musical communities and have identified groups of singers—whether formally organized as choirs or not—as communities (e.g., Lortat-Jacob 2006, 91–94; Balén 2009, 36–37; Duchan 2012, 180). However, as Greg Barz (2006, 27) points out, "the concept of 'community' . . . while central to many contemporary and historical ethnographic studies, is seldom treated sufficiently." Kay Kaufman Shelemay's (2011) award-winning article about musical collectives is an exception to this trend. Shelemay begins by offering a straightforward definition: "A musical community is a social entity, an outcome of a combination of social and musical processes, rendering those who participate in making or listening to music aware of a connection among themselves" (365). Shelemay then delineates three processes that generate musical communities: processes of descent, processes of dissent, and processes of affinity.

All three processes are at work across the GALA organization. Choruses that may best be characterized as "affinity communities" are present; these are groups to which singers are initially attracted because of their preference for singing a certain kind of repertoire. One analogous affinity community in the broader choral music scene is the barbershop quartet: Gage Averill (2003, 16, 154) calls barbershop quartets "affinity formations," explaining that "lyric content is of real importance in motivating contemporary participation in barbershop harmony." Across GALA choruses, the clearest examples of affinity communities are the Lavender Light Gospel Choir of New York City, which focuses on African American sacred music, and Coro Allegro, which describes itself as "Boston's classical chorus," and which specializes in what artistic directors call "standard rep," or Western art music. Maria-Elena Grant, a long-time member of Lavender Light, explained that this chorus has a much larger proportion of African American singers than other GALA choruses because of these singers' affinity for performing the music they grew up with in their churches: "We attract people because of what we sing" (interview, October 29, 2011). Darryl Hollister, accompanist for Coro Allegro, pointed out that the chorus has a significant number of straight singers (more than 25 percent, he estimated) and attributed this fact to the widespread interest in Western art music in the Boston area. Singers of all sexual orientations are therefore interested in a choir that performs this repertoire (interview, June 30, 2014).

Processes of dissent also draw people to GALA choruses. Shelemay (2011, 370) explains that "dissent communities do generally emerge through acts of resistance against an existing collectivity . . . individuals involved in processes of dissent quite regularly draw on musical performance as a mechanism to enlist others in their cause." The GALA Choruses organization focuses consistently on its mission of "changing the world through song"—a point I explore at length in chapter 6—and some of its artistic directors and singers say that it is precisely their desire to support this cause that motivates them to participate in their local chorus. For them, singing in a GALA chorus allows them to express their dissent against heteronormativity and to promote expanded rights for LGBT people.

GALA artistic directors and leaders who articulated reasons that could be glossed as dissent or an act of resistance included Jane Ramseyer-Miller, who is now the artistic director of GALA Choruses. Ramseyer-Miller began her GALA career as artistic director of the Calliope Women's Chorus in Saint Paul, Minnesota. She said that she was eager to work with Calliope because she "liked how they were focused on peace and justice and mission" (interview, November 1, 2011). In other words, Ramseyer-Miller came to this musical community through a process of dissent—dissenting from the norms so prevalent in the United States, dominated as it is by the military-industrial complex, and norms that Ramseyer-Miller opposed due (in part) to her Mennonite background. Both the founding and the current artistic directors of the New York City Gay Men's Chorus, Gary Miller and Charlie Beale, and the current director of the Gay Men's Chorus of Los Angeles, Joe Nadeau, referenced "political" motives, an idea that many GALA chorus singers found uncomfortable (as I explain in chapter 6). Miller said bluntly, "My motivation was political. I loved the idea that there was something positive to do as a gay man, with gay men who shared my interest" (interview, June 27, 2014). Nadeau stated, "What I love about being part of a GALA chorus is that it combines my teaching skills with my desire to make a difference politically in the LGBT community" (interview, February 20, 2011). Beale, one of the most eloquent advocates of the idea that GALA is a mission-driven organization, explained that he first worked with the London Gay Men's Chorus (in the United Kingdom) "as a way of harnessing my skill set to a political project." Since then, he pointed out, his involvement in GALA has become his full-time career: "It's about music and campaigning" (interview, August 16, 2011). Catherine Roma, the founder and longtime artistic director of MUSE, Cincinnati's Women's Choir (and former artistic director of ANNA Crusis in Philadelphia), told me that she started MUSE as a way for women to work on women's issues together, and that "my politics of peace and justice are very important to me" (interview, January 19, 2012). Amy Moore served as national director of membership for the GALA organization from 1998 to 2001; she began her involvement with GALA as a singer in the Lesbian and Gay Chorus of Washington, DC, which intrigued her because "the chorus used Western art music to lift us out of oppression, when [that music] has been a tool of oppression." Moore summarized her GALA involvement by saying, "I was always into the movement to change the world, not just to be part of a wall of choral sound" (interview, February 16, 2012).

Singers, too, explained their motivations for participating in local GALA choruses in ways that justify categorizing them as dissenters or resisters—and this tendency seemed to be especially pronounced among women singers. For example, Linda Krasienko told me that one of her "top motivators" is "to support the mission" of her chorus, Windsong, Cleveland's Feminist Chorus adding that she enjoys fundraising and raising awareness (interview, November 25, 2014). Krasienko pointed out that she is so motivated to support GALA's mission that she also volunteers for the gay men's chorus in her city, the North Coast Men's Chorus. Sharon Donning said that when she joined her mixed chorus, "I believed very heavily in what the chorus stood for, and still stands for," and she followed that remark by partially quoting the mission statement of the West Coast Singers (interview, April 24, 2012). These women and others like them said that their primary motivation for joining and staying involved with their choruses was to enact their own political commitments—that is, to resist the homophobia and injustice that permeates society in the United States and Canada.[7] I also interviewed a man who finally left the San Francisco Gay Men's Chorus because the chorus did not dissent strongly enough, in his opinion: "I was much more political [than the other San Francisco Gay Men's Chorus singers]. If there is a gay chorus, it must have a mission. And I felt that people in San Francisco didn't care all that much about what they represented. I wanted the chorus to do outreach in little towns in California, where we could really make a difference in someone's life. I wanted to go to places where we would challenge beliefs and assumptions. Instead, the chorus flew to Australia for Mardi Gras. So [I realized] I just wasn't aligned with their values" (Fred Fishman, interview April 25, 2012).

Ultimately, he explained, "I am an outlier, and this is partly why I don't currently belong to a GALA chorus—I have a different political perspective."

My own research confirmed this singer's view: he and the others named in the paragraph above constitute a minority in GALA circles; the majority of GALA singers are not primarily motivated to become involved by a process of dissent. When I discussed singers' motivations with Ben Riggs, the artistic director of the Twin Cities Gay Men's Chorus (Minneapolis, Minnesota) and formerly the artistic director of the Denver Gay Men's Chorus (Denver, Colorado), Riggs argued strongly against the notion that most GALA singers join their choruses to commit an act of resistance, as Shelemay would have it. "I know that most new singers who come to the chorus don't join to be political activists. I think there has to be a deeper reason why people keep getting together to sing. . . . People are looking to connect, mostly. Not to change the world, not to commit a political act" (interview, August 15, 2013). In chapters 7 and 8 of this book, I explore at length how GALA leaders and rank-and-file singers pursue their collective mission of fostering social change; this "dissenting" ethos is a powerful force that pervades GALA choruses. Choristers come to embrace this ethos over time, as their artistic directors and fellow singers encourage them to think of their participation as serving a mission to create social change. However, as Riggs contended, at the beginning of their GALA experience, as singers seek to join local choruses, they are not usually motivated by a desire to do political work. GALA singers most often come to their respective musical communities not through processes of dissent, or even affinity, but rather what Shelemay calls "descent."

Descent communities, according to Shelemay (2011, 367), are "united through what are understood from within to be shared identities."[8] In GALA choruses, the overwhelming majority of singers identify either as lesbian or gay, or as strong allies of lesbian and gay people. Furthermore, they understand and prioritize this shared identity as a basis for joining together. For example, Brandon Dowdy articulated the idea that the Turtle Creek Chorale is a community created through a process of descent by saying: "There's relationships I've made inside the chorus that I know will last a lifetime. There's no science to the way we build relationships, there's no formula to how it's supposed to work. But we all have a common focus in music making. And we all have a common background, growing up gay and marginalized. Almost everybody has been discriminated against—I would say 99 percent of us. Also, most of us grew up in strongly religious backgrounds. Many of [my fellow choristers] come from Southern Baptist families. That kind of upbringing goes into your soul. There's no bouncing out of that. It takes a whole lifetime to come to terms with it. And we all share that commonality" (interview, August 11, 2012). Ciaran Krueger pointed out that singers in the Buffalo Gay Men's Chorus go out to eat together after every single rehearsal, and that each week between five and twenty men share in this communal meal. He also noted that many singers have found lifelong friends and life partners among their fellow choristers. Krueger attributed these developments to the conscious efforts of the singers to promote an atmosphere that is "safe, accepting, supporting," and he noted that this atmosphere ultimately derives from "the understanding that they have a shared experience in their lives" (interview, January 28, 2012).

This shared LGBT identity—and the common life experience it implies—is what initially draws the majority of GALA participants together. Most people who described in specific detail how they came to be involved in their GALA chorus told me that they joined the community as the result of a personal invitation or recommendation, and that the invitation was issued because the interlocutor knew, or assumed, that my interviewee identified as gay, lesbian, or transgender, or as an ally. As Donald Butchko, a baritone in the North Coast Men's Chorus, put it, "It seems like people join because they know someone. . . . There's just one or two degrees of separation between most of the people in the chorus" (interview, September 25, 2014). Here are just a few examples: Hugh Gabrielson explained that he attended a Labor Day party at the home of an older gay man; this man encouraged him to audition for Coro Allegro, to which he has now belonged for two decades (interview, August 22, 2016). Aditya Adiredja met a man on a gay dating site; this man took him to a concert performed by Reveille and Reverb,[9] where Adiredja was impressed by the choruses' "beautiful sound: they sounded amazing" (interview, December 20, 2016). Octavio Partida, another Reveille chorister, received a recommendation to join the group from a fraternity brother at the University of Arizona; the fraternity consisted of "gay, bi, trans, and progressive men" (interview, November 7, 2016). Both Joe Nadeau and Kaeden Kass (now a singer in the Cincinnati Men's Chorus) were encouraged by staff members at their respective universities to seek out GALA choruses after graduation. In each case, the staff member knew that the young student identified as gay (Nadeau) or as a transgender man (Kass) and made the suggestion specifically for that reason.[10] Finally, Ben Riggs explained that he was asked to take the position of artistic director of the Denver Gay Men's Chorus. The chorus sought him out—in part—because he was gay. In reflecting on his acceptance of this invitation, Riggs said, "I don't think I would have done it otherwise," meaning, if he were not gay (interview, August 15, 2013).

Among women, this sense of shared identity as a basis for an invitation to join a GALA chorus extends to straight allies. Veronica Crowe-Carpenter was invited to join Windsong, Cleveland's Feminist Chorus, by a woman she met "at a women's feminist meeting" (interview, November 2, 2014). Crowe-Carpenter explained to me that Windsong's membership includes approximately 25 percent straight women, and that the rest identify as either bisexual or lesbian, but that "everyone is a feminist" in this chorus. Jeannie Holton is a straight woman; she had a straight friend who was a member of Crescendo: The Tampa Bay Women's Chorus (in Florida), and this woman urged her to join, knowing that Holton was "entrenched in the women's community" (interview, January 15, 2013). Alyssa Stone, a straight woman who is a volunteer board member for the Lesbian/Gay Chorus of San Francisco, was invited to join the board by the current treasurer; the treasurer knew that she was already "super, super involved in the LGBT community" (interview, June 25, 2012).

The Significance of the Chorus Community

GALA attracts middle-class participants—discussed further in chapter 4 of this book—as is exemplified by a certain aspirational subset of its singers. These men and women have moved to new cities, as adults, in order to pursue career opportunities. In these cases especially, my interlocutors expressed great appreciation for the friendships they found in their local choruses. As Katie Eadie of the Kansas City Women's Chorus explained, it can be challenging to develop new friendships as an adult. She said that she appreciates the meet-ups and parties that frequently occur outside of rehearsals: "The chorus brings people together without that awkward searching. It's kind of like dating, like, how do you approach someone?" (interview, August 10, 2016). Aditya Adiredja moved to Tucson to take a faculty position at the University of Arizona. He summarized the importance of the Reveille Men's Chorus by saying, "When I moved to Tucson I was alone. . . . But at rehearsal I'm in a room with other queer and gay and bi people, and straight allies, and we have trans folks as well, the whole spectrum of nonstraight folks, and it provided me with a group of friends, honestly" (interview, December 20, 2016). Mikal Rasheed, a singer in the Gay Men's Chorus of Washington, DC, said that the friendships he has made are the main motivation for his continued participation in the chorus. These friends, he explained, are people that he sends text messages to, asking "What's going on?" and these friends will then make plans to spend time with him during the weekend (interview, February 9, 2017). This kind of social network is precious to Rasheed, who moved to Washington to take a job at Joint Base Andrews, and whose fiancé works long hours as a television reporter. Brian Tombow explained that he has stopped looking for work outside of Dayton, Ohio, because he values so highly the community he has found in his chorus: "It just felt like we were a family. They are just incredible people. We [he and his husband, who is his fellow chorister] don't want to leave the area, because of our friends in the chorus" (interview, August 17, 2011).

When asked to list the specific actions of their fellow choristers that exemplified their understanding of friendship and community, singers often described gestures of support for choristers in emotional and physical need. Patrick Holcomb, a tenor in the North Coast Men's Chorus, said that after both his father and his brother died, "they were right there with cards and support," and that some choristers drove thirty miles to be with him while he was grieving (interview, September 14, 2014). Jeannie Holton told me that when a Crescendo member became fatally ill, chorus members maintained a constant watch at her bedside, and after her death, they read her will and eventually dispersed her estate (interview, January 15, 2013). Octavio Partida echoed Holcomb, saying that in his chorus "people are right there for you regardless of any situation you might find yourself in" (interview, November 7, 2016). Partida went on to explain that he recently decided to stop drinking; due to the strong sense of "brotherhood" he experiences in his chorus, he shared this decision with his fellow choristers. They told him that they would support him, and one singer, who has himself been sober for thirty years, offered to serve as Partida's mentor in this process. Kaeden Kass explained that shortly after he joined his chorus, he found himself suddenly and urgently in need of housing. He posted a message on Facebook and was moved to see that "so many" choristers offered him a place to stay; ultimately he lived rent free with one of them for some months (interview, February 9, 2016).

These kinds of actions—providing comfort during mourning, expressing support for personal struggles like addiction, being present through the end of life, offering shelter—inspired the many comments I heard either comparing GALA choruses to family, or stating that choruses are in fact families of a sort (see also Robertson 1989, 240).[11] Jeannie Holton, for example, said that due to Crescendo's actions after her fellow chorister fell ill and died, "I realized then, this isn't just a chorus, it's a family" (interview, January 15, 2013). Eric Unhold described his chorus by commenting, "As I say all the time to new members, 'It's a family.' The sense of brotherhood, of belonging, of community, is so intense. My life would be so different . . . if it weren't for the chorus. It is truly the center of my social and support network" (interview, October 13, 2014). Peter Criswell, who has long experience with various community choirs, contrasted participating in gay men's choruses to singing in a college choir: "There's an uber-social aspect to the gay men's chorus. To me this [gay chorus] experience is much more like a family. In every place I've lived, the chorus members have become my friends" (interview, January 8, 2013). The family trope is even sometimes invoked publicly; for example, the Dayton Gay Men's Chorus concert on July 6, 2016, included a spoken testimonial section in between songs. The narrator expressed his love for the chorus and finished with, "We're so much more than just a chorus—we're a family, and we all belong."[12]

In fairness, I must acknowledge that this appreciation for the sense of community that GALA choruses foster, while widespread, is not universal. In rare instances, singers expressed the opposite view, saying that they felt that they were not particularly loved or supported by the other singers in their choruses. Henry Chau told me that the Philadelphia Gay Men's Chorus is "the most clique-ish organization I've ever been a part of," and that only four of the approximately 130 singers even bothered to say hello to him when he returned to the chorus after a hiatus due to illness (interview, December 13, 2016). And David Greene said that while he does have some friends in his chorus, he is not particularly confident of the depth of their commitment to the friendship. He recalled that he once sent an email to the group asking for help with moving; only one person responded (interview, October 10, 2014). These men's opinions are exceptions, however, to the general consensus that creating a sense of supportive community—like a family—is something that GALA choruses do well, and do consistently.

The use of the family analogy is not unusual among adults who group together voluntarily. Joshua S. Duchan (2012, 95) claims that it is rather common in collegiate a cappella groups, for example, who often compare their choirs to families, fraternities, or sororities. The award-winning journalist and chronicler of gay male life Frank Browning (1993, 38) points out that gay men share a desire for family with all Americans, who are seeing their families disintegrate under financial and social pressures, the emotional distance created by frequent moves, and so on. Nevertheless, I argue that family is a uniquely resonant idea for LGBT people because so many of them have lost the sense of unconditional acceptance that is supposed to be guaranteed in their families of origin. As Sharon P. Holland (2005, xii) puts it, for some LGBT people, "home is a four letter word." Scholars Kath Weston (1991), Gilbert Herdt (1992a), and Bernadette Barton (2012)—who conducted ethnographic research in widely separated regions of the United States, across a thirty-year span—found that some of their lesbian and gay informants expressed a fear of physical violence and even death at the hands of their families of origin ("They would kill me!"), should they ever reveal their sexual orientation. Herdt (1992a, 56) documented that some young people in his Chicago study actually did experience a social death when their parents said, "You're dead to me," and then cut off all contact with their children. Barton (2012, 55) found that religious families, especially, taught their children that being gay or lesbian is the worst sin someone can commit: "[Their children] received the impression that to be a homosexual was more terrible, more destructive, more deserving of censure than being a drug addict, a domestic abuser, a rapist, a pedophile, a criminal or a pregnant teen."

Ilan H. Meyer and Laura Dean (198, 173), experts in stress and illness among minority populations, including especially sexual minorities, found that internalized homophobia is associated with many mental health problems. Meyer and Dean argue that self-identified gay groups are deeply important because they constitute communities with which gay people can affiliate. This affiliation allows the members to "benefit from the ameliorative sense of cohesiveness [and combat] the negative effects of internalized homophobia" (180). Psychologist John C. Gonsiorek (1995, 38) similarly argues for the importance of LGBT communities. He asserts that lesbian and gay people often suffer a "narcissistic injury" in childhood as a result of a continuing discourse in which their sexuality is disparaged. He argues that "a positive, ongoing gay/lesbian social support network" is crucial to healing this injury; the support network, or community, functions as the loving, affirming parent the injured adult needs. "Simply put, a positive, affirming community heals the wounds of external oppression" (39).

Small wonder, then, that GALA choristers prize and valorize the friends and familial communities they find in their LGBT-identified choruses. As Robert Frederick said, "Coming from a family that turned their back on me when I came out, this [belonging to the Dayton Gay Men's Chorus] means a lot to me" (interview, August 17, 2011). Patrick Holcomb provided a vivid example of how his chorus community assists him in healing from homophobic oppression. At the age of thirty-one, Holcomb was the victim of a hate crime (as was briefly referenced in chapter 1). After leaving a bar that had been hosting an AIDS fundraiser, he was targeted by three skinheads who lay in wait, determined to kill a gay man. The criminals shot Holcomb and beat him so badly that he lost a kidney and his spleen. "I was initially given a 10 percent chance to live," Holcomb recalls. "So [now] I sing and dance with the chorus because I can. I don't want to be in the shadows. I'm not afraid anymore. And I'm surrounded by people who love and support me. Doing what

I like to do takes away the power of those evil acts. . . . I participate in the chorus as part of my healing process. During rehearsals and performances I'm grounded and happy" (interview, September 14, 2014).

Mike Killen connected the themes of suffering due to his sexual orientation, and finding healing in his chorus community, in his account of how he became involved in his GALA chorus, the Rainbow Harmony Project. Like so many other GALA singers, Killen was invited to join the chorus by a man who was already singing with the group: "He basically hounded me for a year, telling me to stop hiding and come and sing" (interview, September 23, 2016). Killen went on to explain that he was hiding—that is, not singing in public—because the act of singing was linked so strongly to his childhood memories of being bullied in the remote northern town where he grew up. "So I went to Rainbow, although I was terrified, and in the time that I've been with them, I found my voice again. . . . I lived through years of fear of 'sounding like a girl,' when I was growing up. I could tell you stories that would make Oprah cringe. I was assaulted daily in school, people buried me under two inches of snow, rode over me with bicycles, pushed me into lockers. . . . I always just wanted to be accepted. I was terrified that I would be identified as gay." Although Killen was encouraged by a choir teacher to develop his voice, at the time a high tenor, "I felt like I wanted to die when a soprano said, 'You can sing higher than us!' Some chains haven't been broken even yet. When I'm practicing at home, I make my husband go upstairs. But when I sing [in the Rainbow Harmony Project], I'm free. I've got friends in the choir."

It is with this perspective—that GALA choruses provide a crucially important kind of support to LGBT people—that I came to understand some comments choristers made when discussing the role of their chorus in their lives. Aditya Adiredja, for example, said, "Yeah, it's a lot of work. But it's been an amazing thing. To be incredibly dramatic, I would say Reveille saved my life" (interview, December 20, 2016). Tom Fortuna of the North Coast Men's Chorus told me, "I don't miss a practice. . . . I almost have anxiety waiting for chorus [rehearsal] to start on Sunday . . . the inside feeling of freedom when I'm there, the hugging, the little kiss on the cheek" (interview, October 16, 2014). Fortuna continued by describing how he felt during a recent performance: "We had tears in our eyes, and I just felt so overwhelmed to be a part of this and not be ashamed of who I was; it was just phenomenal." Drew Kotchan, a tenor in the Calgary Men's Chorus, explained, "It's healing, it's even joyful sometimes. It's a glorious thing to make music with other people. It has changed my life significantly. It has made a tremendous positive impact on my life" (interview, July 27, 2013).

Women and Men and Inequality

As their comments show, GALA choristers almost unanimously valorize their own choruses as communities of friendship that provide crucial support to their LGBT members. However, when we consider the GALA Choruses organization as a singular community, significant divisions within that community become evident. The rhetoric that celebrates local choruses as "families" and "safe spaces" is far less applicable to GALA Choruses, the international umbrella organization. In this section, I delineate men's and women's choruses, arguing that GALA reveals an unfortunate tendency to disproportionately appreciate men's choruses and, therefore, to prioritize and value men over women.

As historians of LGBT life in the United States have noted, during the 1960s and 1970s, gay men and lesbian women were "rigidly segregated by sex" and usually did not work together (D'Emilio 1992, xli; see also Miller 2006, 346). So-called gay organizations generally comprised men only, while women joined lesbian groups. Moreover, the women-only lesbian organizations became committed to feminism in a way that men's organizations usually did not (Miller 2006, 401). GALA singers who grew up during that era are well aware of this history, and they have seen it play out in their own circles.[13] A number of them told me that they joined mixed choruses—in which men and women sing together—as a way of overcoming the gender separation they had observed. For example, Sharon Donning said that one reason she joined the West Coast Singers was that the group includes both men and women: "I wanted to support this, to show them that we could work together, 'in harmony,' as our mission stated" (interview, April 24, 2012). John Whalen said that mixed choruses like his—One Voice Mixed Chorus of Saint Paul, Minnesota—are "a way of healing the rift [between men and women]," adding that he joined One Voice rather than the Twin Cities Gay Men's Chorus because he "wanted to be a part of bringing gay men and lesbians together" (interview, July 12, 2012). The notion that mixed choruses represent a move toward gender cooperation and, therefore, work against gender separatism appeals even to chorus leaders. David Hodgkins, a straight man who has conducted Coro Allegro for nearly a quarter century, said that he initially became interested in this Boston-based chorus because "They were out! That was the unique thing. They were willing to be publicly identified as gay and lesbian. Also, they were a mixed chorus. At that time, there was a fair amount of enmity between men's and women's choruses" (interview, April 9, 2014). Hodgkins went on to point out that simply singing together was not an immediate panacea. "For the first two years, during rehearsal breaks, I noticed that men and women would separate. And women generally had less money, due to unequal pay, so it was more difficult for them to travel to GALA Festivals. Coro Allegro had to talk about and deal with these tensions."

The patterns that Hodgkins observed inside his mixed chorus are writ large across the GALA organization, in which women's choruses tend to have fewer financial resources than men's choruses do. Not only does this situation make it harder for women's choruses to travel to Festival destinations, it means that women have to do more grunt work to fund their choruses' activities. Veronica Crowe-Carpenter was clear eyed about the difference between her own chorus, Windsong, and the GALA men's chorus in the same city, the North Coast Men's Chorus. "Most women in Windsong are not wealthy. But the North Coast Men's Chorus is backed by big money. You can see this in the venues where we perform: Windsong performs in a church but the NCMC performs at Playhouse Square [the largest performing arts center in the United States outside of New York City].... Our director, assistant director, and pianist are all paid by revenues raised by our chorus. We hold silent auctions during our concerts, and members sell candy bars and fair-trade coffee [as fundraisers]. Some of our members even recycle tin cans for money" (interview, November 2, 2014).

Understandably, the financial inequality between men's and women's choruses, and the exigencies that difference produces, can breed resentment. I recall some angry whispering by women sitting adjacent to me during a fundraiser auction that was held at a 2011 conference of artistic directors.[14] The GALA board members who led the auction emphasized that it was being held to raise money for GALA, and especially to fund travel to the Festival by singers in youth choruses. This laudable goal was presumably shared by all present, but virtually all the bidders who raised their hands were men. The prizes were all vacations in desirable destinations: seven nights in Tuscany went for $2,800, a six-day safari in South Africa was sold for $2,500, and an identical safari went for $2,600. After the auction concluded, the GALA board president asked for donations to the cause; again, all those I saw who raised their hands were men. Eight men promised to donate $250 each, and four promised $500 each. The men's generosity was no doubt appreciated by the women I overheard, but what bothered them was the glaring display of gender inequality. The auction made painfully clear that women generally have less disposable income than men, and that they are therefore less able to publicly and lavishly demonstrate their largesse.

At the same gathering of GALA artistic directors, dozens of conductors attended reading sessions. A reading session is an occasion during which attendees sing through newly published musical scores to get a sense for how the songs are intended to sound. They are, in effect, a kind of marketing for music publishers. Participation in the reading sessions vividly demonstrated GALA's gender priorities. While the reading sessions focusing on TTBB (tenor-tenor-baritone-bass) repertoire for men's choruses were very well attended—attracting dozens of participants—only nine people showed up to a reading session of SATB (soprano-alto-tenor-bass) repertoire.[15] SATB songs are intended to be sung by mixed choruses of men and women. And only two conductors came to the reading session for SSAA (soprano-soprano-alto-alto) repertoire—that is, repertoire for women's choruses. The SSAA reading session was canceled because a minimum of four singers would have been needed to sing the four voice parts. The inescapable conclusion was that GALA artistic directors, considered as a collective, have less interest in women's choruses than in men's choruses.

The same kind of lack of support for, or disinterest in, women's choruses is evident at the GALA Festival. At the Festival, the largest men's choruses draw the biggest numbers of their peers to listen. Women's choruses, on the other hand, even those that are deeply respected as veterans who have con-tributed significantly to the GALA movement, have smaller audiences. This trend is particularly noticeable when prominent men's and women's choruses perform one after another. On July 10, 2012, for example, the Portland Gay Men's Chorus (of Oregon) and MUSE, Cincinnati's Women's Choir, per-formed back-to-back Coffee Concerts, during which each group was the only chorus scheduled to perform. In other words, listeners could either choose to attend these concerts, or choose to hear no singing whatsoever. At 9:30 a.m., for the concert by the Portland Gay Men's Chorus (entitled *A Young Person's Guide to the Gay Men's Chorus*), the venue was completely full. At 11:00 a.m., the concert venue next door, which hosted the MUSE concert (*Tweet2Roar: MUSE Celebrates 29*), was approximately half full. This relative attendance was notable because MUSE's artistic director, Catherine Roma, was awarded the GALA Choruses Lifetime Achievement Award in 2012, and this concert was the first event in her last year with the group. MUSE and Roma are deeply respected across GALA—a number of my interlocu-tors urged me to speak with Roma when I began doing the research for this book—and therefore it was striking that Festival delegates would not fill a hall even for a milestone concert such as this one. Later that day, the concert venue that had been filled at 9:30 a.m. (in anticipation of the concert by the Portland Gay Men's Chorus) was only approximately 25 percent full for the performance by another storied women's chorus, ANNA Crusis Women's Choir of Philadelphia. The announcer valorized the group, pointing out that ANNA Crusis is "the most tenured" GALA chorus, meaning that it is the oldest chorus in the GALA organization and is celebrated on the GALA website as the first GALA chorus to be founded. The announcer even said, "We wouldn't have GALA choruses if it wasn't for them."[16] His remarks reflect the respect that many GALA participants claim to have for ANNA Crusis; however, these same people did not appear in large numbers to hear the group sing.

Incidents such as these reveal a GALA-wide value system: consistently, the biggest GALA choruses are the all-male choruses, and they receive the most attention and appreciation from GALA choristers at large. As Amy Moore said, "There is a 'bigger is better' focus on vocal excellence in GALA" (interview, February 16, 2012). The former artistic director of Moore's mixed chorus, the Lesbian and Gay Chorus of Washington, DC, shared Moore's perspective. "There was a sense that the mixed choruses and women's choruses were slowly becoming more professional, but the men's choruses were where it was at," said Regina Carlow (interview, September 15, 2012). Fred Fishman, who has sung with Carlow and Moore's chorus as well as the Lesbian/Gay Chorus of San Francisco, recalled that the San Francisco Gay Men's Chorus was openly acknowledged as the "granddaddy" GALA chorus in that city: "The Lesbian/Gay Chorus of San Francisco was always the ugly stepchild to the San Francisco Gay Men's Chorus, which was [viewed as] the *real* gay chorus in town" (interview, April 25, 2012). Ultimately some GALA participants have reluctantly concluded that the organization as a whole is sexist. Jane Hoffman is a former GALA board vice president, and she emphasized during our interview that she did not leave the GALA board "in a snit," but that her experience on the board showed that large men's choruses dominated the agenda: "The weight of the organization was oriented toward the big male chorus. So smaller groups and women's groups felt like their priorities weren't respected.... I got really tired. Why am I as a woman pouring all this energy into an organization that is male dominated and not friendly to women and feminists?" (interview, March 1, 2012).

The GALA organization's leaders are aware of the resentment that GALA's preference for large men's choruses can engender among choristers from mixed choruses and women's choruses. At the Festival in recent years, they have addressed the issue by giving equal time to men's, women's, and mixed choruses during the marquee time slots. For example, during the *Our Legacy, Our Song* concert, held on July 8 during the 2012 Festival, the curated program carefully balanced the time allotted to choruses of all types, including small ensembles, youth choruses, Canadian groups, and so on. This concert was intended to highlight the breadth of GALA's historical repertoire, and the organizers did an excellent job of showing that songs that have since become well known to many GALA singers are songs performed by men, by women, and by mixed groups. Similarly, the July 2 opening concert of the 2016 Festival featured men's, women's, and mixed choruses. Prior to the beginning of the concert, a PowerPoint presentation was shown, and audience members were asked to wave if they come from an SSAA (women's) chorus, a TTBB (men's) chorus, or an SATB (mixed) chorus. By soliciting this active self-representation from the audience, the concert organizers— which is to say, GALA board members—emphasized that all three types of choruses are present, and valued, in GALA circles.

Gender Difference and Governance

GALA's men's choruses differ from choruses that include women—both women's choruses and mixed choruses—in that men's choruses generally have more financial resources and receive more attention from their peers. However, the distinguishing factor mentioned most often by the GALA participants whom I interviewed was the approach to chorus governance. When men talked to me about this topic, they tended to attribute the different approaches to a kind of gender essentialism. While I reject the idea—no matter how eloquently and amusingly argued by some of my male interlocutors—that women are inherently disposed to behave in certain ways just because they are women, I also acknowledge the pattern my research revealed. In GALA, groups of women, or groups that include women, do seem to more consistently prioritize feminist values, and this concern is often—but not always—made manifest in the authority structures and decision-making processes they pursue.

Men whom I interviewed made memorable comments about the differences between men and women, and they linked these imputed gender differences to two different modes of governance that are present across the GALA organization. One mode was variously called "hierarchical" or even "patriarchal," and the other was "consensus" (Tim Seelig, interview, September 15, 2011). While I found in my research that GALA choruses rarely adhere to either mode of governance in its purest form, the idea that there are two representative modes of government, and that men appreciate the hierarchical mode whereas women desire the consensus mode, is widespread among GALA men. Both artistic directors and singers stated that men "want to be told what to do" (Joe Nadeau, interview, February 22, 2011; Tim Seelig, interview, September 15, 2011), but women "want to have extensive discussions of every point" (Matthew Gillespie, interview, January 5, 2013). Men described this dichotomy by saying that men want to "cut to the chase," and women "love to process" (Roger Bourland, interview, December 10, 2012), or by saying that "women tend to question authority more [than men]" (Dennis Coleman, interview, September 24, 2011; Vic Hooper, interview, September 9, 2011). John Quillin put it cogently: "Men are task-oriented, but women want to talk about why the task is important," adding that "sometimes it's hard for men to understand women's pain" (interview, March 29, 2011). Or as Hugh Gabrielson more humorously commented, in a tale of organizing a dinner at a French restaurant for his tenor section: "Imagine if it had been the alto section! I'd have had to organize it six months in advance and accommodate eighteen different dietary restrictions" (interview, August 22, 2016).

Fascinated by the widespread agreement among the men of GALA about this divide in governance, I put the assertion to Catherine Roma, an important advocate for women's choruses in GALA. "Women bring up issues and men don't like it, that's true," she acknowledged (interview, January 19, 2012). "Women are the ones who tend to say, 'Men dominate this movement.' ... It's important to identify differences between men and women and to get the cultural contexts of our singing, and how we function in the world. Men without children may have more discretionary income [than women with children]. That's a fact that affects people's lives." Roma further affirmed that women's choruses tend to value a "feminist model of governance," one focused on decision-making by consensus: "This would drive GALA men crazy!" Indeed, the women who sing in choruses that are committed to consensus find the situation to be—if not "crazy"—challenging. Singers from ANNA Crusis spoke lightheartedly but sincerely about the downsides of consensus: making decisions takes a long time, they said, and forging partnerships with other community organizations is difficult because it is sometimes unclear who will make a commitment on behalf of the group.[17]

The idea that women like to discuss issues at length, and therefore value a consensus mode of governance, is mirrored by the idea that men do not want to engage in protracted discussions, and therefore desire a strong leader who will make decisions on behalf of the group. Nearly two decades ago, Paul Attinello (1994, 322) studied five large, urban, gay men's choruses; he asserted that the choruses were "highly authoritarian," and that all power in these groups rested with the conductor; even when an elected board existed, Attinello said, the board usually voted to confirm the conductor's wishes. This structure may still be true in the kinds of choruses Attinello studied. During the 2012 Festival, I rode in an elevator with three men who were wearing their GALA chorus T-shirts and criticizing the artistic director of their chorus, saying that he was "very authoritarian" and a "micromanager." One of them related angrily that he had overheard the artistic director saying, "'My boys sang well last night.' My *boys*!" When I engaged these men in conversation, the singers defended the artistic director. They pointed out that this conductor—and his peers who conduct similar choruses—has tremendous musical skills and produces (musically) outstanding work. They even asserted that perhaps the directors of such choruses are obliged to behave in this way in order to successfully direct two hundred or more men.[18] Brendan Dowdy, who sang under the baton of Tim Seelig, a self-identified advocate of hierarchical choral governance,[19] exemplified the attitude that supporters of hierarchy have: "We know that what comes from the podium is what we're supposed to do. Maybe all two hundred people don't agree, but we all get on board for the sake of the brotherhood" (interview, August 11, 2012).

Women's choruses manifest their commitment to feminist values (and by extension, to a consensus form of governance) most clearly in performance, when they rotate the job of conductor among various singers. Bread and Roses Feminist Singers of Washington, DC, for example, went for some years without any conductor, allowing choristers to volunteer to serve as leader for various pieces (Shannon Wyss, interview, May 23, 2012). I have observed this rotation of conducting responsibilities among choristers in a handful of other cases, including Windsong, Cleveland's Feminist Chorus; the Rainbow Women's Chorus of San Jose, California; and ANNA Crusis.[20] As Christopher Small (1998, 86) points out, conductors have been accorded increasing status and money over the past century; a conductor is granted "a heroic stature as focus for the imagination of those who sit in the audience . . . he is the incarnation of power in the modern sense." Carol E. Robertson (1989, 240) similarly notes that "In the Western conservatory tradition, the role of the conductor is seen as paramount within the decision-making hierarchy. Indeed, the conductor's role takes on a totalitarian orientation that makes an adjustment to group decision making painful, for few conductors would be willing to settle musical interpretations with persons of less formal training and performance experience than themselves." Diffusing the power of the conductor is therefore a radical, hierarchy-leveling move, and a way for women's choruses to enact, and publicly present, their feminist commitments.

Sharing Power with Choristers

With that said, even women's choruses that espouse feminism do not adhere at all times to an entirely consensus-driven model of governance. As scholars have found among other women's organizations, such as battered women's shelters, the difficulties inherent in relying on consensus have compelled these organizations to move away from "pure consensus-based decision-making"; most now use a "modified hierarchy" mode of governance (Reinelt 1995, 90; see also Kinney 2010, 94). Similarly, GALA choruses that are putative hierarchies—meaning that the artistic director appears to be front and center both figuratively and literally—often diffuse the power of the artistic director among the singers and board members. The locus of power that mattered most to my interlocutors, and that I focus on here, was not the conducting podium but rather the office desk or kitchen table at which chorus repertoire is selected. For many GALA singers, the question of who determines which songs the chorus will sing is much more relevant than who eventually conducts those songs.

As a singer in the Gateway Men's Chorus (of St. Louis, Missouri) explained, the ability to select a chorus's repertoire is "a form of artistic power." The songs are "the juice," he said, the issue that everybody in a chorus really cares about.[21] And by examining who wields this power, we can see that men's and women's choruses do not always conform to stereotypes. In Windsong, Cleveland's Feminist Chorus, for example, the artistic director selects concert themes and songs to fit those themes, and invites individuals to sing solos (Veronica Crowe-Carpenter, interview, November 2, 2014). Linda Krasienko, an alto in that chorus, said frankly that she appreciates this practice because it shortens the decision-making process and thereby preserves rehearsal time (interview, November 25, 2014). On the other hand, the Gateway Men's Chorus, a supposedly more hierarchical chorus, holds a "pitch session" twice per year, during which all singers are welcome to suggest repertoire to the artistic director.[22]

GALA choruses—including men's choruses—often invite rank-and-file singers to weigh in on, or even determine, the answer to the question that matters more than almost any other: what songs shall the chorus sing? Many choruses convene a music selection committee, and this committee, rather than the artistic director alone, selects the repertoire that the chorus will sing. In most cases, all singers are welcome to volunteer to sit on this committee. These committees are variously called the music and artistic development committee, the artistic direction committee, or the artistic advisory committee.[23] Artistic directors have varying relationships with their music selection committees. For example, Jody Malone of Singing OUT explained, "I do not care at all for any hierarchical authority, so I'm always willing to open discussion and decisions to the choir. Being gay, many [chorus] members have come from oppression, and they are not interested in being oppressed by an artistic director" (interview, October 13, 2011). Singing

OUT's music advisory committee uses a checklist to guide decisions about repertoire, ensuring the proposal of one familiar song, one French or foreign song, one Broadway selection, one "really gay" song, and so on, for each concert. The artistic advisory committee of the Gay Men's Chorus of Washington, DC, meets weekly to vet repertoire suggestions given by choristers; this committee picks the concert themes and proposes a list of songs to fit each theme. The chorus's artistic director subsequently whittles down the list of songs and makes the final decision about the repertoire to be performed (Derek Smith, interview, September 2, 2016). In the Rainbow Harmony Project, the music team picks the concert themes, repertoire, and soloists, but always in conjunction with the artistic director (Mike Killen, interview, September 23, 2016). The artistic director of The Quire chooses a set of songs from the chorus's library and presents these songs to the group's board for approval—which is understood to be forthcoming (Nancy Bell, interview, November 18, 2016).

Even some of the most hierarchical artistic directors in GALA circles—better said, those who are assumed to be deeply committed to hierarchical governance—have come to value the idea of sharing artistic power with their choristers. Tim Seelig, for example, said that he has become a better leader, specifically "more willing to listen," as he has worked with choirs in which administrative responsibilities are "evened out" across the groups (interview, September 14, 2011). Gary Miller said that he initially thought of the music advisory committee (MAD committee) of the New York City Gay Men's Chorus, "as just the *mad* committee. At first I was insulted that I had to consult with them" (interview, June 27, 2014). Ultimately, though, Miller said, he saw the sharing of power with the MAD committee as a good thing because it forced him to make the case for his own repertoire choices, choices that the committee did not always support.

The hierarchical mode—we might say the traditional mode—of governance that prevails in many community choirs does still have its defenders in GALA circles. The most articulate advocate of hierarchy, and critic of consensus, is Dennis Coleman, the well-loved artistic director of both the Seattle Men's Chorus and the Seattle Women's Chorus. Coleman pointed out that he used the exact same form of governance in both choruses; in both cases, he crafted an artistic vision for each concert and expected choristers to fulfill it. Coleman, like many GALA insiders, deeply values choral excellence (see chapter 1), and he argued that allowing time for all to come to agreement on decisions hinders this excellence. "A consensus model simply doesn't work," he said (interview, September 24, 2011). "There's not enough time to rehearse if you have discussions during rehearsal time. And choruses with music advisory committees don't have as coherent programs [as do choruses in which concerts are programmed by the artistic director alone]." Anne Bush, a singer in Coleman's women's chorus, is a wholehearted supporter: "Dennis doesn't believe in committees for repertoire. And I agree, because generally it seems that there is a clear focus for each concert. Dennis has a vision for the whole show" (interview, August 1, 2012). Other singers in Bush's chorus also support Coleman's hierarchical style of governance, as they made evident in their choice of attire during the 2016 Festival, where I saw a number of them wearing "Keep Calm and Trust Dennis" T-shirts.[24]

With that said, many GALA choruses intentionally grant power to choristers in a variety of ways. Choristers vote on the hiring of new artistic directors, populate the volunteer boards that make decisions about fundraising and spending, and even determine which performance invitations the chorus will accept. Importantly, many chorus leaders welcome suggestions from choristers, and—when these suggestions involve the repertoire—choristers value the adoption of their suggestions deeply. One example: after only a few months of singing with the Rochester Gay Men's Chorus, chorister Neka Zimmerman approached the artistic director and asked that the group make a change to a song that they have performed at every Christmas concert for many years. There is a section in this song during which singers recite the names of people they want to honor; in the past it has been names of victims of AIDS, and more recently, names of now-deceased choristers. Zimmerman asked whether the chorus could instead recite the names of transgender women of color who were killed in 2016; he was delighted when this request was accepted. "In general," he said, "our artistic director is pretty open to suggestions" (interview, December 19, 2016). Zimmerman also pointed out that not all the singers were satisfied with another change that was made: the chorus decided to sing "God rest ye merry gentlefolk" (rather than "gentlemen"), and some objected to changing the lyrics of a "classic." These singers were allowed to "sit out," to leave the stage during the performance of this song and return for the rest of the concert. Sitting out, or stepping out as it is sometimes called, is a way in which GALA choristers are welcome to publicly dissent from artistic directors' decisions—in other words, to assert their own opinions in the most important forum in which choruses operate. Choristers take this step when they have some objection to a song, usually to the lyrics or its extramusical associations, and especially when the song is sacred music from the Christian tradition. GALA choristers are thus permitted to enter and exit their choruses at their own volition, in front of a watching audience, without endangering their standing in their choruses.

Conclusion

In this chapter we saw that GALA choristers are motivated to participate in their local choruses for a variety of reasons, their desire to make music and to find community chief among them. By most accounts, choruses do an admirable job of providing a loving community—what singers in men's choristers, especially, often characterize as a family—to their choristers. The GALA Choruses organization as a whole, however, is marked by a pronounced gender difference; although the rhetoric is consistently in favor of gender equality, the actions of large numbers of GALA participants demonstrate that they have more interest in (and possibly more respect for) men's choruses than for either mixed choruses or women's choruses. Men's choruses, and the choristers who populate them, have more financial resources than do women's choruses, a fact that makes a profound difference in the kind of performances a chorus is able to present and the opportunities it can offer to its singers. The gender difference is especially evident in participants' perceptions of how choruses are governed—perceptions that are not necessarily supported by the negotiations of power evident in choristers' interactions with their artistic directors. In sum, the realities of the gender hierarchy are reflected in GALA Choruses' operations at the local and international levels. In the next chapter, we will see that other constructions of sameness and difference, particularly concerning ethnicity and gender, also impact GALA choruses, challenging insiders' own assertions that they are committed to diversity and inclusion.

3 • Diversity and Its Discontents

On June 3, 2017, at the Victoria Theatre in downtown Dayton, Ohio, the Dayton Gay Men's Chorus and the Dayton Contemporary Dance Company premiered a new work titled *Together We Must*. This five-movement work, approximately thirty minutes in length, was written for TTBB (tenor-tenor-baritone-bass) choir, spoken word soloist, a small complement of accompanying instruments, and nine dancers. Before the performance began, a representative of the chorus explained to the audience that *Together We Must* grew out of a day-long workshop held in 2016, during which the chorus and the dance company "discussed racism and homophobia in our communities." Kathy Clark, the artistic director of the chorus, composed the music, and members of the dance company choreographed the dance.

The performance was remarkable because it demonstrated, in a number of different ways, the success and strength of a representative (and rather small) GALA chorus. First, it exhibited the artistic competence of the Dayton Gay Men's Chorus: *Together We Must* is a long and complex work, and during this first public presentation of it, the choristers sang with skill and confidence, performing the piece entirely from memory. Second, the performance was evidence of the financial vitality of the chorus, which attracted three sponsors, including the Ohio Arts Council, to fund the creation of the new work. Third, the concert was proof positive that the chorus has a dedicated following in the Dayton area; the Victoria Theatre seats 1,154 people, and it was almost full. No discounts for students or senior citizens were offered, so all those who purchased tickets paid twenty or twenty-five dollars to attend. The audience turnout was particularly noteworthy because on the same evening, at exactly the same time and directly across the road from the Victoria Theatre, the Dayton Philharmonic Orchestra and the Dayton Philharmonic Chorus performed Mozart's *Requiem*.[1] Fans of choral music, therefore, had another option; they could have gone next door to hear a familiar and beloved staple of the choral repertoire performed by professional musicians. The fact that so many people chose to attend the concert of the Dayton Gay Men's Chorus is evidence of the interest the chorus attracts in the Dayton region.

I highlight the chorus' performance of *Together We Must* here for another reason. The performance and presentation of this work, given by a GALA chorus together with a dance company that "is rooted in the African American experience" (Dayton Contemporary Dance Company n.d.)—illuminates the argument I make in this chapter. GALA choruses are sincere in pursuing their mission of building a society that is more tolerant of human diversity, including, of course, diversity of sexual orientation and gender expression. However, GALA's commitment to diversity and inclusion is tested in its own backyard. *Together We Must* directly addressed racism and homophobia, communicating the message that "together we must" rise above the forces of exclusion and oppression to create a more inclusive community. The two ensembles shared the stage equally and were equally applauded by the audience. At the same time, among the thirty-seven singers onstage that evening, only three were African American; the membership of the chorus was generally unrepresentative of the local population (as I will explain below). Perhaps even more telling, the large audience was overwhelmingly White; there were very few people of color visible in the crowd. Despite the fact that a historically Black dance company, one with deep roots in the city of Dayton, was featured on the program, the performance did not attract a well-integrated audience. Although the chorus spent months preparing for and advertising this concert, the event ultimately featured a visibly White community choir, singing to a White audience.

The Whiteness of GALA

Why are GALA choruses not more inclusive? Asked another way, why do these choruses not more faithfully reflect the diversity of the communities in which they are located? GALA insiders have struggled with these questions for decades, and I discussed them with many interlocutors while researching this book. "Tell me about diversity in your chorus," provoked rich discussions of many dimensions of diversity, most often beginning with the notion of ethnic diversity.

The relative lack of ethnic diversity in GALA choruses is exemplified by the Dayton Gay Men's Chorus. According to US Census statistics collected in 2010, people who self-identify as White account for 51.7 percent of the population of the city (United States Census Bureau 2019). Self-identified Black or African American people make up 42.9 percent of the population. Yet, over the decade during which I have attended its concerts and interviewed its choristers, the Dayton Gay Men's Chorus has never included more than three African American men, out of a total of roughly thirty singers. The situation in Dayton is largely representative of the GALA organization as a whole. GALA choruses are composed mostly of self-identified White or Caucasian people—that is, people of European descent who speak English as their first language. This observation holds true both at the level of specific choruses, and among the senior leadership of the GALA organization. To be sure, numbers vary according to region and fluctuate year to year.[2] Choruses located in large cities on the coasts of the United States and Canada tend to have larger percentages of singers who self-identify as people of color, whereas choruses from smaller towns, and those located in the interior of the continent, are more uniformly White. The artistic directors of the choruses, the membership of the GALA Choruses board, and the paid staff members of the GALA Choruses organization are almost all White people.

GALA Choruses does not release information about the ethnic makeup of its member choruses, and therefore my assertions about the Whiteness of GALA are based on two previous studies and on my own observations. Paul Attinello (1994) surveyed singers in three large gay men's choruses. He received 172 questionnaire responses; 93 percent of those who responded identified themselves as White (329). Marvin Latimer (2008) conducted a similar study, collecting demographic information from eighty-seven singers of the Heartland Men's Chorus of Kansas City, Missouri. He found that 96.5 percent of them were White (26). My own research, conducted in the 2010s, suggests that the majority of GALA participants are still White. During the interviews I conducted with GALA insiders, I asked each person, "What is your ethnic identity?" Twenty-three of the twenty-five artistic directors answered White or Caucasian or some analogue (such as Ukrainian Canadian). Thirty-nine of the fifty-six singers gave the same or similar answers (including "Anglo-Saxon mutt").[3]

I also attempted to get an overview of ethnic diversity in GALA by sitting in the audience at GALA chorus performances. Between 2011 and 2016, I attended as many performances as I could in my home state of Ohio, as well as the 2012 and 2016 GALA Festivals. During most performances I counted the total number of singers onstage and then the number of singers who appeared to be people of color. My findings are summarized in table 1. As the table shows, I had difficulty counting the total number of singers in choruses of more than fifty singers. But the general pattern was clear: the singers of color were rather easily distinguished from the whole because there were so few of them. In the table I note the few choruses in which the number of people of color appeared to exceed 15 percent of the total number of singers.

My observations of chorus demographics were limited by a number of factors. First, I found it difficult to see some singers because of where they stood onstage. Second, the stage lights sometimes distorted my visual perception of singers' faces. Third and most importantly, I did not have the opportunity to ask each of the thousands of singers I observed which ethnic identity they claim. Nevertheless, I offer these observations here because—as I discovered during my research—this rather unscientific analysis, conducted from an audience member's seat, is exactly the kind of analysis that other people conduct when they draw conclusions about the ethnic makeup of GALA groups. For example, Cory Barrett told me that the Denver Gay Men's Chorus is "a White men's group—you can see it when they perform!" (interview, January 3, 2017). He explained that he found himself counting at the chorus's concerts and had seen between ten and fifteen people of color out of a total of two hundred singers. Similarly, Aditya Adiredja explained that he was favorably impressed by the Reveille Men's Chorus of Tucson, Arizona. Before he formally joined the group, he attended a concert and was glad that he could see singers of color onstage—"and they weren't all stuck in the background!" (interview, December 20, 2016).

We can draw a few conclusions from my data. First, in the overwhelming majority of GALA choruses, the singers of color appear to account for fewer than 15 percent of choristers. In fact, the most common situation among GALA choruses is to have zero singers of color. The next most common situation is to have one singer of color, and the third most common situation is to have two. Among those few choruses for which singers of color account for at least 20 percent of choristers, two are women's choruses in large cities. The longtime artistic director of MUSE, Cincinnati Women's Choir, Catherine Roma, is quoted later in this chapter as an exception to GALA's usual approach to ethnic diversity; clearly, Roma's idea about attracting ethnically diverse singers deserves a hearing. The third anomalous chorus, Confluence (from the Willamette Valley, Oregon), for which singers of color accounted for a record 23.5 percent of choristers in its 2016 Festival performance, also has an artistic director who is African American, a rarity in GALA circles. From this small amount of data, we can tentatively conclude that artistic directors who are intentional about attracting singers of color, or who embody ethnic diversity themselves, are an important factor in their choruses' success in diversifying the membership.

Table 1. Author's Observations of Singers of Color in GALA Chorus Performances, 2012–2016

Name of chorus*	Occasion	Total number of singers	Total number of singers who appeared to be people of color (percentage)*
Heartland Men's Chorus	2012 Festival	142	6
Gateway Men's Chorus	2012 Festival	29	0
Rainbow Women's Chorus	2012 Festival	19	1
Sound Circle	2012 Festival	16	0
Lesbian/Gay Chorus of San Francisco	2012 Festival	a large group	0
Orlando Gay Chorus	2012 Festival	a large group	12
Gay Men's Chorus of Los Angeles	2012 Festival	a large group	at least 12
Resonance Women's Chorus	2012 Festival	a large group	2
Sacramento Gay Men's Chorus	2012 Festival	34	2
Calgary Men's Chorus	2012 Festival	a large group	0
Quarryland Men's Chorus	2012 Festival	18	0
Gay Men's Chorus of Charlotte	2012 Festival	16	0
MUSE	2012 Festival	44	10 (23%)
Perfect Harmony	2012 Festival	a large group	0
Kansas City Women's Chorus	2012 Festival	35	7 (20%)
ANNA Crusis	2012 Festival	25	4 (16%)
Buffalo Gay Men's Chorus	2012 Festival	45	2
Philadelphia Gay Men's Chorus	2012 Festival	a large group	7
Coastliners	2014 Gay Games	10	0
Good Company	2014 Gay Games	28	1
Windsong	2014 Gay Games	30	1
North Coast Men's Chorus	2014 Gay Games	approx. 50	7
Calgary Men's Chorus	2016 rehearsal	31	5 (16%)
Columbus Gay Men's Chorus	2016 Festival	50	1
Confluence	2016 Festival	17	4 (23.5%)
Vocal Harmonies	2016 Festival	24	2
Common Chords	2016 Festival	11	1
Ovation	2016 Festival	12	0
Illuminati	2016 Festival	29	0
Rainbow Harmony Project	2016 Festival	21	1
One Voice Calgary	2016 Festival	20	0
Sistrum	2016 Festival	18	0
River City Mixed Chorus	2016 Festival	65	1
Singing Out Las Cruces	2016 Festival	20	1
Portland Gay Men's Chorus	2016 Festival	approx. 145	1
Windy City Gay Chorus	2016 Festival	56	2
Harrisburg Gay Men's Chorus	2016 Festival	11	0
Desert Voices	2016 Festival	28	2
Richmond Men's Chorus	2016 Festival	23	1
Gay Men's Chorus of South Florida	2016 Festival	80	7
West Coast Singers	2016 Festival	49	2
Dayton Gay Men's Chorus	2016 Festival	26	0
Rainbow Chorale	2016 Festival	23	1
Una Voce	2016 Festival	33	6 (18%)

* Choruses arranged in order of performance at each event.

*The last column includes in parentheses a percentage for people of color to total number of singers only if it is greater than 15 percent.

*A "large group" indicates that I was unable to complete the count, but the number was very large, more than 50 singers.

Addressing the Issue of Ethnic Diversity

I addressed the lack of ethnic diversity in GALA groups with many of my interlocutors; they expressed varying levels of concern and described taking different actions in response. Maria-Elena Grant of the Lavender Light Gospel Choir of New York City told me that, upon attending her first GALA-level meeting in 1994, she was struck by the fact that all the board members were White. Her response, as a British Jamaican, was to nominate herself for the GALA board; she received a "huge vote" and went on to serve on the GALA board for some years (interview, October 29, 2011). Aditya Adiredja, who is a Chinese-Indonesian American citizen, told me that he is "cautiously optimistic" that the pervasive Whiteness of GALA may change. For now, he said, he wants to "occupy the space"; "you have to pick your battles" as a person of color in a predominantly White organization (interview, December 20, 2016). Steve Milloy, an African American score arranger and artistic director for a number of GALA choruses, insisted that GALA must take action to build ethnic diversity in the ranks: "In order to have a voice in the twenty-first century—beyond 'We're here, we're queer'—we *have* to pay attention to and reach out to people of color; if we don't we look like pompous asses" (interview, July 16, 2011).

In 2010, Milloy, who was then the assistant director of the Cincinnati Men's Chorus, sent an email to the GALA listserv, asking, "How many African American conductors are there in GALA?" (interview, July 16, 2011). He received only one response. This incident—which received serious attention, based on the number of times I heard about it from other readers of the listserv—may be indicative of a broader reluctance to discuss the lack of ethnic diversity in GALA circles. During my research I encountered some GALA insiders who seemed rather uninterested in the diversity question. For example, Fred Poland of the Dayton Gay Men's Chorus said that, while the chorus's board did exert some pressure to recruit "minority" singers, he himself felt that the concern was "a bit misplaced," saying that the chorus already represents a minority population—that is, gay men (interview, June 16, 2011). Patrick Holcomb of the North Coast Men's Chorus of Cleveland, Ohio, seemed nonplussed when I asked him about ethnic diversity in his chorus: "Everybody's welcome. . . . I couldn't tell you how many culturally diverse people we have . . . they're just members of the chorus, brothers. I never even thought about it" (interview, September 14, 2014).

The clearest and most disturbing example of resistance to ethnic diversity that I discovered in my research—specifically, resistance to the notion that non-White perspectives should be honored in GALA circles—was recounted in depth by Diane Benjamin (interview, February 10, 2012).[4] Benjamin was the accompanist for Calliope Women's Chorus of Minneapolis, Minnesota, and she served on the GALA Choruses board from 1992 to 1994. Her story begins in 1992, the five hundredth anniversary of the arrival of Christopher Columbus in the Americas. Various commemorations and protests took place across the continent in recognition of the impact of this event. Calliope Women's Chorus presented a concert in collaboration with a Native women's drumming circle, "to celebrate five hundred years of Native peoples' survival." The concert featured, among other songs, a new composition cowritten by a chorister who was an Anishinaabe Ojibwe woman. Calliope, by consensus, decided to sing three songs from this concert at the 1992 GALA Festival, held in Denver, Colorado. At the Festival, Calliope heard the Columbus Gay Men's Chorus, of Columbus, Ohio, perform; Benjamin's best recollection is that the chorus sang "a jokey show-tune type song [about Christopher Columbus], with a line in it about seeing the savages on the shore."[5]

Calliope's singers had several long discussions about the men's chorus's song; they eventually decided (again by consensus) to use their own performance time to make a statement in response. As Benjamin recalled, "[The statement] was quite mild; we specifically did not name the Columbus Gay Men's Chorus. We just asked GALA not to condone these kinds of lyrics. We then called for a moment of silence in acknowledgment of the genocide [perpetrated by Christopher Columbus and his successors], and then we sang our last song." The reaction was intense: some audience members booed Calliope, some walked out, and one person yelled "Your singing is great but your politics suck!" As Benjamin pointed out, this audience behavior was especially shocking in the context of a GALA Festival, where audiences are generally overwhelmingly supportive of all performances (as discussed in chapter 1 of this book). For the rest of the 1992 Festival week, Calliope choristers faced angry remarks from other Festival delegates, who claimed that Calliope had behaved inappropriately by criticizing, however implicitly, another choir while onstage. "The reaction we got was really disproportionate to what occurred," Benjamin said.

Benjamin herself continued to serve on the GALA board. She and her fellow choristers were shocked when, in October 1992—that is, around the time of Columbus Day—each of them received a personally addressed form letter from an anonymous "member of the Columbus Gay Men's Chorus." Benjamin recalled the message of the letter as "'How dare you, you bitches?' It was very misogynistic language, hate mail basically." Looking back, Benjamin reflected, "Perhaps Calliope could have raised our disagreement privately with the Columbus Gay Men's Chorus . . . but the reaction really showed the racism and intolerance in GALA. Even in a group that prides itself on inclusion and openness, when you scratch the surface, things come out."

At the time of the writing of this book, the story recounted above is twenty-five years in the past. And as I explain further below, GALA Choruses has engaged in a number of diversity initiatives during its four decades of existence. Diane Benjamin herself "worked on diversity issues" while serving on the GALA board in the early 1990s (interview, February 10, 2012). While I conducted ethnographic research on GALA from 2011 to 2016, I discovered tangible evidence that both leaders and rank-and-file singers are discussing GALA's relative lack of ethnic diversity, and actively working to make the movement more inclusive. With that said, at this point, GALA remains a White-majority organization.

GALA Choruses is, of course, not exceptional in this regard. Rather, GALA's Whiteness reflects the pervasive Whiteness of the two scenes to which GALA is most strongly tied: the gay and lesbian community and the amateur choral music groups of the United States and Canada. As other scholars have noted, the public face of the gay and lesbian community is White. AIDS Coalition to Unleash Power (ACT UP), for example, one of the best known and most influential gay rights organizations of the 1990s, had a "largely white, male, middle-class membership" and "attempted, without great success, to recruit African Americans and Latinos" (Rimmerman 2002, 106). Neither the mainstream nor the gay press has done much to challenge the notion that gay people are White people. The lesbian and gay characters appearing in advertisements, television shows, and movies are almost always played by White actors, and the perceived "white homogeneity of the American gay movement" is a problem of long standing (Browning 1993, 196; see also Almaguer 1993, 263). And, as Alexandra Chasin (2000, 60), points out, "race is, with shockingly few exceptions, not addressed as a theme in issue after issue of periodical after periodical of the white-run gay press."

If gay identity is correlated with White identity, especially for men—an idea I heard articulated during my own fieldwork[6]—then choral singing, perhaps even more powerfully, is a White-majority activity. Community choirs in both the United States and Canada are composed largely of White singers and are led by White directors, and these choirs sing to mostly White audiences. As Jean-Louis Bleau, former artistic director of the Calgary Men's Chorus, described it to me: the Canadian choral scene is "kind of a whitewash" (interview, June 24, 2016). Cindy Bell (2004, 43), who compared a number of studies of community choirs in the United States, found that "minorities are disproportionately underrepresented in community singing with sources revealing 85–96% of the adult singers to be White." Further, Chorus America's study of choral music audiences, which included data from audiences for three different GALA choruses, revealed that 86 percent of audience members self-identified as White or Caucasian (Brown et al. 2016, 21). GALA choruses, therefore, are not exceptional in their lack of ethnic diversity; indeed, when considered as either part of the gay rights movement or part of the community choir scene, they reflect broader demographic trends.

Accounting for GALA's Lack of Ethnic Diversity

With that said, I agree with scholar Charles I. Nero's (2005, 231) contention that it is insufficient for scholars to acknowledge that a particular scene is disproportionately White without advancing an explanation for this imbalance. Nero himself asked, "Why are gay ghettos white?" and offered two answers based on his ethnographic study of a so-called gay ghetto in New Orleans: specifically, the cost of housing favors White home buyers, who typically have more money to spend, and a racially insensitive and even offensive atmosphere in the neighborhood discourages African Americans from wanting to live there. In what follows, I advance several explanations for why GALA choruses are predominantly White, noting that some of these explanations were suggested to me by concerned GALA insiders who have thought deeply about the question.

First, participating in a GALA chorus costs money. Singers usually have to pay annual membership fees and purchase uniforms, at a minimum, and they are encouraged to spend thousands of dollars traveling to the quadrennial GALA Festival and to other choral festivals around the world. (The GALA Choruses website maintains a listing of worldwide festivals; in 2017 and 2018 these festivals included Cromatica in Naples, Hand in Hand Asia in Seoul, and Various Voices in Munich.) Given that socioeconomic class intersects powerfully with ethnic identity in both the United States and Canada, people of color are less likely to be able to afford to participate in a GALA chorus than White people are (Wilson and Rodgers 2016; National Council of Welfare 2012). Second, rehearsal location may be a "barrier to entry," as one of my interlocutors called it (Octavio Partida, interview, November 7, 2016).[7] If rehearsals are held in a predominantly White neighborhood, people of color may feel unwelcome. As Charles Nero discovered, and as Diane Benjamin's story showed, discourse in White locales—even predominantly gay and lesbian scenes, which promote themselves as bastions of freedom—

may reinforce racist messages (Green 2007, 766–67). Also, rehearsal locations may be relatively inaccessible to people of color. Residential segregation remains a real and potent factor in American cities, influencing life outcomes for residents of neighborhoods (Greene, Turner, and Gourevitch 2017). People of color are most likely to live in neighborhoods dominated by other people of color, and separate from neighborhoods that are predominantly White. People of color who live in a neighborhood far from their local GALA chorus's rehearsal location must therefore confront the possibility of a long journey by car or public transportation; the long commute may discourage them from participating in the chorus.

Third, as is explained in chapter 2, GALA singers most often become involved with their local GALA chorus by being invited to join by a current chorister. Current singers and artistic directors are mostly White, and they issue invitations mostly to other White people; thus, GALA choruses continue to attract a preponderance of White singers. Maria-Elena Grant expressed this idea gracefully when she pointed out that GALA was founded by White people in the late 1970s and remains predominantly White today: "Everything takes on the shape of its roots" (interview, October 29, 2011). Grant's, and my own, inference about who gets invited to join GALA choruses is supported by the Public Religion Research Institute's 2013 American Values Survey (Cox, Navarro-Rivera and Jones 2013). The survey was self-administered online; a nationally representative sample of 2,317 adults responded. The survey aimed to "measure Americans' core social networks." The survey designers defined a member of one's core social network as a person "with whom they 'discussed important matters' in the previous six months regardless of the nature of the relationship or the frequency of interaction." Survey respondents were able to name up to seven members of their core social network. The results revealed that significant numbers of Americans have racially homogeneous social networks; a large minority (46 percent) of self-identified Hispanic people reported that their social networks were entirely composed of other Hispanic people, and a majority (65 percent) of self-identified Black Americans reported that their social networks, too, consisted only of other Black people. But the survey's most striking finding was that "fully three-quarters (75%) of white Americans report that the network of people with whom they discuss important matters is entirely white, with no minority presence." In other words, in twenty-first-century America, three-quarters of White people—who constitute the large majority of the population of GALA—discuss important matters only with other White people. One such important matter might be, we can imagine, what a friend's sexual orientation or gender identification is, whether that friend has any interest in choral singing, and whether that friend might want to join a local GALA chorus. To the extent that GALA choruses grow because current participants encourage members of their own social networks to join, we can see that GALA's Whiteness becomes self-perpetuating. Because GALA choruses are filled with White people, and because those people may never discuss important matters with people of color, invitations to join choruses (and to diversify the chorus membership) are not often issued to Black, Hispanic, Asian, Native, and other Americans.

Cost of participation, rehearsal location, and the lack of an invitation likely account for part of the reason why GALA choruses fail to include representative numbers of singers of color. But the biggest challenge to building ethnically diverse choruses is that—according to GALA insiders I interviewed—for many people of color, joining a chorus is tantamount to claiming membership in the LGBT community. And an LGBT identity is understood to conflict in some way with certain ethnic identities (see also E. Hayes 2010, 59). As was mentioned above, ubiquitous media images reinforce the notion that gay equals White; the result is that people of color who experience same-sex desire may decline to identify themselves as gay. Ethnomusicologist Alisha Lola Jones (2016, 221) discovered that several African American men who consented to interviews with her referred to themselves as "homosexual" because "the term 'gay' . . . often registered . . . as signifying dominant White social and cultural experiences." Professor of social work Michael LaSala (2010, 225) identified a similar phenomenon among Caribbean immigrants in the United States, and ethnic studies scholar Tomás Almaguer (1993) observed it with Chicano men. Almaguer noted that "in the Mexican/Latin American context there is no cultural equivalent to the modern gay man" (257). Chicano men who do identify as gay, therefore, are understood to have adopted a "foreign" sexual practice and are referred to as *internationales* (262). As a result, self-identified gay organizations may struggle to attract members who do not self-identify as White.

The GALA singers of color I interviewed for this project clearly transcended this supposed divide; they identified themselves to me as gay or lesbian *and* as African American, Hispanic, Chinese American, and so on. Nevertheless they—along with some of the White singers I interviewed—claimed that embracing both an LGBT identity and a non-White ethnic identity is uniquely difficult, because one faces the prospect of being exiled from one's ethnically identified community when one comes out as gay or lesbian (John Whalen, interview, January 3, 2013). As one African American woman put it during a discussion on racial diversity at the 2016 GALA Festival, "Black and gay just don't go together."[8] Her own life experience was testament to this assertion: she shared that she was excommunicated from her predominantly Black Baptist church, after decades of service in various church ministries, when she revealed that she is a lesbian. Anthropologist Kath Weston (1991, 134) concluded, similarly, "Whites without a strong ethnic identification often described coming out as a transition from no community *into* community, whereas people of color were more likely to focus on conflicts *between* identities, instead of expressing a sense of relief and arrival."

One branch of the literature examining the intersection of homosexual identity and various ethnic identities focuses in particular on African American gay men and lesbians. Homosexuality in Black communities has been called "the greatest sexual taboo in the African Diaspora" (Constantine-Simms 2000b, 76). Therefore—according to this line of thinking—one can choose to participate in the Black community, or one can publicly identify as gay or lesbian, but not both (Green 2007, 758). As ethnomusicologist Eileen M. Hayes (2010, 60) found in her study of race, sexual politics, and the women's music scene, in which a number of Black lesbian musicians requested that she not disclose their names, these individuals were mindful of this very dynamic as they traversed different music communities in making their livings as professional musicians.[9] African American studies and performance studies scholar E. Patrick Johnson (2009), one of the most eloquent chroniclers of Black gay experiences, wrote in a deeply revealing book chapter that he himself struggles to be open about his gay identity when he visits with his African American extended family. Johnson recounted that he does not mention his (male) partner when he is at home, and he tempers his response when asked when he is going to marry a nice girl and have children (63). Johnson argues that he is representative of many Black gay men and lesbians who participate in a "complicity of silence," declining to "*name* that identity or *flaunt* that transgression" in order to maintain their place in the Black community (55).

Still more scholarly accounts reveal another possible explanation for the underrepresentation of African American men, specifically, in GALA choruses: these men have another place to sing, a place in which they can celebrate their homosexuality (albeit in guarded ways) and simultaneously participate in the historical and ongoing musical contributions of the African American community. More simply said, they are welcome to sing in Black church choirs.[10] Being a gay man in a Black church choir is a somewhat problematic position to hold because most Black evangelical churches condemn homosexuality as a sin and preach against it (Green 2007, 761–63). Scholars have repeatedly critiqued music ministries in Black evangelical churches for benefiting from the unpaid labor of gay men and lesbian women, whom they publicly condemn; this duality is the "central contradiction of Black church practice" (E. Hayes 2010, 119; see also Hawkeswood 1996, 39–40; Johnson 2009, 55; Jones 2016, 225). Indeed the position of gay and lesbian musicians in Black churches is reminiscent of the racial injustice the Black church has always contested: "Like blacks who accepted a place of inferiority in order to stay within white racist churches and institutions, black lesbians and gays must stay in a place of inferiority to remain in black churches" (Griffin 2000, 116–17).

Nevertheless, the Black church choir continues to be a place where gay men can and do sing. In his study of gay Black men in Harlem, New York, William G. Hawkeswood (1996) found that the church was central to his informants' lives. These men told Hawkeswood that they found gay friends among their fellow congregants, and especially among the choristers: "All the choir boys are sissies . . . there's a strong network of us in the church" (111). E. Patrick Johnson (2008, 184) explains why gay men are especially committed to singing in their church choirs: "The choir provides a medium to express one's sexuality through the theatricality already built into the church service . . . [singing in the choir is a way] to express and affirm our queerness without ever naming our sexuality." In church choirs, men wear choir robes, a uniform that is like a dress (that is, like a feminine garment). Men often sing high notes (high pitches are usually associated with female singers), and male soloists are lauded for being able to improvise in their falsetto range, producing notes that are an octave or more above middle C. Perhaps most importantly, male singers are expected to move their bodies while singing, often using big, energetic gestures. To say it another way, they are encouraged to perform stereotypically feminine traits and to do so flamboyantly—although their movements are interpreted not as affirming a singer's homosexuality but rather his anointing by the Holy Spirit (Johnson 2008, 184).

GALA's Diversity Initiatives

The GALA Choruses organization has taken up a number of initiatives during its nearly four decades of existence in order to address the lack of both gender and ethnic diversity among its member choruses. Some people interviewed for this book played central roles in these efforts. Catherine Roma, founding director of MUSE, Cincinnati's Women's Choir, was asked to join the GALA board in 1986 in order to promote the inclusion of more women's choruses in the GALA Festival (interview, January 19, 2012), and Maria-Elena Grant served on a diversity committee in the 1990s (interview, October 29, 2011). Most recently, GALA's leadership engaged in a sustained effort to gather information and generate new ideas in response to concerns that were raised after the 2012 Festival (Cory Barrett, interview, January 3, 2017).[11] Jane Ramseyer-Miller, the artistic director of GALA Choruses, convened an ad hoc diversity and inclusion workgroup; singers and artistic directors in this workgroup met monthly, via phone conference, for nearly three years.

The workgroup's discussions focused largely on how the GALA organization could promote more inclusion of both transgender singers and people of color. This initiative resulted in a number of changes and new events at the 2016 Festival. To provide a more welcoming space to transgender people, the 2016 Festival featured a gender-neutral bathroom in the central concert hall, and a handout encouraged Festival attendees to refer to choirs by the voice parts they included (e.g., soprano, alto, tenor, baritone, or bass) rather than as "men's choruses" or as "women's choruses."[12] To welcome and celebrate people of color, the 2016 Festival included a People of Color Gathering. Those who attended the gathering received free food and wine and—more importantly—had the chance to be part of a critical mass of people of color, a marked change from their usual Festival experience of being individuals who constitute a visible minority.[13]

To underline GALA's support for both transgender people and people of color, the 2016 Festival organizers created concert blocks to showcase music performed and created by people from both groups. The Gender Blender concert, held on July 5, 2016, began with three songs that explicitly referenced transgender experiences; the concert also included several video messages from supportive celebrities like Broadway musical star Kristen Chenoweth, and personal testimonies from GALA composers and singers who spoke about being transgender and their experiences of transitioning. One of the Festival's opening concerts, held on July 2, 2016, had a special emphasis on ethnic diversity, featuring a number of spirituals and other Black-identified songs such as "Glory" from the soundtrack of the 2014 movie *Selma*.[14] The Mosaico concert of July 4, 2016, was entirely devoted to performers of color and included the People of Color Festival Chorus, a pickup group created just for the Festival. All these concerts were very well attended, and the Mosaico concert was sold out. Festival organizers also provided two workshops that were so well attended that attendees who arrived late had to stand. The July 3, 2016, workshop was titled "The Art of Gullah Stick-Pounding"; it was an interactive music-making session intended to help participants understand some of the music culture of the Gullah people of the Carolina sea islands.[15] The "Introduction to Trans Singing" workshop held on July 4,

2016, was a group discussion that included specific and helpful advice for singers who are using testosterone or estrogen to transition.

The open table sessions that GALA sponsored at the 2016 Festival were more intimate, by design. These sessions, which allowed for two hours of open discussion on various themes, were held in a designated safe space that included refreshments and supplies for simple arts and crafts. The first open table I attended, on July 3, 2016, addressed the question, "How can GALA be more inclusive? And especially, how can GALA attract more people of color?" The eight people there shared their remarks and listened to each other respectfully, creating what I experienced as a kind and listening atmosphere. I attended another open table session on July 4, 2016; the stated topic for the session was "Dating and Relationships," but the twenty people who participated spoke mostly about the challenges of being a transgender singer in a GALA chorus—"an outsider among outsiders," as one attendee phrased it. At both workshops, I was impressed by how effectively the discussion facilitators encouraged a variety of people to speak and to express a range of perspectives. In sum, having personally experienced GALA's recent efforts to build diversity, I came away from the 2016 Festival convinced that GALA's senior leadership is sincerely committed to including and honoring the wide range of people in its ranks and is open to making changes to undergird this commitment.

Diversity at the Local Level

The international GALA Choruses organization is evidently attempting to transform its quadrennial Festival so that the Festival will valorize viewpoints and cultural contributions of people beyond GALA's (White, cisgender male, gay) demographic majority. That said, diversity initiatives are usually enacted, and their impact is usually felt, at the local chorus level. As Cory Barrett, who participated in the ad hoc diversity and inclusion workgroup, pointed out, the GALA organization has control only over the Festival (interview, January 3, 2017). Member choruses run their own affairs, and the GALA leadership can only offer recommendations and training opportunities. In my discussions with people across the United States and Canada, I found that while there is some cynicism about the GALA organization's commitment to diversity, rank-and-file participants were almost unanimous in commending their own local chorus's diversity initiatives.

Julio Avila, who was the board president of Perfect Harmony Men's Chorus of Madison, Wisconsin, for two years, exemplified this kind of divided opinion. When I asked him about diversity in GALA, he expressed frustration: "They're not even talking about it!" (interview, February 27, 2012). He said that he "struggled" with the international GALA organization, in part because the leadership did not effectively communicate its plans regarding diversity. On the other hand, Avila was extremely positive about Perfect Harmony's work in this regard. At the time of our interview, the board was formulating plans to reach out to Madison-area groups including the Urban League and the Latino Chamber of Commerce and was considering allowing video applications for membership (in addition to paper applications), to be more welcoming to new singers with learning and physical disabilities. Avila summarized his experience with Perfect Harmony by saying, "I could never repay [this chorus] for what they've done for me. They have given me a new understanding of servant leadership. [My time as board president] has been the best year and a half of my life" (interview, February 27, 2012).

Jill Strachan is another excellent example. Strachan was a founding singer in the Lesbian and Gay Chorus of Washington, DC, and she served on the GALA Choruses board from 1993 to 1999. She gave years of volunteer labor to the GALA organization, working to build more respect for women and for mixed choruses within the movement. She reluctantly concluded that, "GALA Choruses was always stuck in being politically correct, but it could never be cutting edge. And the reason for that is that GALA was founded and is maintained by White gay men. And so there's a conservatism at the heart of the movement" (interview, March 2, 2012). Strachan criticized the tokenism that allowed GALA leaders to valorize Lavender Light Gospel Choir—GALA's only predominantly African American chorus—by showcasing this choir at the Festival, while simultaneously maintaining a structure that consistently marginalized women and people of color. At the same time, Strachan remained proud of the diversity initiatives pursued by her own chorus. She pointed out that the Lesbian and Gay Chorus of Washington, DC, was the first among GALA groups to sing South African freedom songs, a repertoire it presented to GALA audiences at the 1989 Festival. The chorus was also a consistent proponent of consensus governance for local choruses, a model that was centrally concerned with respecting the opinions of all choristers (for more on consensus governance, see chapter 2). In Strachan's view, the Lesbian and Gay Chorus of Washington, DC, lived out its commitment to diversity and inclusion, but that fact made the group an exception in the larger GALA organization: "We never intended to be controversial, but within GALA we were definitely considered strange."

Other GALA insiders who spoke to me exclusively about their local choruses were enthusiastic in endorsing their choruses' efforts to build diversity or, at least, to build respect for the idea of diversity. For example, Kaeden Kass, a transgender singer in the Cincinnati Men's Chorus, said that he was "surprised in a good way by the level of enthusiastic support" for an impor tant change to the chorus' description of itself (interview, February 9, 2017). The Cincinnati Men's Chorus had long described itself—online and in verbal introductions before performances—as "gay men and their straight allies." However, in an effort to show respect and welcome for people beyond its demographic majority, the chorus changed this language to "individuals identifying as male, whether gay, bisexual, transgender, or straight allies." Kass said he was "pleased and proud" that the chorus board held formal discussions about this issue and then put the proposal to a meeting of the entire chorus; the proposal passed unanimously. Vic Hooper, who served as artistic director of Rainbow Harmony Project in Winnipeg, Canada, told me, "This group is all about diversity"; therefore, he allowed choristers who could not memorize certain songs to use their scores during concerts, even though the chorus's general standard was that all music must be performed from memory (interview, September 9, 2011). Dennis Coleman, the longtime artistic director of the Seattle Men's Chorus, told me that he was proud that the chorus generally had greater proportions of African Americans in its ranks than did the surrounding city population (interview, September 24, 2011). Coleman attributed this achievement to the fact that the Seattle Men's Chorus intentionally programmed music composed by, and of interest to, African Americans; the chorus once devoted an entire concert to Black gospel repertoire, and it employed a guest artistic director who was an expert in Black gospel music to lead rehearsals. The chorus also sponsored a quartet of African American singers that was "very successful" according to Coleman; the quartet performed at the 2012 GALA Festival.

Still other GALA insiders were optimistic about their local chorus's commitment to progressive change and spoke with hope about upcoming initiatives. Octavio Partida, who identifies as Hispanic, told me that he is confident that the leadership of his chorus, the Reveille Men's Chorus of Tucson, Arizona, is sincere in "reaching out to diverse communities, to bring them to our choir" (interview, November 7, 2016). For example, in fall 2016 the chorus engaged in honest discussion about an issue I outlined above: location. Reveille rehearses on the East Side of Tucson, but the majority of the city's Hispanic population lives on the South Side. Partida was confident that choristers would consider changing the locations of their outreach and fundraising activities, if not their rehearsal spot, in order to make meaningful contacts with the Hispanic community. Mikal Rasheed said that he is the only Muslim (to his knowledge) in the Gay Men's Chorus of Washington, DC. At the time of our interview, he was looking forward to participating in an inter-faith "listening session" organized by his chorus. Rasheed was confident that the chorus was "trying to be sensitive to *all* faiths, and atheists" because he had already seen that commitment in action via the chorus's programming choices (interview, February 9, 2017). He mentioned a recent holiday concert that had included songs celebrating Hanukkah, Kwanzaa, and the winter solstice. Rasheed said that the concert sent "a really beautiful message of inclusion. As a Muslim I never felt like the Other, even at the holiday concert. The GMC is phenomenal! They take a lot of time to include people of different faith traditions, emphasizing the common threads."

The diversity initiative that my interlocutors mentioned most often was programming—that is, the choice of songs that (GALA insiders believed) would celebrate and attract people of color. Indeed, this advice was given at GALA's 2011 annual leadership conference; during a workshop on "What kind of programming will connect with audiences?" participants agreed that programming "ethnic" songs is important to attract members of ethnic minority groups.[16] Chorus America's 2016 study of choral music audiences also takes this view. The authors of the study wrote that anecdotal evidence collected in their survey suggested that programming affects the racial diversity of choral music audiences; that is, works associated with a particular ethnic group tend to draw larger numbers of people from that group as audience members (Brown et al. 2016, 22). "All of this is intuitive and validates . . . one of the central tenets of decades of audience research—that the audience is a reflection of what's onstage. Artistic directors curate programs, and, in so doing, curate audiences" (27).

Dennis Coleman and Mikal Rasheed both agreed with this approach: they linked their choruses' presentation of particular songs and concert themes to their ability to attract and retain singers and audience members who identify as something other than White and Christian. Jean-Louis Bleau explained it thus: "In my programming I try to prioritize songs in other languages [i.e., other than English]. We're trying, even if we don't pronounce all the words right—because music opens doors to understanding" (interview, June 24, 2016). Maria-Elena Grant and Steve Milloy both insisted that singing Black-identified songs such as spirituals is crucial if choruses want to attract African American singers. Milloy referenced both the importance of programming and the challenge of Black identity's presumed link to heterosexuality when he explained, "People always ask me, 'How can we attract more African Americans?' and I say, 'Go back in the closet and sing gospel!'" (interview, July 16, 2011).

Some of my interlocutors, however, questioned the logic of the idea that programming is the key to building a more diverse GALA. Jane Hoffman, a former board member of GALA Choruses who participated in efforts such as bringing in a diversity training expert to address an annual leadership conference, said that "the lack of intentionality just drove me bananas . . . you don't sing gospel just so Black people will come!" (interview, March 1, 2012). Dorian Osborne, an African American singer in the Dayton Gay Men's Chorus, thought that this kind of targeted programming could even backfire. He himself is a passionate fan of Kirk Franklin and other contemporary gospel music artists, but he wanted his chorus to avoid singing gospel songs, specifically because it is a gay-identified chorus: "My family would see that as a form of mockery" (interview, August 16, 2011). Catherine Roma acknowledged that it is "very hard for GALA to recruit people of color" (interview, January 19, 2012). She explained that MUSE was more successful than most GALA groups at including women of color, especially African American women, because the choir did not settle for programming as its primary strategy: "What you have to do is *show up* at events in those communities. You have to go to them, not just wait for them to come to you. You have to show an interest in order to become more diverse." MUSE has lived out this belief by performing at a variety of events around the Cincinnati area, for a total of twenty-five to thirty concerts per year. MUSE has sung at a fundraiser for breast cancer treatment, at a memorial for victims of domestic abuse, and at the graduation ceremony for Off the Streets, a program for women victims of sex trafficking. Large GALA choruses that have enough singers to populate "run-out" groups (small ensembles) also present significant numbers of concerts in response to community invitations. However, the most common diversity initiative discussed in GALA circles is strategic programming for concerts to which audience members are supposed to come—as opposed to programming for events to which GALA choruses will go.

One Dimension of Local Diversity: Transgender Singers

In the second decade of the twenty-first century, transgender singers and ensembles became more prominent in GALA circles, at the same time that transgender people became more visible in the United States and Canada at large.[17] GALA Choruses saw the founding of choruses intended specifically for transgender singers, including Phoenix, Colorado's Trans Community Choir; the Trans Chorus of Los Angeles; and the Butterfly Music Transgender Chorus (in Boston, Massachusetts).[18] Both Phoenix and the Trans Chorus of Los Angeles benefited from tangible support offered by other GALA choruses: Phoenix was joined by singers from Resonance Women's Chorus of Boulder for early performances, for example, and the artistic director of the Trans Chorus of Los Angeles described the Gay Men's Chorus of Los Angeles as "the birth parents" of her chorus.[19] Phoenix and the Trans Chorus of Los Angeles also both performed at the 2016 GALA Festival (Phoenix was then known as the Colorado Trans Chorale), and both received enthusiastic receptions. As discussed above, during the 2016 Festival the GALA leadership demonstrated its willingness to respond to concerns expressed by transgender singers, by encouraging the use of gender-free terminology to identify types of choruses (SSAA [soprano-soprano-alto-alto], TTBB [tenor-tenor-baritone-bass], or SATB [soprano-alto-tenor-bass]), by providing a gender-neutral bathroom in the main venue, by hosting open table sessions, and by including concert blocks designed to celebrate transgender people and the music they create.

While transgender visibility in GALA is a relatively new phenomenon, transgender singers' participation in GALA choruses is not.[20] Transgender singers have found both joys and challenges in GALA choruses. For some, this opportunity has been rewarding because it is a relief from the vocal dysphoria they experienced when they were younger. Gender dysphoria refers to the emotional distress experienced by transgender people as a result of the dissonance between their true gender (that is, the gender they know themselves to be) and the gender assigned to them at birth (based on physical characteristics including genitalia). Vocal dysphoria is a term I heard at a GALA workshop, and it was used to describe the distress that young transgender people feel when they hear their own voices, especially their singing voices. Kaeden Kass described this feeling of vocal dysphoria: "Before I transitioned I was super uncomfortable with my voice." As a teenager, he sang in the low alto range, "but still, my voice felt separate from me. I liked to sing, but only alone in my room with the door locked. I was mortified a couple of times when my parents overheard" (interview, February 9, 2017). As part of his transition process, Kass began taking testosterone while attending university, and his voice deepened considerably. Kass now sings tenor and baritone parts in the Cincinnati Men's Chorus, participates in the chorus's small ensemble called Männerchor, and volunteers as assistant director of Diverse City, a local youth chorus. Kass's commitment to choral singing is connected to the joy he feels in using his singing voice, a voice that now matches his male gender identity.

Transgender singers spoke to me about finding a place of safety and acceptance in their GALA choruses, a sense of security that mattered deeply to them. Specifically, they found that their GALA choruses are communities in which they can openly inhabit their gender—that is, their true gender, as opposed to the one assigned at birth. For example, Neka Zimmerman, a transgender man, told me that he feels "very accepted" in the Rochester Gay Men's Chorus, and that his fellow choristers were uniformly supportive when he "came out as trans" after singing his first concert with the group (interview, December 19, 2016). Mitchell Hunter told me that while he "totally supports" the creation of new transgender choirs, he himself values the opportunity to sing with the Seattle Men's Chorus because being included as an equal in an all-male group affirms his true, male, identity.[21] Similarly, Kaeden Kass explained that his participation in the Cincinnati Men's Chorus constituted "the first time I went into a male space and was accepted as a gay male. . . . It was the first time I was accepted into a group of men" (interview, February 9, 2017). This experience was especially important to Kass because it contrasted powerfully with his experience as a transgender university student: Kass had tried out for his university's all-male glee club, but after the audition the artistic director's response was, "Have you thought about trying out for the all-women's ensemble?" Kass pointed out that he had sung low alto parts in high school (meaning that he was capable of singing in the tenor range), that he identified as male, and that he wished to wear the men's uniform during concerts. However, the glee club director "just didn't get it."

Stephanie Dykes, a transgender woman, said, "My experience with both the Gay Men's Chorus of Charlotte and the Windy City Gay Chorus has been thoroughly positive. . . . The Windy City Gay Chorus and Aria [a Chicago-based SSAA chorus now known as the Windy City Treble Quire] perform together, and I have experienced acceptance from the women of Aria as well" (interview, April 25, 2011). Dykes explained that when she asked whether she might change into her concert uniform in the Aria dressing room, the Aria singers welcomed her without question into this women-identified space; also, Dykes enjoyed going out for drinks with the Aria women after a joint rehearsal. Another transgender woman, whom I heard about secondhand, is "out" as a woman only during the rehearsals and performances of her mixed chorus, which I will not name here. This woman changes her clothes in the women's washroom before rehearsal begins, and then changes back into men's attire afterward. "In society, he's closeted," explained the artistic director of the choir, "he's a divorced father of five. Choir is the only safe place for her to be a woman" (anonymous, interview, October 13, 2011).

Joining an existing GALA chorus, especially if that chorus identifies as a single-gender (men's or women's) chorus, can also pose challenges for transgender singers and their fellow choristers. "This is so controversial!" said Jane Ramseyer-Miller, who has a broad understanding of what goes on in GALA circles because of her international leadership role in GALA Choruses.[22] My own research revealed a number of controversies involving transgender singers, and I also observed creative ways in which choruses, especially artistic directors, addressed those controversies. For example, a transitioning singer in the Rainbow Harmony Project asked the other choristers to use their new name, the name associated with the gender to which the singer was transitioning. The choristers agreed to this request, but two weeks later, another singer mistakenly referred to the transitioning singer by their deadname. The transitioning singer was offended, and the artistic director had to do some emotional labor to repair the breach; she explained to the transitioning singer that the incorrect name use had been a mistake, and encouraged the other singer to apologize (Mike Killen, interview, September 23, 2016). Another "controversy," according to Amanda Cenzer, was a 2014 discussion among the singers in Aria about the group's name.[23] The choristers eventually agreed to change the name of the group from Aria: Windy City Women's Ensemble to the Windy City Treble Quire. The name change reflects the reality that a number of singers in the chorus do not identify as women, although all its singers perform in the soprano and alto ranges. However, according to Cenzer, who sings with this chorus, some older choristers valued the history associated with the previous name, which was chosen when "women's ensemble" was code for "lesbian ensemble." These older singers were reluctant to make a change in order to accommodate the concerns of transgender singers.

The controversies (or rather, challenges) that I heard about most often centered on one particular potential dispute: the relative importance of homogeneity. Choral leaders, and many rank-and-file singers in GALA, value homogeneity both in look and in sound, and transgender singers may disrupt that homogeneous ideal. The two challenges my interlocutors discussed most frequently were, first, transgender singers' desire to wear the uniform of their true gender, even if that uniform did not "match" their voice part; and second, transgender singers' wish to join the section coded to their gender identity, even if they could not sing in the range associated with that section.

In order to understand why both of these challenges rose to the level of controversy, it is necessary to understand how voice parts in community choirs are organized. Voice parts, or sections, are designated as soprano, alto, tenor, baritone, and bass, with gradations within these parts in certain cases (soprano, alto, and tenor are often subdivided into two or more parts). The parts are listed this way because they correspond to the range of the pitches, or notes, sung by the singers in that section: sopranos sing the highest pitches, altos sing the next highest, and so on—the basses sing the lowest pitches. Furthermore, singers in each section usually sit together in rehearsal and stand together in performance, so they are both physically and sonically proximate. For the past hundred-plus years of choral singing in the United States and Canada, soprano and alto parts have been consistently sung by women, and tenor, baritone, and bass parts have been consistently sung by men. As scholars have pointed out, vocal range has long been understood as a primary marker of gender identity, although we need not look far for evidence that vocal ranges—and understandings of vocal capabilities—are socially constructed (Cusick 1999, 29; Jarmen-Ivens 2011, 3, 106).[24] Men can learn to sing high pitches in what is called their "falsetto" range, and countertenors (men who sing in the alto or mezzo-soprano range) have recently found great commercial success among classical music fans (Levin n.d.). Nevertheless, the idea that women sing higher pitches and men sing lower pitches is entrenched among choral singers, so much so that the words soprano and alto are understood to be interchangeable with "women," and the words tenor, baritone, and bass are interchangeable with "men." Thus women's choruses perform songs notated in the soprano and alto ranges—often with subdivisions of each part, written as SSAA—and men's choruses perform songs notated in the tenor, baritone, and bass ranges, written as TTBB. Further, during performances those singing the TTBB voice parts usually wear uniforms coded as male, often tuxedos, and those singing the SSAA parts usually wear uniforms coded as female, such as long skirts.[25]

When an adult transgender person transitions, they usually take hormones associated with the gender to which they are transitioning. People in the process of transitioning to a female identity take estrogen, and people transitioning to a male identity take testosterone. Both hormones have powerful effects on the human body over time, creating physical changes in the body that are strongly associated with traditional gender markers; for example, testosterone provokes the growth of facial hair, and estrogen provokes the growth of breasts. However, the two hormones do not have equivalent effects on one's voice. While testosterone does have the effect of lowering one's vocal range, estrogen does not raise one's vocal range. In other words, if a person transitions from female to male, taking testosterone, that person will likely eventually possess a voice that can sing in the tenor, baritone, or bass range. However, if a person transitions from male to female, the estrogen they take will not allow them to sing notes high enough to be designated alto or soprano. Therefore a transgender man will likely to be able to sing in a men's TTBB chorus (which accounts for the majority of GALA choruses). However, a transgender woman will have a harder time finding a place in a women's SSAA chorus, and in a mixed SATB chorus a transgender woman will still only be able to comfortably sing the male-coded voice parts.

This context of the traditional expectations surrounding voice parts or sections, as well as the unequal vocal outcomes for singers who transition between genders, allows us to better understand the challenges posed to artistic directors and transgender singers in the choral music scene. Again, while GALA chorus leaders make much use of the word *diversity*, and many GALA insiders genuinely value various dimensions of diversity, these choruses stand firmly in the Western art music choral tradition. And this tradition values homogeneity in performance.

Artistic directors usually expect all singers in a section, or an entire chorus, to present a homogeneous appearance. Indeed, this expectation of homogeneity of appearance—more commonly glossed as wearing a uniform—is a flashpoint for controversy in choruses. Matthew Gillespie, a singer and board member with the Calgary Men's Chorus, recalled that choristers have "stomped out" of rehearsals due to disagreements over pant styles and even the relative shininess of a belt buckle (interview, January 5, 2013). Tara Napoleone-Clifford, an alto in the Kansas City Women's Chorus, said that after extensive discussions regarding uniforms, the chorus president "said she was ready to kill people over this!" (interview, June 30, 2011). While uniforms are a touchy subject for any chorister, they can pose a particular problem for transgender singers. Singers who sing in a male-coded range—tenor, baritone, or bass—but who identify as women often wish to wear the female-coded uniform of the group (the reverse scenario, although less common, is also true). If the transgender singer in the male section wears a dress, for example, she will not match the tuxedo-wearing singers with whom she is standing during the performance.

The Gay Men's Chorus of Washington, DC, faced and rose to this challenge. The group includes a singer who wears female-coded attire, including a wig and high-heeled shoes, for concerts. A new artistic director joined the chorus, unaware of this custom. The singer arrived at a concert wearing a long black gown. The artistic director refused to allow the singer to perform because her clothing did not match the group's tuxedo uniform. However, the artistic director and the singer were subsequently able to compromise; the singer now wears a tuxedo top, a long black skirt, and high-heeled shoes (Derek Smith, interview, September 2, 2016). In this way, the singer is able to affirm her gender identity with female-coded clothing, while still "matching" the other choristers; the long black skirt resembles tuxedo trousers, and the shoes are hidden beneath the skirt. I observed another graceful resolution to the uniform controversy: the Rainbow Chorale of Delaware, an SATB mixed chorus, performed in a unisex uniform at the 2016 GALA Festival. All singers wore a dusty rose-colored dress shirt and black dress pants. Most men in the group tucked their shirt in, and most women did not; that was the only way in which gender was differentiated through the chorus's uniform.[26] According to its website, the Rainbow Chorale of Delaware also uses a more traditional, gendered set of two uniforms (tuxedos and all-black outfits). However, the tuxedo style is worn by both men and women, and the all-black outfit is worn with either a skirt or pants.

Homogeneity of sound is a more salient and more sensitive issue in GALA choruses. In chapter 1 of this book, I described the qualifications of GALA's artistic directors and the training they receive in the Western art music tradition. Suffice it to say here that this tradition values what is often called a "blended" sound. Christopher Small (1998, 120) references "blend" in his description of the ideal sound of a symphony orchestra, the instrumental analogue to the concert choir: "It is perfectly coordinated and unified, the sound of a hundred or more musicians all blended into one huge instrument." GALA artistic directors also referenced this term when I asked them about including transgender singers in their choruses. For example, Carol Sirianni, artistic director of the GLASS Youth Choir of Surrey, British Columbia, said, "My policy is, the sound of the choir comes first. You must be able to blend with your section" (interview, October 9, 2011). To somewhat oversimplify, in this context to "blend" means to sing the same pitches, in the same range, as the other singers in one's section. In other words, if one belongs to the soprano section, one must sing the same notes as all other sopranos—and be able to produce those notes without noticeably straining one's voice. A handout distributed at a 2016 GALA Festival workshop titled "Creating Choirs that Welcome Trans* and Gender-Queer Singers" emphasized this priority: "Assign voice sections for each singer dependent on their voice range and voice color. . . . You may encounter a transwoman who wants to sing alto or soprano. . . . But, unless she's lucky enough to be a countertenor or has the finances to undergo a new vocal adjustment surgery, singing in a treble range is likely an unrealistic goal. . . . It is all right to be clear that you assign all singers to sections based on vocal range" (this document was authored by Jane Ramseyer-Miller, "with assistance from singers in a variety of GALA choruses").

The transgender men I interviewed were all happy with their singing voices post-transition and glad to sing in their local GALA choruses. I was able to interview only one transgender woman, and she is still happy with her baritone vocal range. Stephanie Dykes won a "Male Vocalist of the Year" award when she was a teenager, and as an adult she continues to embrace both her male-coded singing voice and her female gender identity (interview, April 25, 2011). However, other indications (such as the handout quoted above) made clear to me that the position of transgender women in GALA can be complicated.

Identification with a voice part is not only about singing notes in a certain range, it is also about belonging to a social group. It is not an accident that, when asked about their role in their GALA chorus, the dozens of singers I interviewed for this project answered by identifying strongly with their voice part. Over and over people said, "I am a baritone" or "I am a soprano" (as opposed to "I sing baritone" or "I sing soprano"). When a transgender woman says that she wants to join the alto section, she is not necessarily intending to provoke a controversy; she is making a statement about her own gender and about the gender of the people with whom she wishes to be included (Adam Adler, interview, July 11, 2014). Singing in a section means, as we have seen, sitting and standing with a specific group of singers, matching one's voice to theirs, wearing the uniform associated the gender of the group, and even spending time with them outside of rehearsal.[27] As one transgender woman stated during a 2016 GALA Festival workshop, "Chorus isn't just a place I go to sing, it's a place I go to socialize."[28]

One solution to the conundrum outlined here (transgender women's wish to belong to sections that do not match their vocal range) was proposed by Mitchell Hunter during another 2016 GALA Festival workshop.[29] If MTF (male-to-female transgender) singers wish to sing in SSAA choruses, he asked, can the directors of such choruses simply compose a bass line for each song, adding to the choral arrangements? The answer is, of course, yes—but it virtually never happens. GALA's artistic directors are increasingly coming to their positions with extensive training in the Western art music tradition, usually acquired at a university or conservatory. One of the unspoken but powerfully influential ideas inculcated by this tradition is that the musical score (the notation written by the composer of the song) is a "sacred and unalterable text," a "sacred object, not to be tampered with" (Small 1998, 115, 118). In chapter 5 of this book I describe the dissenting views among GALA insiders around changing song words; suffice it to say here that changing lyrics is problematic. And changing musical sounds—for example, by adding a bass line to an SSAA arrangement—is never even considered. Among adherents of the Western choral music tradition, changing an existing score is virtually unthinkable.

With that said, some of GALA's artistic directors are embracing other ways of including, and even showcasing, gender diversity in their choruses. Stephanie Dykes, who now lives in Chicago, was happy to visit her previous home of North Carolina in 2011 in order to sing a concert with the Gay Men's Chorus of Charlotte and the Common Woman Chorus of Durham. The artistic director of the Gay Men's Chorus of Charlotte, John Quillin, wrote a solo line for Dykes to sing in her baritone range. The words of the song are a celebration of an aging woman ("I am becoming the woman I wanted"); Dykes sang these words by herself, at the very beginning of the performance, highlighting both her low vocal range and her other, female-associated, physical characteristics. This concert was an important opportunity for Dykes, the first time she had ever sung "a song with a specific transgender message" (interview, April 25, 2011).[30] Similarly, the West Coast Singers of Los Angeles used solo performances to celebrate gender diversity when performing at the 2016 Festival. Like many other mixed choruses, the West Coast Singers wore two gendered uniforms: tuxedos and a sequined black blouse with black trousers or skirts. Two different soloists sang solos in the female-identified alto and mezzo-soprano range, and both were attired in the male-identified tuxedo uniform.

Conclusion

In this chapter I argued that GALA choruses are largely White and largely cisgender organizations. Despite well-meaning initiatives to address the lack of diversity in their ranks—initiatives that may bear fruit in coming decades—GALA choruses are at this point collectives that articulate sincere commitments to diversity and inclusion, but that remain generally homogeneous in terms of ethnicity and gender expression. As the next chapter of this book will show, the demographic majority of GALA choristers are not only White and cisgender but also middle class. This intersection of ethnic, gender, and class identifications results in choruses that are largely homonormative, which is evident not only in the way they appear to others, but also in the values they themselves often proclaim.

4 • Homonormativity

GALA Choruses as Middle-Class Organizations

During the years I spent writing this book, I sometimes shared various facets of the research with my students at the University of Dayton. Once, in an effort to show a group of students that GALA choruses perform many different kinds of choral repertoire, including sacred music—meaning music referencing the Christian tradition—I played a video of the San Francisco Gay Men's Chorus singing Randol Alan Bass's "Gloria" (San Francisco Gay Men's Chorus 2011). I chose the video for a couple of pragmatic reasons, including that it had rather higher production values than many other GALA chorus videos archived online, and because students at my Catholic university would recognize the words of the Latin Mass that are sung in "Gloria." After showing the video I asked for student comments. One young woman spoke, I suspect, for many of her peers: "I wouldn't have known they were gay."[1] And why would she? What she saw in the video was a group of gender-conforming men wearing tuxedos, relatively expensive uniforms that reinforced their maleness. These men sang words taken from the liturgy of the Roman Catholic Church. This student reacted just as she has been socialized to do; she saw a group of men behaving as mainstream choral singers do, all across the United States and Canada, and assumed they were heterosexual. The choristers who sang in the video did nothing to challenge that assumption; this particular performance conformed to all the conventions of a choral recital (see chapter 5) and tacitly reinforced the presumptions of the heteronormative society of the United States and Canada.

In this chapter I argue that GALA choruses and performances, like that described above, are largely homonormative. They often—although not always—present themselves publicly in ways that reinforce the idea that LGBT people are "normal," which is to say that they are just like heterosexual people. Further, I argue that their homonormativity is strongly related to GALA singers' socioeconomic status. GALA choruses are populated by middle-class people. This basic fact influences not only some of their performance norms but also their commitment to the goals of the mainstream gay rights movement, goals that are articulated by cisgender middle-class White people, usually Christians or post-Christians, who are just like the majority of GALA choristers themselves.

Homonormativity

Homonormativity is a way of thinking and behaving among LGBT people that affirms the dominant assumptions of mainstream (heteronormative) society in Canada and the United States. It asserts that LGBT people can be "normal," that they can behave in ways that society valorizes as good and acceptable. In short, homonormativity rests on the presumptions of heteronormativity, which is "a system of norms connected with a particular form of life" (Halperin 2012, 450). Heteronormativity "is about how policies, institutions, individuals, and society in general have normalized heterosexuality—along with monogamy and patriarchy—to the point that everyone is (first) assumed to be heterosexual" (Walks 2014, 125). It universalizes the idea that everyone is, or should be, heterosexual, and then articulates and validates a "normal" kind of adulthood to which heterosexual people are expected to aspire. Heteronormativity's vision of a normal adulthood focuses on a stable, loving couple who share property, finances, children, and sexual activity; the two members of the couple share with each other exclusively, and not with others (Halperin 2012, 450). This vision has been so successful in persuading people about what is normal that home ownership, for example, has become synonymous with the American Dream. To summarize: heteronormativity valorizes middle-class married people and marginalizes those who do not conform to this ideal. But "normal" is not a neutral concept, nor even a historically rooted one; it developed during the nineteenth century with the science of statistics, and since then, it has been the domain of the already powerful, who have used it to define their own behaviors and preferences (Warner 1999, 54). To promote what is normal in the United States and Canada, therefore, is to promote the value system of the most powerful group—that is, cisgender, White, middle-class and upper-income men. That GALA choruses advance this understanding of normality is unsurprising because the largest population within the GALA organization, from which most of its thought leaders come, is that of cisgender, White, middle-class men. By advancing heteronormativity's version of what is normal, GALA promotes homonormativity.

Homonormativity, following heteronormativity, upholds the idea that two men or two women can commit to each other in a long-lasting domestic partnership, sharing a home and a bank account, and parenting children. In short, homonormativity argues that members of sexual minorities are just like the majority heterosexuals, but for the negligible difference of their sexual orientation. Importantly, representatives of homonormativity, such as the gay characters on popular television shows, do not challenge gender norms and are usually cisgender. Cisgender gay and lesbian people, in this way of understanding, are conventional citizens in the American and Canadian middle class, and they should be recognized as equal members of it. Homonormativity thus leads logically to the argument that same-sex marriage should be sanctioned by the law of the land. As we shall see in what follows, GALA choruses work hard to promote same-sex marriage. They also sing Christian, or sacred, songs—that is, the music of the religious tradition that has sanctified marriage and that is dominant among White, middle-class people in the United States and Canada.

GALA Choruses as Middle-Class Organizations

"The growth of amateur choral singing in secular settings belongs to the massive political and social reconfiguration that resulted from the Enlightenment and the growth of bourgeois culture" (Ahlquist 2006c, 266). Community choirs are, at their heart, voluntary associations, with which individuals (not families or other traditional social groups) affiliate themselves. They are populated by singers who not only perceive themselves as individuals exercising freedom of choice, but who also have the leisure time and disposable income to devote hours each week to their choirs. Community choirs, in other words, are middle-class organizations, and have been since their emergence in the nineteenth century. Recent studies that have identified the markers of middle-class identity in community choir members confirm that in the twenty-first century, the overwhelming majority of adults participating in community choirs are high school graduates; a 2003 survey from Chorus America showed that 45 percent of community choir singers in the United States have earned graduate degrees (Bell 2004, 42–43). As choral music scholar Cindy L. Bell (2004, 43) points out, "it is difficult to draw conclusions" about income levels among community choir members, in part because "incomes evolve over time and geography." However, the same Chorus America survey, the most recent and most broadly based survey of singers in the United States, stated that as of 2003, 63 percent of them earned at least $50,000 per year (Chorus America 2003). My own interview sample of fifty-six GALA chorus singers, in both the United States and Canada, demonstrated that almost all of them worked in, or were retired from, what could be called a white-collar job—or a "white-coat job," in the case of those employed in health care. Reported professions included software developer, clinical psychologist, manager of luxury apartments, attorney, marketing manager, and nurse practitioner. There were only three exceptions: one singer was unemployed at the time of our interview, and two others worked at what might be considered manual labor (as a nanny and as a postal carrier, respectively). To summarize, most GALA singers—just like singers in other community choirs—belong to the American and Canadian middle class, with the education, the professional experiences, the income, and the lifestyle markers common to that class.

For American gay men, and—I argue—for American lesbian women as well, class and sexual identity intersect. The public gay identity (Barrett and Pollack 2005, 437) is "implicitly . . . middle class, respectable, private, dependable, and most deeply, male" (Valentine 2007, 202). GALA's demographics reflect the truth embedded in the stereotype: the largest and most influential choruses are men's choruses, mostly populated by White, middle-class men. GALA singers' middle-class status makes their choir participation possible for a number of reasons. Just as for singers in other community choirs, their participation in leisure activities is "facilitated by the sorts of relatively flexible work schedules associated with professional and white-collar occupations" (Barrett and Pollack 2005, 439), and they have the financial means to pay their membership dues and travel costs. But perhaps most importantly for GALA singers, their class position makes the claiming of a gay identity less costly in social terms (Cantù 2011, 159–62). As a survey of men who have sex with men found, "both higher education and higher income are related to increasing odds of labeling oneself as gay" and of "belonging to a gay group" (Barrett and Pollack 2005, 447, 450). Said another way, the more firmly embedded a same-sex-oriented person is in the middle class, the more likely that person is to self-identify as gay or lesbian and to participate in a gay-identified organization such as a GALA chorus.

For some GALA choristers, the opportunity to mingle with successful members of the middle class—"professionals"—is part of what attracts them to their local chorus. Jeannie Holton, speaking about Crescendo: The Tampa Bay Women's Chorus (in Florida), explained that she was the owner of a tech company, and that as a professional, she related well to the other professional women (such as doctors and nurses) in the chorus. "There is a sense of community among them that is a real privilege to be a part of" Holton said (interview, January 15, 2013). She pointed out later that Crescendo offered financial assistance (including paying for airfare and hotel costs) to any singer in the chorus who could not afford to attend the 2012 Festival and also paid for uniforms for singers who could not purchase them. The idea that her chorus was sensitive to the needs of people not enjoying the privileges of the middle class was important to Holton, as it was to Tara Napoleone-Clifford, who sings alto in the Kansas City Women's Chorus (in Missouri). "I really appreciate that there are lots of professionals in my chorus," said Napoleone-Clifford, explaining that she has met lawyers, accountants, and veterinarians through singing in her chorus. "But I've met people from all walks of life. We come together as women, not because we're particularly classist" (interview, June 30, 2011).

However, Napoleone-Clifford was concerned that middle-class privilege sometimes blinkered the decision-makers in the Kansas City Women's Chorus: "There are lots of working people in the chorus who can't afford to go to our fundraisers." Expensive fundraising dinners are not the only challenge; even the generous "scholarships" offered by many choruses, such as Holton described, require that singers identify themselves as needy in order to qualify. One interlocutor who shall remain nameless here told me that he did not attend the 2016 Festival because he could not afford to go. Although he works full time, his salary is relatively small, and he inhabits a high-cost-of-living city. When I said, "But your chorus offered scholarships for anyone who needed them!" he replied, "Yes—but that means that you have to go and ask the board for it." For this man, a White middle-aged man who holds a white-collar job, the prospect of admitting that he could not afford to spend two thousand dollars on a chorus trip was more painful than missing the trip. The idea of telling his chorus leaders that he did not possess a crucial marker of middle-class identity—and thereby outing himself as an outlier in the middle-class chorus community—was unacceptable. His story is a reminder that any generalization about any group of people is problematic.

Having made that point, I reassert that most GALA participants are members of the middle class, which means that they not only have access to a certain kind of privileged social position but also espouse certain values around sexuality and religious expression. Like the White lesbian Christians studied by Krista McQueeny (2009, 160), GALA singers pursue a "normalizing strategy [that] emphasizes their similarity to straight Christians and distances them from the perceived promiscuity of the [gay and] lesbian world." They are what a number of other scholars have called the "good gays" (Bersani 1995, 42). The good gays, says Arlene Stein (2001, 226), are those who are "virtually normal," a phrase that cites the title of Andrew Sullivan's 1995 book on the politics of homosexuality. They are the gay men and lesbian women who "embrace conventional gender roles, who live quiet lives, who keep their sexuality to themselves, and who make no public demands on that basis" (Stein 2001, 107). Sandra Faiman-Silva (2004, 114) and Michael Warner (1999, 114) position the "good gays" against "sexual rebels" and "bad queers," respectively; the foils to the "good gays" are those LGBTQ persons who "challenge basic heternormativity, the heterosexual family, public vs. private conduct, and sexual propriety boundaries" (Faiman-Silva 2004, 114). Good gays, like the GALA choristers who are the subject of this book, are disdained by the likes of Warner because they make themselves acceptable to the heteronormative mainstream and, most tellingly, to the straight White Christians who are their fellow travelers in the middle class. They do so by affirming monogamous love and by referencing Christian teachings in the songs that they sing.

Monogamy

In asserting that GALA choruses are middle-class organizations, I argue not that every singer in every GALA chorus self-identifies as a middle-class person, but rather that GALA culture—the behavioral norms and commonly shared beliefs of its members—is marked by a middle-class ethos. For example, GALA singers and artistic directors, like the "middle-class suburban gays" studied by Frederick R. Lynch (1992, 191), are "politely verbal in social settings," as I discovered during hundreds of hours of interviews and observations of rehearsals and meetings. They also generally maintain "middle-class standards against 'excessive' appetites" (191). Specifically, they usually decline to lend their corporate approval to the idea of multiple, anonymous sexual encounters and, instead, publicly affirm monogamy (Gamson 2005, 10).

This tendency became very evident during the period I was conducting research for this book, a time in which marriage equality laws were being debated at the state and federal level across the United States. For example, in 2014, the North Coast Men's Chorus of Cleveland, Ohio, sang Eric Helmuth's "Finally Here" while photos of choristers with their partners were projected on a screen behind them. The song includes the lyrics, "When you love from deep within / it can never be wrong." Various GALA choruses proclaimed the same message at rallies and public events in support of same-sex marriage. In 2012, the Philadelphia Gay Men's Chorus commissioned and premiered a multimovement work called *Raise Our Voice*.[2] "Two Hearts," a song in this work, clearly evokes middle-class economic norms ("A dog, a cat, and a baby / A house out in the burbs") and also a monogamous partnership ("It was twenty years ago, that fateful night we met.... Now we're two hearts beating as one"). The song reveals that the narrator met his partner at a gay chorus rehearsal. The Twin Cities Gay Men's Chorus performed a song titled "Marry Us" throughout the 2011–12 concert season "as our part in taking a stand against the [Minnesota antigay] marriage amendment" (Twin Cities Gay Men's Chorus 2012). Presentations of the song concluded with choristers who are in long-term monogamous relationships coming to the front of the stage, holding hands. Partners of singers who were in the audience were also encouraged to come onstage at this point. One Voice Mixed Chorus, also located in Minnesota, sang at both a Mennonite church and at a Jewish synagogue during this campaign; and Ovation, One Voice's small ensemble, performed in support of the amendment at no fewer than twenty-five churches (John Whalen, interview, January 3, 2013). Similarly, the GALA Choruses organization combined concertizing and affirmation of same-sex marriage during the 2012 Festival. At the final concert, organizers presented a male couple who had first met at the Festival in Tampa in 1996.[3] The couple danced together and spoke about their courtship and marriage proposal. The master of ceremonies then asked all couples in the audience who had met at the GALA Festival in prior years to stand, and these couples were honored with thunderous applause.

In supporting same-sex marriage, White middle-class gay men and lesbians—such as the majority of GALA members—effectively consolidate their middle-class status. Scholar Devon Carbado (2013, 832) notes that the same-sex marriage media campaign in the United States placed cisgender, middle-class, White men and women at the center of its public representations; these "normatively masculine white men" and women were described as good citizens and hardworking people who were "just like everybody else" but for their sexual orientation. By expressing their desire to marry, the public faces of the campaign emphasized how "normal" they were; in other words, they highlighted one more similarity between themselves and the White heterosexuals atop the privilege pyramid of American society. Eventually winning the right to marry, White middle-class gay men and lesbians "moved from the periphery of white privilege to its core.... The homonormativity of the gay rights marriage-equality campaign instantiates a naturalization process through which white gay men are incorporated into a white mainstream identity. This incorporation moves them from a kind of first-class white citizens-in-waiting status to first-class white citizens proper" (Carbado 2013, 835–36). Singing in support of same-sex marriage, therefore, can be understood as both a logical outcome of GALA choristers' position in the middle class and as an action that solidifies their position in that same privileged class.

Hooking Up and Dating

While GALA choruses do publicly valorize monogamy, I make no claim that all GALA singers consistently practice monogamy and disdain promiscuity. In fact, the GALA Festival has become known as a meeting place for sexual encounters—so much so that some GALA bears (gay men with large body frames and plentiful body hair) agree to stay in the same hotel during the Festival, and that hotel's pool is then called "bear soup" (Dennis Coleman, interview, September 24, 2011). Few interlocutors talked openly with me about this phenomenon, however. One woman said that during her first Festival (in Tampa, Florida, in 1996), "I had daylong romances with a handful of people, all week" (Jane Hoffman, interview, March 1, 2012). Another person, a man, said that he did not participate in any of this behavior himself. However, he told me that during the 2016 Festival, both he and his fellow choristers were approached by strangers: "There was definitely some cruising going on. It ranged from being propositioned, subtly, to people who come up to you and tell you exactly what they'd like to do with you. There are guys who go to the Festival—and women are just as bad—to get as many notches on their belt as possible" (Mike Killen, interview, September 23, 2016). This man went on to say that "Growler [a dating app for bears] was going crazy there"—a claim I heard from others as well.[4]

To the extent that hooking up at the Festival is an observable phenomenon, it seems to involve mostly men. During the 2016 Festival, I observed male participants checking gay dating apps on their phones and showing photos to each other, and other men, sitting beside a large window, openly ogling and commenting on the physical attributes of the men walking past the window. I also heard a story about a male singer who was seen "making out hard core" with another man. When his fellow chorister, presumably a supporter of monogamy, challenged him about this behavior, the singer allegedly replied, "It's the Festival! I've got a boyfriend but we're allowed to make out with other people [here]."[5] The story seemed credible because on the previous day, July 5,

2016, GALA Choruses executive director Robin Godfrey sent the following email to all registered attendees at the Festival:

> Dear GALA Festival Delegates,
>
> Our hotel partners for Festival 2016 have indicated there have been numerous incidents of inappropriate sexual behavior is [sic] public spaces in the hotels. Please remember that we are the face of the LGBT choral movement here in Denver and need to conduct ourselves appropriately in public.

Hilariously, later that afternoon the Harrisburg Gay Men's Chorus (of Pennsylvania) prefaced its performance by saying that its song was dedicated to "those engaging in inappropriate sexual behavior at GALA."[6] The chorus then sang Bennie Benjamin and George David Weiss's "Cross over the Bridge," a lightheartedly moralistic song that addresses a male listener: "If you broke as many hearts as ripples in a stream / Brother, here's the only way you can be redeemed / Cross over the bridge.... Leave your fickle past behind you, and true romance will find you."

Although the quadrennial Festival is an exception, my interlocutors reported that local choruses are generally *not* perceived as hookup sites, or as scenes that encourage casual sexual encounters. In fact, some individuals took pains to emphasize that their local chorus was not a venue for hookups. When Robert Frederick described the social events regularly organized by his chorus, the Dayton Gay Men's Chorus, he pointed out that they "truly are social events, not hookup opportunities" (interview, August 17, 2011). Similarly, Katie Eadie stated that she was not seeking hookup opportunities when she joined the Kansas City Women's Chorus, nor has she felt any pressure to engage in such activity with anyone in the chorus (interview, August 10, 2016). Gary Miller, the founding director of the New York City Gay Men's Chorus, said that from the chorus's earliest days, singers enjoyed much social time together, but that the chorus was "not a pickup scene; no, no, no, no, my God, no!" (interview, June 27, 2014). When I asked Patrick Holcomb of the North Coast Men's Chorus this question directly, he was thoughtful: "Are they [my fellow choristers] hooking up? I don't know, and I don't care, to be honest. There's a lot of flirtation and comments, joking and stuff, but no explicit, obvious interactions" (interview, September 14, 2014). Holcomb went on to explain that some singers in the chorus regularly go out for drinks after rehearsals; when he joins this group, "they're inclusive." Socializing among GALA singers, in other words, is not a prelude to sexual activity. The hookup-free ethos of GALA choruses is evident to outsiders; in fact, it can be a factor that draws people to a local chorus. For example, Scott Meier said that he joined the Dayton Gay Men's Chorus in 2008 because he was "looking to meet people who don't sleep around or get into trouble" (interview, August 2, 2011).

GALA insiders differentiate between hooking up and dating, that is, spending time together with a view to possibly establishing a long-term relationship. As Joe Buches, artistic director of the Philadelphia Gay Men's Chorus, explained: "It's common for chorus members to date. But you don't want it to be a hookup, because you're going to have to see these people every week" (interview, March 27, 2012). Dating is acceptable in GALA circles, and it often leads to the creation of couples, those who (legally married or not) are celebrated in the performances described above. Some singers and artistic directors pay attention to this phenomenon and counted off for me the number of married or committed couples in their local choruses. For example, David Greene told me that "there are about twelve couples" in the North Coast Men's Chorus. Greene is not a member of one of these couples. He—like others I interviewed—was somewhat wistful about the fact that he had not found a long-term partner in the chorus: "There's a hundred gay men there. If I meet a partner, great. And if not, okay. And it has turned out to be okay" (interview, October 10, 2014).[7]

In the past, some choruses discouraged—or attempted to discourage—both hookups and dating. Eric Unhold recalled that the North Coast Men's Chorus handbook used to say, "The chorus is not a dating service," in order to clarify the purpose of the chorus (interview, October 13, 2014). In that case, dating was discouraged but not explicitly forbidden. The Perfect Harmony Men's Chorus of Madison, Wisconsin, by contrast, has an explicit policy forbidding "fraternization" between board members and singers, in order to prevent conflicts of interest for board members (Julio Avila, interview, February 27, 2012). Years ago, says longtime chorister Maria-Elena Grant, the Lavender Light Gospel Choir had a rule forbidding dating: "But people broke it!" (interview, October 29, 2011). Grant pointed out that the rule had a rational basis. "The problem is, if a couple breaks up, the chorus almost always loses a member," she said.

Rules and policies about romantic and sexual activity between choristers may still be on the books, but in GALA choruses today, hooking up is either well hidden or contained to the quadrennial Festival, dating is common, and couplehood is valorized. But what GALA insiders value most, it seems, is their chorus's fostering of unconditional friendship. As Patrick Holcomb said, "Some of the best friends I have now are from the chorus. . . . Everybody's accepted! If you can't sing [well], sing softly!" (interview, September 14, 2014). "A lot of the members [of my chorus] have found lifelong friends in the chorus" claimed Ciaran Krueger, artistic director of the Buffalo Gay Men's Chorus (interview, January 28, 2012). Drew Kotchan, who joined the Calgary Men's Chorus at age fifty, told me that he was "pleasantly surprised at how warm some of the young people have been" (interview, May 31, 2016). Kotchan was relieved that in the chorus "there was no troll/twink divide," meaning no obvious groupings of younger or older singers, and no sense that the older men were attempting to troll, or pressure, the younger men for sex. Instead, Kotchan said, "in the choir I've found a real warmth and welcoming." Steven Hankle, a straight man who sang bass-baritone with the San Francisco Gay Men's Chorus, lightheartedly related that shortly after he joined, some of his fellow choristers asked him whether he was *sure* he was not gay (interview, July 5, 2018). More soberly he added, "But I didn't feel any pressure to flirt or engage in dating. They weren't pressuring me to do anything. All the men were very respectful."

The GALA Chorus: Not like a Gay Bar

When GALA insiders spoke to me about the nature of the relationships that they have found, and that they value, in their local choruses, they often contrasted the chorus's atmosphere, or ethos, with that of a bar. Indeed GALA's middle-class singers and artistic directors are markedly negative in their perception of the bar scene. It represents a place where "excessive appetites" (à la Lynch) are indulged, and such indulgence, for many GALA participants, is immoral, unhealthy, or both. Al Fischer, artistic director of the Gateway Men's Chorus in St. Louis, Missouri, summarized this contrast by saying, "It's not a big old sex orgy at the Gateway Men's Chorus. It's not like a smoky, noisy, bar; it's a healthy, positive place. It's a lighter, healthier, happier place" (interview, January 31, 2012). Eric Unhold described the North Coast Men's Chorus as "a more positive face of the gay community, as opposed to going out to gay clubs, gay bars." Because he perceived the chorus this way, he was eager to join it when he moved to Cleveland in 2000: "I wanted to have a positive, uplifting, supportive way to meet other gay people" (interview, October 13, 2014). Darryl Hollister, accompanist for Coro Allegro in Boston, Massachusetts, described the chorus as "an aboveboard alternative" to a gay bar (interview, June 30, 2014). Evidently the notion that GALA choruses are not like gay bars goes back to GALA's earliest days; when John Reed Sims, founder of the San Francisco Gay Men's Chorus, died in 1984, his obituary celebrated the fact that, through the chorus, he offered "an alternative to the baths and the bars" (Vermillion 2009).

Not only is the contrast between the gay chorus and the gay bar pronounced, but GALA insiders actively value the distinction. Therefore, when the Dayton Gay Men's Chorus was seeking new singers some years ago, its members debated whether they ought to place informational posters in local gay bars. "Do we want the chorus [to be] associated with bars?" some singers, and the artistic director, asked (David Brown, interview, n.d. 2011). Ultimately, the chorus did place the posters in gay bars, but the uneasiness about doing so underlined the singers' unwillingness to identify with the bar scene. GALA performances also sometimes underline GALA's corporate dissociation from gay bars. For example, the Twin Cities Gay Men's Chorus show called *Out of My Range*, by Michael Shaieb, is based on interviews with choristers "sharing their experiences of coming out, living authentically, and how the Chorus was a part of that" (Jeffrey Heine, email to author, January 31, 2019). In one scene in this show, a man goes from a bar—where he is lonely—to a chorus rehearsal, where he is welcomed.[8] The song "Come On With Us" clearly expresses the contrast between the chorus and the bar, explaining that in the chorus, acceptance is unconditional and not based on sexual attractiveness: "We don't care where you're from, or what you believe / If you curl your hair or shave your head or just put a weave in / We range from thinner to fatter / But your voice is the only place size doesn't matter!"

Scholars have long identified bars as important locations where LGBT people are able to congregate in large numbers; from the 1950s through the 1980s, bars were "central social institutions in the gay community" (Newton 1972, 59; see also Miller 2006, 290). In recent decades, attendance at bars has declined for both straight and LGBT people; Robert D. Putnam (2000, 101) calculates that bar attendance decreased among all Americans by 40 to 50 percent between the years 1980 and 2000. Still, gay bars and nightclubs retain a hold on the imagination of many LGBT people, and scholars have analyzed these locations in a variety of ways, starting from the premise that gay bars and clubs are "vital sites for the construction of gay/queer identities and communities" (Taylor 2012, 187; see also Barrett and Pollack 2005, 446; Boisvert 2000, 69–70; Johnson 2000; Warner 1999, 169). Why then do GALA choristers privately and publicly disavow gay bars? One reason is that, in the past, alcohol-fueled violence was commonplace at gay and lesbian bars (Miller 2006, 294). Another is that regular attendance at bars, which are most lively late at night, requires "an after-hours lifestyle that often interferes with other aspects" of middle-class workers' lives, including nine-to-five jobs and schooling (Hawkeswood 1996, 135).

Most importantly—and the reason that GALA choristers referenced during interviews with me—gay bars and nightclubs promote a ruthless kind of judgment of others based on stereotypes about physical attractiveness (David Greene, interview, October 10, 2014). As the scholarship shows, this ethos is especially present in spaces frequented by gay men. Adam Isaiah Green (2011) conducted an ethnographic study of seventy gay men who frequented gay bars, nightclubs, coffee shops, and bathhouses in a gay neighborhood in Toronto, Canada. His study showed that interactions between men in these stereotypical gay scenes were marked by what the men called "comparing," "competing," and "judging." All of the men participating in these scenes, hoping for either a short-term sexual encounter or an introduction to a possible long-term partner, were evaluated, and in turn evaluated the others, according to their "erotic capital." This capital is determined by one's age, racial or ethnic background, weight, height, musculature, and amount of body hair. Men who wanted to increase their capital in this hypercompetitive scene often engaged in "deceptive front work," or lying, about aspects of their erotic capital. Green's study reveals in devastating detail how unkindly the men with low erotic capital were treated by others, to whom they were expected to show deference.

GALA choruses, at their best, offer friendship rather than judgment based on a narrow understanding of sexual attractiveness. And it is precisely this aspect of their culture that has attracted people to the choruses over the years. Sue Fink, founding artistic director of the Los Angeles Women's Community Chorus, said, "To me, the whole choral movement was about creating community, creating a place that wasn't derogatory, wasn't involved with alcohol and bars, about making people feel proud of themselves" (interview, March 12, 2012). Eric Aufdengarten of the Heartland Men's Chorus of Kansas City, Missouri, was struck by the fact that at the chorus's annual orientation for new members, these new singers commonly answered the "What brought you here?" question by saying that they want to meet new people, particularly outside of bars. "At the chorus, you get to meet people *not* as potential sex partners, or as potential anything," Aufdengarten argued. "Our common ground is singing" (interview, October 25, 2011). Hugh Gabrielson, a tenor in Coro Allegro, told me he is not interested in going to gay bars. He connected his participation in his chorus to his "search for deeper, more meaningful contacts with other gay men" (interview, August 22, 2016). Steve Milloy, a singer in two different GALA choruses, said that he joined the chorus as a young man because he "wanted to have camaraderie with my fellow gay brothers outside of the bar scene and cruising sites. That scene didn't offer spiritual fulfillment or true friendship" (interview, July 16, 2011).

The GALA Chorus: Like a Church

When GALA insiders did make an analogy, comparing their chorus to another institution, they most often said it was like a church, a scene that contrasts sharply with that of a bar. For example, Eric Helmuth said about the Boston Gay Men's Chorus, "It was like church! You have the same celebration of sameness and community and you have this outreach component" (interview, August 10, 2012).[9] Artistic directors who had backgrounds in church music or who were practicing Christians used this analogy most commonly. Dennis Coleman, artistic director of the Seattle Men's Chorus and the Seattle Women's Chorus and former Southern Baptist music minister, has repeatedly made the argument that GALA choruses resemble evangelical churches, and he seems to have convinced other artistic directors of his view. Miguel Felipe, former artistic director of the Maine Gay Men's Chorus, and Joe Nadeau, artistic director of the Heartland Men's Chorus and the Kansas City Women's Chorus, both cited Coleman as they explained the analogy to me: GALA choruses and churches both meet weekly, are led by charismatic authority figures, and are committed to transmitting a message (Felipe, interview, July 31, 2013; Nadeau, interview, February 20, 2011). Scholar Janice L. Kinney (2010) makes a related argument about feminist women's choruses, concluding that these choruses function as churches. Kinney sees the church analogy applying in a number of ways, including some that are discussed at length in this book, such as providing a sense of community for choristers, and fostering shared beliefs about the mission of the group. Most importantly, for Kinney, women's choruses are like churches because "they provide the specific disciplines necessary to allow spiritual experiences to happen. They support and enable those experiences; the chorus's reason for existence—making music—is itself a vehicle for producing feelings of connectedness, bonding, and 'flow'" (126).

GALA artistic directors evoked the church analogy by comparing their own work to that of the clergy and by using terms usually associated with evangelical Christianity—even if they did so reluctantly. Gary Miller said, "I hate to say it, but I felt it was a calling, a mission, something I was born to do" (interview, June 27, 2014). Jody Malone, of Singing OUT in Toronto, Ontario, told me, "It's more than a choir, it's like a ministry." She pointed out that, just like churches are supposed to do, her chorus accepts all who wish to sing, including people who use wheelchairs, people struggling with mental illness, and those who cannot afford to pay the membership dues. "I am the choir's first straight artistic director, and I consider it an honor that they entrust me with this calling," Malone said (interview, October 13, 2011). Rich

Cook went even further, claiming that as a GALA artistic director, he not only resembles a minister, he is in fact a minister: "When I started [MenAlive,] the Orange County Gay Men's Chorus, I felt that it was a ministry, that God was giving me another chance to glorify Him and to help people with the talents and energy he gave me" (interview, May 14, 2012).

Ben Riggs, a graduate of Wheaton College (an evangelical Protestant institution in the United States), now works as the artistic director of the Twin Cities Gay Men's Chorus. Riggs has a long history as a church musician, and he agrees with the comparison of GALA choruses to churches. "[A GALA chorus] is like church, obviously. It improves [the choristers'] lives and the lives of those around. Because they're getting together to do something so positive, week in and week out. It's the same as church, and more, because you end up being even more pastoral" (interview, August 15, 2013). Riggs shared that he struggled with this aspect of his work because he never trained to be a pastor. However, he embraced the idea—relayed to him by yet another GALA artistic director—that "each rehearsal is a Sunday morning." He had seen GALA leaders give what amount to sermons, talking about pieces of music before rehearsing them. Riggs decided he was not equipped to give sermons, so instead he introduced the Three-Minute Share to his rehearsals. During the Three-Minute Share, choristers can volunteer to speak about any topic they choose, and usually what they share is "very personal." Riggs explained that the Three-Minute Share is directly inspired by the "testimony time" so common in evangelical churches, when lay people speak briefly about their life experiences.

GALA Choruses and Sacred Music

The evocation of church by GALA leaders is particularly interesting because Christian churches have historically taught that homosexuality is a sin, and—in many cases—they have made their LGBT congregants feel deeply unwelcome. Many GALA singers who grew up in church-going families "felt very battered by the church," as two of my interlocutors said (Jill Strachan, interview, March 2, 2012; Eve Campbell, interview, January 7, 2011). To give just one example: Robert Frederick, who now sings baritone in the Dayton Gay Men's Chorus, grew up in the United Methodist Church and sang in his church's choir. He vividly remembers a sermon delivered by his pastor, when Frederick was just sixteen years old, in which the pastor commanded, "If anyone here is homosexual, leave at the end of the service" (interview, August 17, 2011). Today, Frederick says that he is not a member of any religious organization, but that he is "a strong believer in a supreme being."

Of the ninety-seven GALA insiders I interviewed between 2010 and 2016, twenty-three interlocutors (23.7 percent) identified themselves as "religiously unaffiliated," to use the Pew Research Center's (2012) terminology— that is, they said that they were either atheist or agnostic, or that they followed no particular faith tradition. The religiously unaffiliated are somewhat more represented in the GALA organization than in the United States population at large, of which they constituted just under 20 percent in 2016. The one-in-four "religious nones" in my interview sample does not include another large group of GALA insiders who responded like Robert Frederick did when I asked him about his religious faith. People in this group said things like "I'm an on-the-fence Christian" (Charlie Beale, interview, August 16, 2011), "With me, there's believing without a lot of practicing" (Jody Malone, October 13, 2011), "I believe in a higher power" (Derek Smith, interview, September 2, 2016), "I'm spiritual but not religious" (Guy Hebert, interview, May 11, 2014), "I'm semi-Catholic, I guess" (Patrick Holcomb, interview, September 14, 2014), and "I have an expanded view now" (Maria-Elena Grant, interview, October 29, 2011). This subsection of my interview sample also does not include the two Buddhists, the three Jews, and the two pagans in the pool, nor the people who said they attend Christian churches even though they are not believers in the Christian faith.

With that said, various GALA choruses sing sacred music—songs with lyrics that reference religious, almost always Christian, beliefs—with great regularity. And there are people across the organization, both Christians and "nones," who are deeply glad that their choruses afford them the opportunity to sing sacred music. For some, this repertoire is a way to stake a claim to the Christian heritage outside of homophobic church structures. For example, Maria-Elena Grant is a longtime and fervent participant in her chorus specifically because the chorus sings African American sacred music: "Lavender Light prevents the Black church from being the only one who owns Black sacred music" (interview, October 29, 2011).[10] For others, sacred music is simply music that they enjoy. Frances Bird, who now identifies as a "none," said that she is happy to participate in the Glammaphones (of Wellington, New Zealand) because the chorus "sings sacred music, which is my favorite" (interview, March 8, 2014). Adam Coatney, another "none" and a tenor in the Dayton Gay Men's Chorus, told me that his first preference is to sing Christian hymns: "The appeal, for me, is musical, not faith based. They're so beautifully written, they're 'hallowed' songs" (interview, August 4, 2011). For still others, singing sacred music with their GALA chorus is an important part of their own spiritual practice. Tom Fortuna, a bass in the North Coast Men's Chorus, said "I have such a strong belief in a power greater than myself. And I live not a religious, but a spiritual life, today. Singing religious music brings that out. I don't go to church, but performing sacred music, especially at Christmas concerts, it's a really important part of my spiritual life: standing on the stage, singing praise to God. . . . I wish the chorus would sing *more* hymns and spirituals" (interview, October 16, 2014).

My own view is that GALA choruses sing sacred music for reasons that extend beyond the preferences of singers and artistic directors. Sacred music is part of the "standard repertoire" of the Western choral music tradition, and because GALA choruses are committed to sustaining that tradition, it is logical for them to sing that music. More specifically, the highly educated artistic directors that GALA choruses are hiring with increasing frequency (see chapter 1) are trained to value many sacred music pieces as staples, even as outstanding examples, of the repertoire; since they seek to achieve musical excellence (as defined by the Western academy), they want to encourage their choristers to sing these "masterworks." But most importantly for my analysis, sacred music performance underlines the homonormativity of GALA choruses. By singing this "standard repertoire," GALA choruses emphasize that they are just like other community choirs. Like the White middle-class singers in community choirs (who are surely not all Christians), they can sing songs with lyrics that they do not personally affirm, in the service of a great musical tradition to which they all belong. That tradition prioritizes music of the Christian faith—a faith that promotes practices, like monogamy, for which GALA choristers are eager to demonstrate their own shared regard. In singing sacred music, I argue, GALA singers once again emphasize their similarity to other White middle-class musicians, publicly performing their "normality."

Strategies for Programming Sacred Music

Singing sacred music goes back to the early days of GALA's history. As the GALA website documents, the second gay chorus ever established was the Gotham Male Chorus; it was founded in 1977 in New York City and specialized in "Gregorian chant and Renaissance music"—which is to say, sacred music (GALA Choruses n.d.b.). The San Francisco Gay Men's Chorus, which was founded just one year later, had its first, and impromptu, public performance at the vigil held for Harvey Milk, where the chorus sang "Thou, Lord Our Refuge" (San Francisco Gay Men's Chorus n.d.)

Indeed, some GALA choruses today sing nothing but sacred music; examples include Lavender Light of New York City, and Illuminati, the sacred music ensemble of the Columbus Gay Men's Chorus. However, tension around the programming of sacred music persists across the GALA organization. GALA's artistic directors know that their choruses include singers like Tom Fortuna, who would love to sing more sacred music, but also singers like Robert Frederick, who experienced trauma or heartbreak in the church. Although choristers' music choices are not always the conductors' top priority, programming decisions are certainly made with the sensitivities of singers in mind. Regarding sacred music, artistic directors take various approaches.

Some artistic directors simply do not program any sacred music. This position is in the minority, nearly forty years into GALA's history. These artistic directors are usually following the mandate expressed in their chorus's constitution or bylaws, which were developed with respect for singers who had been rejected by their church congregations. For example, Billy Sauerland, the artistic director of the Lesbian/Gay Chorus of San Francisco, said that his chorus's bylaws call for "no religious music of any kind."[11] As an example of how he fulfilled this requirement, Sauerland said that when he programmed a Bach chorale, he rewrote the words to remove all religious references.

The majority of GALA's artistic directors, however, program sacred music in the same way that artistic directors of other community choirs do. At the 2012 Festival, I spent some time noting the sacred songs I heard; examples included African American spirituals, settings of the Catholic Mass (in Latin and in English), and "Judah and His Maccabees," by Karen Hart (referencing Jewish history and beliefs). Indeed, one whole concert block, called "Songs of the Soul" was entirely devoted to sacred music. These many sacred songs were presented by their performers without explanation or any hint of apology; GALA singers and conductors were comfortable singing such songs in front of their GALA colleagues. I have also observed artistic directors presenting sacred songs at GALA reading sessions, again without seeming to feel the need to justify such songs to their fellow artistic directors. At one session I attended, a participant advocated for a song by noted contemporary Christian artist Michael W. Smith, and no one present expressed any objection.[12] Some GALA choruses have even presented concerts with contemporary Christian artists as featured soloists; for example, the Cincinnati Men's Chorus gave a concert called *Glory! Journey for the Spirit* with Andraé Crouch in 1998 (Cincinnati Men's Chorus n.d.), and in 2013 the Turtle Creek Chorale in Dallas, Texas, featured Sandi Patty at its *Inspiration and Hope* concert (Turtle Creek Chorale n.d.). Concerts like these, focusing on marquee Christian artists, are exceptional, but the regular programming of sacred music is normative for GALA choruses.

And yet, the singing of sacred music is not entirely unproblematic. In fact, controversies over religious song texts still arise from time to time. Members of Resonance Women's Chorus of Boulder, Colorado, reported that their chorus lost six singers when the artistic director, Sue Coffee, decided to program a "Jesus piece"; apparently long discussions with the chorus's leadership did not bring about resolution, and these choristers left the chorus over this issue.[13] Chorus leaders are therefore sensitive to the possibility that their programming of sacred music may raise conflict, and they often provide ways for choristers to opt out of sacred songs. For example, the Rainbow Harmony Project of Winnipeg, Canada, allows singers either to sing sacred songs but remain silent during words like God and Jesus, or to sit off to the side while the other choristers perform sacred songs (Mike Killen, interview, September 23, 2016). Singing OUT allows choristers to skip any performances given at churches because these performances include sacred songs (Jody Malone, interview, October 13, 2011).

In a related move, chorus leaders sometimes provide rationalizations for the singing of sacred music, in order to lessen any cognitive dissonance their choristers might feel. The artistic director of Reveille Men's Chorus in Tucson, Arizona, explained to his singers that they would perform sacred music as a way of fulfilling their mission. As Octavio Partida, one of Reveille's choristers, explained: "There's a 'disagreement' in our chorus about religious music. For some, it reminds them of a bad time . . . but this isn't an open topic of conversation, it's not openly debated. Everyone has a lot of trust in our conductor, because he explained that the point of singing religious music is to do outreach to religious people" (interview, November 7, 2016). Jane Hoffman remembered that the Lesbian and Gay Chorus of Washington, DC, had "huge discussions" over programming African American spirituals; ultimately choristers decided to understand these songs as "containing coded language, just like gay people used to have" (interview, March 1, 2012).[14] The Lesbian and Gay Chorus of Washington, DC, also performed Gabriel Fauré's *Requiem*, which, as Hoffman recalled, "pissed off a lot of people [in the chorus]." Hoffman explained that the chorus's justification for performing this setting of the Catholic Mass for the dead was, "Gay people have always existed, have died, and have had funerals. So we can find a way to connect to it."

GALA conductors—like public school music educators, who walk a similarly fine line when considering whether to program sacred music—also choose songs that reference the Christian tradition without ever explicitly mentioning God or Jesus. In this way they can satisfy their singers and listeners who want to hear or perform songs that evoke the Christian faith, while avoiding offending those singers who might otherwise decide to sit out. I have heard multiple GALA choruses perform the hymn "How Can I Keep from Singing," and the spiritual "Walk Together Children." Each of these songs uses well-known Christian terminology, such as "a new creation," "a great camp meeting," and "the promised land," and each has a long history of being sung by Christian congregations, but neither uses the words God or Jesus. Similarly, Larry Folk's song "Gathering of Friends" references the Christian belief in heaven ("There is music on that hillside / There are angels in a song that never ends") but never mentions the deity; this song was performed to enthusiastic applause by Captain Smartypants, the small ensemble of the Seattle Men's Chorus, at the 2012 Festival. Another example, one that has been performed by numerous choruses since it was commissioned from composer Joseph M. Martin to celebrate artistic director Tim Seelig's twentieth anniversary with the Turtle Creek Chorale, is called "Love Has Always Been Our Song." This song's lyrics contain a phrase commonly used in Christian circles ("We'll be faithful to our call") and gesture toward Biblical language ("We have raised a thousand alleluias"), but the song never mentions God or Jesus. "Love Has Always Been Our Song" is beloved by GALA choruses because it also contains a clear statement of their commitment to their mission (see chapter 6): "We'll change the world with voices raised as one."

Finally, GALA conductors sometimes program innovative songs that combine Christian ideas with affirmations of same-sex attraction. One such song, which was performed in the 2012 GALA Festival "Songs of the Soul" concert block, is Ron Sexsmith's "God Loves Everyone." The lyrics in this song both proclaim Christian dogma ("We're all worthy of His grace") and affirm the equality of LGBT people ("There are no gates in Heaven / Everyone gets in, queer or straight"). Similarly, Barbara Fried and Alex Rybeck's "Together This Christmas" references both the Nativity story ("Carols, stars and kings / The gift each shepherd brings") and a loving same-sex relationship ("Writing the cards, signing both our names / Showing our friends we two are now a pair, with happiness to share"). "Together This Christmas" is performed by the Albany Gay Men's Chorus (in Albany, New York) and the Gay Men's Chorus of South Florida. Another, rather witty, example is performed by Windsong, Cleveland's Feminist Chorus, and is titled "Faith Comes Out of the Closet" (with words by Farrell Collins and music by Nancy Vedder-Shults). It tells the story of a woman named Faith and implies—though it does not state explicitly—that after coming out, Faith will "meet a lover" of the same gender. Most interestingly, this song incorporates references to a Bible verse ("Sure Faith could move a mountain but she's far too tired to start," evoking Matthew 17:20) and to "Amazing Grace," one of Christianity's best-known hymns ("She's raising money for PFLAG, AIDS research, the Old Dyke's Home / Yes Faith has brought us safe thus far, and Faith will lead us on").

In singing songs that affirm both Christian teaching and same-sex love, GALA choruses engage in what scholar Krista McQueeny (2009, 167–68) calls "moralizing." When LGBT people moralize, McQueeny says, they "advance homosexuality as a basis for moral identity . . . defining gay and lesbian inclusion as an act of Christian love, true to Jesus' example, not as a rejection of Christian tradition or a political position" (168). McQueeny's research subjects were self-identified Christians, and as we have seen, many GALA choristers are not. However, GALA choruses do effectively moralize. By singing the songs of Christianity, GALA singers proclaim that they are—or ought to be—included in the religious faith that has historically been embraced by middle-class people in the United States and Canada. In so doing they emphasize their resemblance to the "normal" members of that class, once again demonstrating their commitment to homonormativity.

Conclusion

This chapter has emphasized the homonormativity of GALA choruses, which is, as I argue, the logical outgrowth of GALA choristers' status as White, cisgender, middle-class subjects. This is, of course, not the whole story. We saw in chapter 3 that people who do not identify as White, and those who do not identify as cisgender, do participate in GALA choruses, and that the GALA Choruses organization has made repeated attempts to increase the ethnic and gender diversity in its ranks. In chapter 5, I explain that GALA choruses' performances often extend far beyond the homonormative examples highlighted here. In short, while public presentations by GALA choruses often affirm the values upheld by heteronormative society, they also often contest those same values, either subtly or boldly.

5 • Disidentifying

The Music and Performance Practices of
GALA Choruses

On July 8, 2012, Harmony: A Colorado Chorale was onstage at the Ellie
Caulkins Opera House in Denver, Colorado. This mixed chorus presented
an excellent choral performance; its choristers' warm vocal tone, precise
intonation and pronunciation, rhythmically tight ensemble coordination,
and expressive use of varying levels of volume and rates of speed all reflected
the chorale's commitment to the highest standards of the Western choral
music tradition. The performance also transcended the bounds of that tradition, showing a significant degree of innovation in the songs it included and
in the way those songs were presented to the audience. For example, the second song was a choral arrangement of an American folk tune titled "Cindy";
Harmony's version included square dancers wearing uniform shirts emblazoned with one of the best-known symbols of Gay Pride, the rainbow flag.
The dancers danced in pairs, some of whom were same-sex couples. The performance continued with "America the Beautiful," another standard, this
one from the American patriotic repertoire. Harmony's presentation of it,
however, conveyed a message not usually heard in mainstream performances.
The message was reiterated by choristers who recited spoken testimonies
between the verses of the song: a man said that he was rejected by his family
because of his sexual orientation but found love and family in the chorale; a
woman told of her love of her lesbian mother; a bisexual woman and a transgender woman shared their stories; and finally a lesbian woman who said
that she did not want to go to gay bars explained that she was able to come
out when she eventually joined the chorale. America is beautiful, this perfor-

mance explained, because people from sexual and gender minorities engage in the pursuit of happiness within it. The final song of the performance extended this message even further. "Color Out of Colorado" name checks various American cities and states and asserts that LGBT people are essential to the greatness of those places: "You can't take the sissy out of Mississippi. . . . You can't have New York City without Queens. . . . Who'll keep Santa fey? / Yes we're proud to state / We make this country great / You need us to make the USA."[1]

Harmony: A Colorado Chorale's concert was an exemplar of many GALA chorus performances, as this chapter will delineate. These GALA performances vary quite dramatically in their adherence to, or deviation from, the norms of Western choral musicking; they also belong to another performance tradition theorized by performance studies and queer studies scholar José Esteban Muñoz (1999). Muñoz's term for this tradition is *disidentification*; disidentifying is a "survival strategy" practiced by "minority subject[s] in order to negotiate a phobic majoritarian public sphere" (4). As he explains, "The process of disidentification scrambles and reconstructs the encoded message of a cultural text in a fashion that both exposes the encoded message's universalizing exclusionary machination and recircuits its working to account for, include, and empower minority identities and identifications. Thus, disidentification is a step further than cracking open the code of the majority; it proceeds to use this code as raw material for representing a disempowered politics or positionality that has been rendered unthinkable by the dominant culture" (31). Disidentifying is exactly what Harmony: A Colorado Chorale did in its 2012 performance: the chorus sang well-known songs indexing American history and patriotism but "recircuited" them to include gay men, lesbian women, and bisexual and transgender people. With their last song they proclaimed something that has been unthinkable, and therefore unstated, in dominant tellings of the American story; that is, that the country would not exist without "sissies" and other sexual and gender minorities.

Muñoz (1999) focuses on instances of cultural production—painting, film, photography, writing, and theater—created by "queers of color," as examples of disidentification. However, he hastens to point out that all persons in a minority position may pursue disidentification (5). Although most GALA choristers identify as White and middle class, they nevertheless occupy a minority position by virtue of their sexual orientations and/or gender identifications. And what they are doing with their choral performances is, as Muñoz explains, "reading [themselves] and [their] own narrative in a moment, object or subject that is not culturally coded to 'connect' with the disidentifying subject. . . . A disidentifying subject works to hold on to this object and invest it with new life" (12). The choral music scene in the United States and Canada is conservative, and it seeks to sustain an art form whose norms were established some two hundred years ago. Those norms are heteronormative (see chapter 4); they reinforce the male-female gender binary (by requiring gender-coded uniforms, for example) and celebrate the faith tradition that has long permeated the White American middle class. Although LGBT people have no doubt always sung in community choirs, they and their life experiences were—and still are, in many cases—invisible and inaudible to both their fellow choristers and their audiences. When they perform, GALA singers and artistic directors are simultaneously upholding the values of the heteronormative choral music tradition and proclaiming their own narrative within it. As Muñoz would say, they are holding on to Western choral music and—at the same time—investing it with new life. GALA choruses accomplish this dual process in two ways. First, they disidentify explicitly during their concerts by singing "gay songs" that tell the stories of LGBT lives. Second, they disidentify implicitly by prioritizing innovation in their performances. Using the raw material of the Western choral music tradition, they scramble and reconstruct the idea of the choral concert in order to represent their own positionality, celebrating the creativity so frequently found among gay men and lesbian women.

"Gay Songs" and Gay Culture

GALA choruses disidentify with the Western choral music tradition by proclaiming their own narrative in the context of traditional choral music concerts, singing what insiders often gloss as "gay songs." I heard this phrase during my first encounter with a GALA participant. The artistic director of the Dayton Gay Men's Chorus, located in Dayton, Ohio, invited me to the group's upcoming Christmas concert, telling me that the plan was to sing "some traditional carols and some gay pieces" (Jason Schuler, interview, September 16, 2010). Since then, I have discovered that this term is commonly—although not universally—used in GALA circles. For example, Sharon Donning, an alto in the West Coast Singers of Los Angeles, California, shared in 2012 that "at every concert we have at least two numbers that are gay oriented or are made to be." Similarly, the music and artistic direction committee of the Orlando Gay Chorus in Orlando, Florida, chooses pieces according to the theme designated for each concert; however, the artistic director checks each song before approving it, asking "Where's the gay in this song?" (Manny Agon, interview, January 17, 2013).

GALA insiders do not demonstrate strict agreement on the parameters of so-called gay songs. Their divergent understandings mirror those in another community of LGBT musicians. Music journalist Will Grega (1994) interviewed forty-nine gay and lesbian recording artists in the early 1990s, specifically asking twenty-five of them, "What is gay and lesbian music in your definition?" They gave a variety of responses, as did GALA choristers when I asked similar questions. Some of Grega's interlocutors denied that such a category exists, claiming that any distinction between "gay music" and "straight music" is unproductive (24, 68). But twenty of the twenty-five interviewees averred that gay music was a definable category of music, and that it consisted of music created by self-identified gay and lesbian artists, as well as music with lyrics that addressed LGBT lives. Tom McCormack summarized the consensus by defining gay music as "music created by gay and lesbian songwriters/composers that speaks to gay experience" (qtd. in Grega 1994, 46).

An understanding of "gay music" necessitates an understanding of something of the larger "gay culture" of which the music is a part. David M. Halperin's (2012, 62) magnum opus, *How To Be Gay*, acknowledges that queer theory, in its reflexive opposition to essentialism, has led to scholarly disregard for "any cultural patterns or practices that might be distinctive to homosexuals." Nevertheless Halperin argues that gay culture—or, at least, gay White male American culture—can be discerned and learned. To the extent that scholars have agreed on a definition of "gay culture," they have focused on the camp aesthetic as central to forms of gay cultural and artistic expression. Jack Babuscio (1993, 36, 20), for example, argues that gay people both perceive and perform camp because camp is a "product of the gay sensibility" and reflects "an underlying unity of perspective among gays." George Chauncey (1994, 290) calls camp "the most distinctive, and characteristic, cultural style" of gay men. Halperin (2012, 140–211), for his part, devotes some seventy pages to discussing the notion of camp. Camp was authoritatively outlined in the 1970s by Esther Newton (1972, 107), who studied drag queens and explained that camp depends on the incongruous juxtaposition of two seemingly opposed things or ideas, such as is embodied by a man dressed as and acting like a hyperfeminine woman. As Newton points out, any juxtaposition may be campy (high and low social statuses, youth and old age, the profane and the sacred, the cheap and the expensive): "The camp inheres not in the person or thing itself but in the tension between that person or thing and the context or association" (107). The camp ethos is found at all levels of homosexual culture, Newton asserts (105). Frank Browning (1993, 211) agrees: "As variegated as the many gay demimondes may be in the inversion or exaggeration of masculine and feminine display, what unifies them is an ironic sensibility in the construction of mask and costume . . . shared homosexual culture has a trickster nature . . . [this is] the essence of the camp sensibility."

Newton (1993, 46) further explained that incongruity—or irony, as Babuscio and Browning call it—is one of three "strong themes" always present in camp. Camp also includes an element of theatricality, meaning that camp is always performed for an audience, and that the performance is always consciously styled, or shaped, for effect. As Scott Long (1993, 79–80) explains, camp focuses outward and is incomplete without a satisfactory response from a spectator or group of spectators. Finally, camp is humorous. The humor in camp is inherent in the juxtaposition of two incongruous elements, and it serves as political critique. As Newton (1972, 109) wrote, camp involves "laughing at one's incongruous position instead of crying. That is, humor does not cover up, it transforms." In Chauncey's (1994, 290) cogent summary, camp humor is a way to reveal one's anger at the social marginalization experienced by gay and lesbian people. Halperin (2012, 196) explains: "Forgoing your claim to dignity is a small price to pay for undoing the seriousness and authenticity of the naturalized identities and hierarchies of values that debase you."

Camp is thus an expression of an LGBT sensibility that develops in gay and lesbian people as they grow up and realize that their attraction to persons of the same gender is incongruous in a heteronormative society. Further, camp is performative and funny, and its stagey humor is a vehicle for criticizing repressive social norms. In what follows I show that GALA choruses perform a wide range of songs, which I divide into three categories: community songs, contrafacta, and commissioned works. Importantly, GALA insiders cite examples from all three categories when they refer to "gay music." As we shall see, some gay songs exemplify the three strong themes elucidated by scholars of camp and are beloved by GALA singers for that very reason. However, other examples are not campy—they present a sincere rather than ironic message—and yet are equally important in GALA circles and are also considered to be legitimate examples of gay music.

Community Songs

GALA choruses sing what I call community songs; that is, they perform virtually the entire repertoire of other community choirs. Artistic directors with formal academic training sometimes refer to these songs as "standard repertoire."[2] This repertoire is dominated by works in the Western European classical choral tradition, including so-called masterworks by European classical composers like Johannes Brahms and Gabriel Fauré, and newer works based on the same sonic elements: three or four voice part compositions that use triadic tonal harmonies and that are most often accompanied by a piano. GALA choruses also sing other community songs such as arrangements of folk tunes and popular hits, songs popularized in movies and musicals, and so on. Just as other community choirs are increasingly interested in "world music" scores (new compositions, arrangements of folk tunes, and other song material from around the world, usually including words in languages other than English), so are GALA choruses programming world music with increasing frequency. In addition, most GALA choruses perform some sacred music, an important segment of the community songs or standard repertoire (as we saw in chapter 4).

On September 24, 2011, I heard a concert that exemplified GALA's commitment to community songs. Caballeros, now known as the Palm Springs Gay Men's Chorus, presented a recital for the assembled attendees at GALA's annual leadership conference in Palm Springs, California. Under the baton of guest conductor and beloved GALA composer Robert Seeley, the chorus sang pop standards ("Try to Remember [the kind of September]," "I Believe [for every drop of rain that falls]," and "It Don't Mean a Thing [if it ain't got that swing]"), hymns and new and traditional spirituals ("In This Very Room," "Ain't That Good News," and "Blow Gabriel Blow"), and several songs featuring texts of empowerment and hope, although not explicitly gay affirming ("We Shall Overcome," "Wheels of a Dream" from the 1996 musical *Ragtime*, and Gloria and Bill Gaither's "Let Freedom Ring"). On this occasion, GALA was singing to itself; the audience consisted of artistic directors and board members from GALA choruses across the continent. Interestingly, the program—which was warmly received by the audience—was entirely composed of community songs.

GALA insiders argue that when community songs are performed by GALA choruses, they can be termed "gay songs" because the performers of those songs self-identify as LGBT. As Miguel Felipe, the former artistic director of the Maine Gay Men's Chorus, told me, "Music carries, in part, the identity of the performers" (interview, July 31, 2013). Gianluca Ragazzini of Tone Cluster—quite a queer choir (a mixed chorus in Ottawa, Ontario) pointed out that "depending on context," a song might become gay. He said that especially when his chorus sings songs about social change and the surmounting of obstacles, these songs can become gay: "It's considered to be gay music just because we sing it" (interview, March 5, 2012). John Quillin, artistic director of the Gay Men's Chorus of Charlotte, North Carolina, summed it up memorably by saying, "You can stand on a stage and sing 'Mary Had a Little Lamb,' and it would be gay if it was a gay chorus!" (interview, March 29, 2011). My own experience bears these assertions out. I first heard Libby Roderick's song "How Could Anyone [ever tell you / you were anything less than beautiful?]" at a conference for foster parents. In that context, I understood the lyrics to be addressing children whose parents had been unloving or emotionally abusive. However, when I heard the song again—twice—at the 2012 GALA Festival, I wondered whether the lyrics had originally been intended to refer to adult men and women who were suffering social ostracism due to their sexual orientation. I made this association only because I heard the song sung by groups of gay and lesbian singers. Of course, Roderick's lyrics are nonreferential enough to permit very different interpretations. Still, the incident showed me how a song might "become gay" in the ears of listeners by virtue of being performed by LGBT singers.[3]

This phenomenon demonstrates that LGBT choruses can disidentify with mainstream discourse simply by singing the songs that "everyone" sings: in so doing, the singers implicitly proclaim that LGBT people are not deviants on the outskirts of society (or on the margins of the community choir scene) but rather full members who function in the same way (and who sing the same songs) as do the majority. Furthermore, when gay and lesbian singers perform well-known, non-LGBT-referencing songs, they show that music that is unconsciously marked as "straight" can be effectively performed by LGBT people. By performing this repertoire they may destabilize the accepted interpretation of the songs, causing audience members to question the ideas they previously attached to dearly loved music. In short, such performances may counter some notions that homophobic folks hold dear, forcing them to think new thoughts. (This line of reasoning is why listeners sometimes vehemently oppose performances by a GALA chorus, as is described in chapter 1. They react strongly because their own ideas about what is acceptable are contested.) Therefore, when GALA choruses cause a well-known song to "become gay" simply by singing it, they simultaneously communicate that the song is important and that the song can be understood to affirm LGBT perspectives. In short, they disidentify.

David M. Halperin (2012, 421) gestures toward the idea of disidentifying in his discussion of instances when gay men "colonize" mainstream culture. He argues that gay men often "selectively reappropriate" elements of mainstream culture, claiming songs, for example, as expressions of gay sensibility, although the songs' composers likely intended to make no such reference. Halperin points out that this practice is common in gay culture: "Cultural objects that contain no explicit gay themes, that do not represent gay men, that do not invoke same-sex desire, but that afford gay men opportunities for colonizing them and making them over into vehicles of queer affirmation exercise a perennial charm" (112). One such cultural object is the song "Seize the Day" from the 1992 movie musical *Newsies*. This song was the second most commonly performed song at the 2012 GALA Festival in Denver, Colorado; over the course of one week this song was presented by five different choruses. The lyrics of "Seize the Day" reference the main theme of the movie: uniting to stand against oppression. Here a community song not originally intended to refer to gay or lesbian themes was reappropriated by gay and lesbian singers because the lyrics are nonspecific enough to refer both to child laborers in the nineteenth century and to LGBT people in the twenty-first: "Wrongs will be righted / If we're united / Let us seize the day!"

The GALA repertoire is full of community songs that have lyrics or extra-musical associations that allow them to be reinterpreted as gay songs. George Gershwin's "The Man I Love" (featured in the 2015 musical *An American in Paris*) is one example; Stan Hill, former artistic director of the Twin Cities Gay Men's Chorus in Minneapolis, Minnesota, once described this song by saying, "the gayest song in the world is not a gay song" (interview, September 24, 2011). When a group of men sings "The Man I Love" as written—with its open declaration of faith in a future romantic relationship with a man—they claim the song and the sentiment as their own. Similarly, Al Fischer, the artistic director of the Gateway Men's Chorus of St. Louis, Missouri, pointed out that when his choir of gay men sings "I Can Hear the Bells," a song from the 2002 musical *Hairspray*, it is an expression of same-sex desire—and given that it is also a show tune, "it's double gay" he said (interview, January 31, 2012). Jason Schuler explained to me that one of the "gay songs" in the Christmas program of the Dayton Gay Me's Chorus was an a cappella rendering of Pyotr Tchaikovsky's "Dance of the Sugarplum Fairies" (interview, September 16, 2010). This performance consisted only of vocables, not words. However, the fact that "fairy" was included in the title, and the fact that the music is associated with one of the best-known and most spectacular of the classical ballets, afforded his chorus of gay men an "opportunity to colonize" a piece of mainstream culture, à la Halperin, and to present it to the public as a gay artifact. And we can also understand this strategic singing of community songs as instances of disidentification, moments when members of sexual and gender minorities assert that such songs are their own property, and that they communicate their own message.

The examples cited in the above paragraph are, further, campy community songs. What makes them campy? Most obviously, in each case a "straight" song is performed by openly gay men, and the juxtaposition of these two incongruous elements constitutes classic camp. Moreover, the first two examples—like many show tunes—feature lyrics that communicate a tremendous amount of emotion (from "I Can Hear the Bells". "My temperature's climbing / I can't contain my joy / 'Cause I've finally found the boy I've been missing"). Emotional display is traditionally associated with women, not men, and so when men publicly perform such emotions, they take on a (supposedly) feminine quality; the juxtaposition of masculinity and femininity in such songs renders them campy. The camp aesthetic also embraces a political critique of social norms, and GALA's performances of such emotional, campy community songs can be read in just this way. Tim Seelig, the current conductor of the San Francisco Gay Men's Chorus and former artistic director in residence for GALA, told me that despite his extensive formal training and academic experience with the canonical art music repertoire, he embraces "sentimental, gay music" and "funny, flamboyant music: I endured years of abuse at the hands of parents and teachers and friends who said, 'Real men don't behave that way,' and so now I program that music unapologetically" (interview, September 15, 2011). In other words, programming stereotypically campy community songs is a way to resist the limiting social roles imposed by our heteronormative society. Another way to understand Seelig's and his GALA colleagues' choices is to see them as instances of dis-identifying, as moments when GALA singers can assert their own truths in the context of the Western choral music concert, a context that has reinforced heteronormative gender roles for two centuries.

A second important way in which GALA choruses present community songs as campy performances is by including choralography and dance. As Fred Fishman, who has sung with GALA ensembles across the United States, explained, "Choralography can really gayify a piece of music" (interview, April 25, 2012). Choralography consists of coordinated movements (usually of the upper body) performed by some or all choristers while they sing, and may involve the use of extra costumes. These movements serve to emphasize certain lyrics, and the exaggeration is usually very humorous. One typical example is "Ya Got Me" as performed by the Gay Men's Chorus of Los Angeles.[4] At the midpoint of this performance, the singers remove their tuxedo jackets to effect a small costume change. The chorus uses choralography and dance extensively; in the dance portion of their rendition of "The Anvil Chorus," from a Verdi opera, physically strenuous movements by three attractive and shirtless (hypermasculine) young men effectively exaggerate and "gayify" the piece (GMCLA.org 2007). Choralography and dance increase the camp factor in a community song because they emphasize the performative nature of the event. The coordinated motions of the singers are a visual testament to the fact that the performers have consciously shaped and rehearsed their performance, and are seeking to communicate with their audience. A performance that includes movement is more theatrical than a stand-and-sing performance, and as Esther Newton (1972) first explained, theatricality is central to camp.

While the camp aesthetic is important to GALA's repertoire of community songs, campy songs by no means constitute the entirety of this repertoire. Indeed, many GALA performances of community songs are sincere rather than ironic. For example, when GALA choruses perform the American national anthem at local sports events—as many of them have—they intend the performance to be understood as an expression of patriotism and national unity, in the same way that other performers, the audience, and indeed they themselves, understand it. Another example: a number of GALA men's choruses have performed Jake Heggie's operatic *For a Look or a Touch*, a work that tells the stories of gay men who were killed during the Holocaust. Heggie's composition is deeply meaningful to gay men's choruses, as the choristers value the opportunity to recount their own history; this is a gay choral opera that GALA choruses present with utmost sincerity. It is very important, moreover, that such performances be taken as sincere because, as we will see more fully in later chapters, GALA choruses are ultimately committed to their mission of increasing mainstream society's acceptance of LGBT people. They are committed, therefore, to treating seriously themes that most people in the United States and Canada treat seriously, understanding that to mock (or to be perceived as mocking) events such as the Holocaust with campy songs would provoke anger rather than sympathy. So, as Robert Frederick (a baritone singer in the Dayton Gay Men's Chorus) explained, "We're out to change minds . . . without a doubt," adding moments later that it is therefore important that his chorus's Christmas concert, which is performed in a church, be markedly "reserved: It's not the time to camp out; we don't want to offend the public" (interview, August 17, 2011).

Perhaps the clearest example of community songs, or standard repertoire, being performed sincerely can be found in the work of Illuminati, an ensemble of the Columbus Gay Men's Chorus of Columbus, Ohio. Illuminati is dedicated to singing sacred music, and to singing it in churches and at religious celebrations. When its choristers perform well-known hymns at Protestant church services, as they commonly do, they present these hymns in the spirit of reverence that congregation members often attach to the songs. It is of great importance that this ensemble's performances be regarded as sincere, not ironic, since Illuminati's stated mission is to "increase our outreach performances, particularly to religious organizations, while respecting the members' religious beliefs" (Columbus Gay Men's Chorus n.d.). Of course, to be successful in demonstrating respect for the beliefs of its listeners, and to "be a bridge between the LGBT and religious communities," Illuminati must sing the sacred songs of those communities without being seen to poke fun at or make light of those songs.

Contrafacta

Contrafacta are previously composed songs with some number (whether few or many) of the original words changed. Importantly, in this kind of composition the melody, harmony, and rhythm remain intact, so that the tune is recognizable and listeners may attach to it previously understood meanings. We can trace the creation of contrafacta at least as far back as the fifteenth century, when the Italian friar Girolamo Savonarola replaced the lyrics of secular carnival songs with words from sacred texts (Fenlon 2010, 63–65). Martin Luther, the figure at the center of the Protestant Reformation, did the same, creating much-loved Lutheran chorales by writing new words to folk songs and other secular melodies (Bulow 2004, 205). Contrafacta continue to be popular in other countries today, where rock and pop singers perform Anglo-American hit tunes with words in local languages. However, in the contemporary United States and Canada, contrafacta are almost never performed by adult musicians. Fear of violating copyright laws undoubtedly partly accounts for this absence. But more important is the value placed by late-capitalist societies on originality and innovation. Some GALA insiders share this perspective on originality, and therefore—as I will explain further—contrafacta, while common, are not universally embraced by GALA choruses.

When GALA composers and arrangers create contrafacta, they almost always change the words in order to imply some kind of same-sex relationship. This action can be as simple as "changing the pronouns" (as this practice is known in GALA circles); swap "he" for all the instances of "she" in a love song, for example, and the lyrics instantly reference same-sex desire. I heard one such contrafactum in 2010 at the very first GALA concert I ever attended; it was titled "I Saw Daddy Kissing Santa Claus."[5] Another contrafactum that resulted from "changing pronouns" is titled "I Want a Guy!" and was created by a GALA chorus director who simply replaced the fourth word of the original song's title, "I Want a Girl" (field notes, January 7, 2011). The contrafactum continued in this vein, changing one-syllable words referencing female gender to analogous words referencing male gender (substituting "lad" for "girl," for example).[6] Complete contrafacta—in which all the words to a known melody are changed—are quite rare. One well-known GALA example is "Coming Out On Christmas," which is sung to the tune of the Christmas carol "Hark the Herald Angels Sing." The second verse and chorus consist of the following lyrics:

Oh say can you see it now?
Watch my parents have a cow.
Or perhaps, if fate is kind,
They'll insist that they don't mind.
Then they'll say "We always guessed,
After all, look how you're dressed.
Seven earrings in each ear?
We're not quite that dense, my dear."
They'll adore me, anyway,
When I come out on Christmas Day.

In GALA circles, the practice of rewriting lyrics to create contrafacta is common enough that it is a frequent topic of conversation. One of my interlocutors recalled that, when meeting GALA singers and artistic directors from other choruses at Festivals and national conferences, choristers often introduced themselves by asking, "Does your chorus change words?" (Jane Hoffman, interview, March 1, 2012). In addition, candidates for GALA conducting jobs are asked about this practice during interviews (Regina Carlow, interview, September 15, 2012). It is an important question because the practice of changing pronouns is controversial: some artistic directors refuse to do it, either because they are concerned about copyright or because they are reluctant to violate the original composer's intent.[7] However, because the performance of contrafacta is common among GALA choruses, and because it virtually never happens in other community choral organizations, we can claim that these songs are unique to GALA choruses. Moreover, performing contrafacta is another important way in which GALA singers disidentify with the Western choral music tradition.

When I asked GALA interviewees for examples of gay pieces, they most often mentioned contrafacta. These songs are textbook examples of camp: they are created by juxtaposing known melodies with unknown (new) words. These new words usually refer a same-gender relationship, incongruously contrasting with the known melody, which was previously linked to a different and heteronormative set of words. The juxtaposition of words about same-sex love and a melody associated with the straight world—for example, words about coming out as gay juxtaposed with the melody of a Christmas carol (a song that is linked to a religious festival celebrating the birth of a baby to a heterosexual couple)—is unexpected, and therefore humorous. Moreover, the new lyrics in contrafacta serve the political purpose of camp in that the new text highlights how easily words—and ideas—can be changed. In a classic contrafactum, the new words are chosen to fit the rhythm of the existing melody. The one-syllable word "girl," for example, is easily replaced by the one-syllable word "guy," without requiring any melodic pitches to be added or deleted, and a men's chorus can just as easily and pleasingly sing "I Want a Guy" as it can "I Want a Girl." The contrafactum works just as well, musically speaking, as the original song. The underlying lesson here is that original, straight lyrics can easily be rewritten. The original lyrics—and the heterosexual relationships to which they refer—were not "naturally" or organically tied to the melody, and they can be deconstructed as easily as they were first constructed.

Commissions

The third branch of the GALA repertoire consists of new compositions and new arrangements of existing songs, usually commissioned from "GALA-friendly" composers and arrangers; these songs often address LGBT themes.[8] Local choruses, alliances of choruses, and the GALA organization itself have all provided funds to pay composers to write new songs to be premiered by various GALA choruses. Recently, the life of gay rights icon Harvey Milk has become a favorite theme for commissions; the Lesbian/Gay Chorus of San Francisco commissioned *Harvey Milk: A Cantata* (in which all the words come from unpublished writings by Milk) from Jack Curtis Dubowsky in 2012, and a consortium of six GALA choruses commissioned *I Am Harvey Milk* from Andrew Lippa in 2013. Like *I Am Harvey Milk*, many of GALA's best-known commissioned pieces are lengthy multimovement works written for men's choruses.

GALA-commissioned pieces may be campy, and those that interviewees identified to me were usually "funny and flamboyant," to use Tim Seelig's phrase. Eric Lane Barnes is one of the best-known GALA-friendly composers, and he has made something of a specialty of writing humorous, campy songs for various GALA groups. His song "Disclaimer" (commissioned by the Gay Men's Chorus of Charlotte, North Carolina), for example, announces that it will use sound effects such as hand claps and foot stomps in the place of potentially offensive words. It begins: "Instead of saying butthole we'll say

[clap] / Instead of saying boner we'll say [stomp]." The use of sound effects increases the performative aspect of the song, as choristers use their bodies as percussion instruments. Even more importantly, the humor here points to a constricting social reality: certain words are not acceptable at public events like choral concerts because they refer to sex between two men, an act deemed unacceptable—even criminal—in a heteronormative society. Another of Barnes's campy songs, "Parade," was commissioned by One Voice Charlotte (a mixed chorus also in Charlotte, North Carolina). The last line of the chorus of "Parade" is "It's the Gay Pride Parade today!" Each time the chorus is reiterated, this line is longer, due to the insertion of more and more words (e.g., "It's the Gay and Lesbian Pride parade today!"; "It's the Gay and Lesbian, Bisexual and Transgender Community Pride parade today!") The longer text disrupts the rhythm articulated in the first iteration of the chorus and delays the expected harmonic resolution. Again, the unexpected musical gesture here is laugh-out-loud funny, and the campy humor of this moment makes a powerful point: the inclusion of more and more varieties of queer-identifying folks in the gay rights movement is disruptive and sometimes uncomfortable, and the movement (strongly influenced by cisgender White men) has sometimes struggled to live up to its own ideals of inclusivity.

However, many of GALA's commissioned works are not campy; in fact, most commissioned music that GALA insiders discussed with me is sincere rather than ironic. These are gay songs, to be sure—their lyrics clearly reference gay and lesbian themes—but they do not evoke the camp aesthetic. Take for example David Conte's "Elegy for Matthew," a piece that has been widely performed and that was originally commissioned by the New York City Gay Men's Chorus. This song mourns the death of Matthew Shepard, a young gay man who was brutally murdered in 1998. Music reviewer Lewis Foreman (2000) described "Elegy for Matthew" as "direct and touching." The aforementioned Eric Lane Barnes also composes serious music for GALA; his "Am I Welcome Here?," jointly commissioned by the Seattle Men's Chorus and the Cincinnati Gay Men's Chorus, tells the story of a gay man standing outside a church on Christmas Eve, wondering whether he might enter. The *Seattle Times* review of a performance of this piece called it "moving," in direct contrast to the other "fun stuff" on the program (Bargreen 2001).

The reviews of the above pieces indicate that they have been interpreted as serious works that communicate—without irony or humor—some painful aspects of contemporary LGBT life. These songs, along with many others, are well-known and well-loved examples of gay songs that evoke difficulty and pain and are presented without histrionics or the flamboyant excess that characterizes camp. For example, the 1992 piece *Hidden Legacies*, one of GALA's best-known large-scale commissioned works, was written by Roger Bourland in response to a request to honor singers in the Gay Men's Chorus of Los Angeles who had died of AIDS (Bourland, interview, December 10, 2012). Singing this oratorio allowed the choristers to publicly express their grief over the deaths of their friends and lovers. Michael Shaieb's 2008 *Through a Glass, Darkly*, commissioned by the Twin Cities Gay Men's Chorus, treats crystal methamphetamine addiction among gay men. One of this chorus's singers had been found frozen to death in an alley with the drug still in his system, and another chorister, a public school teacher, had been caught stealing from his fellow teachers to support his meth habit (Stan Hill, interview, September 24, 2011). This commission, therefore, allowed the Twin Cities Gay Men's Chorus to communicate directly with their audience about a problem affecting the gay male community.

A number of GALA-friendly composers have created lyrics for lengthy works by interviewing choristers. A famous example of this genre is *Naked Man*, written by Phillip Littell and Robert Seeley in 1996, and performed many times by many choruses since then. The lyrics for *Naked Man* were developed from statements made by sixty singers in the San Francisco Gay Men's Chorus, who were interviewed specifically for the purpose of creating a text for this work. Similarly, the lyrics for *Watershed Stories*, by Canadian composer David Mcintyre, are based on interviews Mcintyre conducted with men and women of the Prairie Pride Chorus in Regina, Saskatchewan (Mcintyre, interview, July 31, 2012). One of the movements tells how a same-sex couple developed their relationship: "We Met Singing in the Choir." The 2012 work *Heartlands*, by Arthur Durkee, was commissioned by the Perfect Harmony Men's Chorus and the City of Festivals Men's Chorus (of Madison and Milwaukee, Wisconsin, respectively). In the 2012 GALA Festival program, the work was described thus:

> *Heartlands* was created by collecting the stories of the members of Perfect Harmony and their families. These stories share the lives of LGBT community through the filter of rural America. They share the joys of life in the Midwest including the beauty of the quiet spaces and having family at the center of your life to the depths of loneliness as one tries to seek out others like themselves without the amenities of our urban centers. In our choruses, where some members drive over 70 miles to get to rehearsal, the final movement When We Sing celebrates the strong community that is created through our, and other, GALA choruses. (GALA Choruses 2012, 131)

Serious works such as the commissioned pieces described previously are crucial to the GALA repertoire because singing in a GALA chorus represents, for GALA singers, an important opportunity to speak or sing about one of their most profoundly felt realities, that is, their sexual and gender identities. When singing such commissioned works, choristers explicitly affirm their gay, lesbian, bisexual, or transgender identities; in other words, these songs constitute precise and concentrated moments of self-revelation during a choral performance. Using Muñoz's terms, these are moments of disidentification. Disidentifying with Western choral musicking—and more broadly, with our heteronormative society—is an important and potentially impactful act, and therefore many of GALA's commissioned songs are correspondingly serious in intent and presentation.

GALA's Contributions to Gay Culture: Beyond Camp

David M. Halperin (2012, 421) concludes *How to Be Gay* by offering the following definition of gay culture: "[it] can refer to new works of literature, film, music, art, drama, dance and performance that are produced by queer people and that reflect on queer experience. Gay culture can also refer to mainstream works created mostly by heterosexual artists, plus some (closeted) ones, that queer people have selectively appropriated and reused for anti-heteronormative purposes." Halperin insists that "gay men routinely cherish non-gay artifacts and cultural forms that realize gay desire instead of denoting it," arguing that they generally show little attraction to literal representations of gay life (112). Accordingly, he spills much ink on Joan Crawford's 1945 movie *Mildred Pierce* and spends virtually no time analyzing the kind of cultural artifact I emphasize in this chapter, that is, songs with lyrics that openly reference LGBT experiences and concerns.

As we have seen, GALA choruses' component of gay culture, their so-called gay songs, includes appropriated mainstream works (community songs), reused mainstream works (contrafacta), and new works (commissioned pieces). The camp aesthetic is central to contrafacta, in which new, same-sex lyrics are juxtaposed with known, "straight" melodies. And camp can be an important part of the performance of community songs; indeed, camp is inherent even in traditional presentations of sentimental love songs, especially when a chorus of men sings a love song with the passionate intensity stereotypically associated with women. The humor that is so central to camp is sometimes evident in pieces that

GALA commissions, and the musical humor found in these campy new songs functions as camp humor always does, to critique repressive social norms. However, camp is not the defining element in all of the gay cul tural artifacts that GALA creates and performs. Indeed, as the examples described above show, performances of both community songs and commissioned works can be deeply serious and sincere. Indeed, GALA insiders insist that these performances be taken at face value. Sincere, rather than ironic, performances of gay songs are of utmost importance to GALA choristers. Such performances allow the singers to tell stories about LGBT lives, to "read their own narrative" into Western choral musicking, and to disidentify with a tradition that they love but that has long marginalized and silenced people like them.

GALA's Performance Practices

My attendance at dozens of GALA chorus performances during the years that I conducted research for this book revealed that GALA chorus concerts are focal points for artistic creativity, and that audience members at these concerts are frequently treated to a range of innovative performance practices. Not all GALA choruses are especially groundbreaking in the way they design and present performances; the general trend is that the bigger the chorus, and the more financial resources it has, the more likely it will perform "shows," as insiders often call them. And therefore innovative shows are most often the purview of men's choruses rather than of women's choruses.

Dennis Coleman, one of GALA's most influential artistic directors, asserted that GALA groups led the trend (now evident among other community choirs) of presenting choral music as a "theatrical event" (interview, September 24, 2011). Indeed, theatrical events—or shows—are a prominent and important part of GALA's developing performance tradition. These shows exemplify the innovative impulse that is central to GALA's concertizing. The biggest shows are especially innovative precisely because they are created by sexual Others, usually gay men. As scholars of gay culture have asserted, members of sexual and gender minorities are often found at the center of innovative artistic endeavors. The development of innovative performance practices is therefore another way in which GALA's LGBT choristers disidentify, reading their own narrative into the Western choral music tradition.

The Spectrum of GALA Performances

The idea that GALA choruses' performance practices vary, and that these variances can be categorized, is well recognized by GALA insiders who have attended a GALA Festival. At the Festival, which occurs in July, choruses present one of their recent programs, usually from the preceding twelve months. Given that the Festival venue does not provide exactly the same logistical possibilities as do the choruses' regular venues, the performances at the Festival are not precisely the same as the performances that occur all over the United States and Canada. However, choruses work hard to showcase a representative sample of their best concertizing at the Festival. The biggest choruses might pay to fly their guest soloists and instrumentalists to the Festival, while smaller choruses—who can only afford to bring their piano accompanists to the Festival—nevertheless wear their costumes and present their choreographed movements just as they did during their hometown performances. Therefore, the performances one sees and hears at the Festival do faithfully reflect the variety of performances presented by GALA choruses. Festival veterans often say that there are two types of choruses. Stephanie Dykes of the Windy City Gay Chorus of Chicago, Illinois, identified these two types as "serious" and "kitschy," adding that "kitschy" meant a chorus that uses a lot of body movement in their performances (interview, April 25, 2011). Joe Nadeau, artistic director of the Heartland Men's Chorus of Kansas City, Missouri, characterized the two types as "stand-and-sing choruses" and "the other kind" (interview, February 20, 2011). However, having witnessed numerous concerts at the GALA Festival in both 2012 and 2016, I believe that GALA concerts are better understood not as constituting two types but as occurring along a spectrum marked by two contrasting poles. Shows exist at one end of the spectrum, and what I am calling "choral recitals" exist at the other end of the spectrum. GALA choruses locate their public concertizing at various points along the spectrum at various times and for various reasons.

Choral recitals represent the most faithful adherence to the Western choral music tradition. The other pole, representing a performance containing the highest number of innovative elements, is a show. The comparative list that follows shows the differences between choral recitals and shows. The most consequential elements are at the top of the list, and the least important differences are at the bottom. Note that the most important distinction between choral recitals and shows, is, in this analysis, the existence of a thematic program, which Chorus America defines as "a program centered around a story or an idea" (Brown et al. 2016, 43). This thematic program, or its absence, drives the inclusion of all other elements. Thus, although GALA insiders most often distinguish between choral recitals and shows by mentioning the presence or absence of choralography (movement of upper bodies only) and dance (movement of small groups about the stage in choreographed routines), I contend that these elements are secondary to the question of thematic program.

1. *Choral Recital*: Songs are not linked by any particular theme or story.
   Show: Songs are all clearly connected to a thematic program.
2. *Choral Recital*: Songs are not preceded by any verbal explanations; songs are listed on a printed program.
   Show: Thematic program is explained through the use of narration, including verbal interludes, voice-overs, and testimonies, and also through the presence of visual aids, such as a screen displaying words and images.
3. *Choral Recital*: Audience applauds, and conductor acknowledges the applause, after every song.
   Show: Sound and action onstage are continuous; conductor implicitly or explicitly discourages applause between songs.
4. *Choral Recital*: Most songs are "standard repertoire," coming from the Western art music tradition.
   Show: Most songs are newly commissioned works, or they come from Broadway musicals and other popular traditions.
5. *Choral Recital*: All songs are sung by the entire chorus.
   Show: Select songs are sung by soloists and by small ensembles.
6. *Choral Recital*: The choristers stand in rows and never move from their standing positions.
   Show: All choristers perform choralography, and select choristers dance.
7. *Choral Recital*: Singers wear a uniform consisting of formal clothing (often a tuxedo for men and a long skirt or dress for women).
   Show: Singers wear various costumes and may change their uniforms during the performance.
8. *Choral Recital*: Singing is accompanied by a piano.
   Show: Singing is accompanied by a piano and a small group of additional instruments.
9. *Choral Recital*: Performance is usually described as a "concert."
   Show: Performance is described using new vocabulary.

As the list implies, shows require more financial resources to stage than do choral recitals. It is therefore unsurprising that large men's choruses, with their larger budgets, are the most likely to mount shows, and that smaller choruses (usually mixed choruses and women's choruses) are more likely to lean toward choral recitals, but this divide is not absolute. One of the most elaborate shows I saw, in 2016, was a work from the Seattle Women's Chorus about the large-scale entry of women into the male-dominated workforce during World War II (described in greater detail in chapter 7). Notably, the Seattle Women's Chorus is a large organization and is affiliated with the Seattle Men's Chorus, one of the best-resourced GALA choruses in the world. Most women's choruses in GALA have much smaller membership numbers and, consequently, fewer financial resources. Further, men's choruses sing plenty of traditional choral recitals, such as the following example, which I observed at the 2016 Festival.

The thirty-one singers of Out Loud: The Colorado Springs Men's Chorus presented an exemplary choral recital in 2016.[9] The songs they sang were not thematically connected. The recital included arrangements of two folk songs that reference the Christian tradition ("Zion's Walls" and "When the Saints Go Marching In"); neither of these songs mention God or Jesus, and therefore they exemplify a common programming strategy used by GALA artistic directors (see chapter 4). These two songs were interspersed with others that had serious and traditional—but unconnected—messages ("Behold Man" and "If Music Be the Food of Love"). The composers of the chorus's selections included luminaries of twentieth-century art music—Aaron Copland, Lucy Simon and Ron Nelson—and a composer of some of GALA's best-known commissioned works, Alan Shorter. Shorter's contribution was a new composition, "Every Dream Begins with a Dreamer." This concert was a kind of absolute art: the songs were presented not because they illuminated a thematic program, but rather because each was beautiful and worth hearing for that reason alone. The preceding sentence is my own interpretation, of course, because no one from Out Loud provided any spoken explanations of the songs. The audience applauded enthusiastically after each song concluded, as expected. The singers wore tuxedos and stood in rows that were carefully organized to maximize the acoustic blend of their voices. They were ably accompanied by a pianist. Interestingly, this concert did not include an ASL interpreter, as is common, but not universal, among GALA chorus performances. In short, the Out Loud performance was a choral recital that epitomized the norms of the Western choral music tradition.

The other end of the spectrum is exemplified by a show titled (Accentu-

ate the) Positive, presented by the New York City Gay Men's Chorus in 2012. This chorus is one of the largest and oldest in GALA, and it presents shows annually. The shows created by large GALA choruses, including *(Accentuate the) Positive*, combine elements in a way that bends genres and frequently necessitates the creation of new, precise terminology. Heartland Men's Chorus, for example, premiered the idea of a "musical documentary" (Joe Nadeau, interview, February 20, 2011). Columbus Men's Chorus called its 2016 show a "musical essay."[10] This use of new vocabulary demonstrates that these performers clearly understand that what they are presenting is innovative and cannot be captured by the word *concert*. Most importantly, these shows are organized around thematic programs that are encapsulated by titles. The New York City Gay Men's Chorus appoints a director for each show; the director writes the script, or the text that delineates the story or theme of the show (Charlie Beale, interview, August 16, 2011).

(Accentuate the) Positive was directed by Jason Cannon, and the show's central theme was "living with HIV/AIDS" (New York City Gay Men's Chorus n.d.). Each song expressed an emotion experienced by a person who is diagnosed HIV positive, and who then must accept this new reality. The show included choral singing, personal testimonies recited by individual choristers, voice-overs (recorded speech played while another action occurred), short acted scenes, and dance.[11] The songs were pulled from a variety of sources, from the standard repertoire to Broadway musicals, and even the music of pop superstar Beyoncé. For example, the chorus sang a staple of the Western choral music canon titled "Sure on This Shining Night,"[12] but this version included a spoken portion, during which a singer explained that he wanted this song to be sung at his funeral. The show moved seamlessly from there to the next song, "Totally Fucked" from the 2006 musical *Spring Awakening*,[13] which was accompanied (at the 2012 Festival) by both a piano and a recorded backup track. "Totally Fucked" was an engaging song that—in the context of this 2012 performance—clearly communicated the emotional state of a man who has just learned that he has HIV. The juxtaposition of high art and popular music, and of confidently prepared music and movement with evocations of difficult and uncomfortable emotions continued throughout the show; the thematic program was emphasized by narrations and acting. The show concluded with "Falling Slowly," a contemporary pop song that was featured in the 2007 movie musical *Once*.[14] Two choristers danced a pas de deux during this song; one dancer clearly had professional ballet training, while the other was something of an amateur. The contrasts evident here (between classical dance and popular music, and between the two dancers' skill levels) reinforced the

message of the show once again: life with HIV/AIDS is a complex human experience that includes powerful and conflicting emotions.

While concerts that align with one end of the spectrum or the other—clear-cut choral recitals and innovative shows—are common among GALA choruses, the reality is that most GALA groups present a variety of performances that fall somewhere in the middle of the spectrum. In other words, most GALA performances include elements from a choral recital and other elements from a show. To give just a few examples: On July 10, 2012, at the GALA Festival, MUSE, Cincinnati's Women's Choir, presented *Tweet-2Roar: MUSE Celebrates 29*. MUSE's artistic director, Catherine Roma, introduced the event by saying that there is a need to "roar" about many social justice issues, and the choir proceeded to sing songs that referenced combatting various kinds of oppression.[15] The songs were therefore thematically connected, but *Tweet2Roar* contained no other elements of a show: rather, the forty-four choristers stood and sang each piece, and no further commentary was provided. On the same day, the Portland Gay Men's Chorus (from Oregon) presented a contrasting example, titled *A Young Person's Guide to the Gay Men's Chorus*.[16] Despite the title, this event had no clear thematic program; all its songs were commissions previously composed for, or arranged for, various GALA choruses, but their messages and emotional tones varied dramatically. For example, the event included Fred Small's "Everything Possible," a gentle affirmation of same-sex love; Slipknot's "Left Behind," a heavy metal song that in this context specifically addressed the AIDS crisis; and an arrangement of ABBA's "Dancing Queen." However, *A Young Person's Guide* was in every other way a typical show. It included choral singing, a song performed by a small ensemble of singers, choralography, choreographed dance routines, and a screen showing images and a video. The screen was used to great effect during "Matthew's Lullaby," a song about the death of Matthew Shepard; while the choir sang, stark photographs of fence posts and razor wire in empty fields were displayed, evoking the place where Shepard died.[17]

GALA choruses' willingness to transcend the norms of the traditional choral recital—although most choruses usually do not (or cannot) mount full-blown shows—is continually evident. At times, the addition of just one innovative element can be powerfully affecting. For example, at the 2016 GALA Festival, the Beijing Queer Chorus presented a formal, traditional choral recital, with songs in Mandarin Chinese and no translation, preventing the largely English-speaking audience from ascertaining a theme. The twelve singers stood in place to sing these songs; the women wore Western-style uniform dresses, and the men wore tuxedos (that is, they wore the standard concert attire for community choirs in the United States and Canada). However, the singers mounted the stage wearing Batman masks, and they sang their first song masked. They then slowly and in unison removed their masks. A chorister subsequently explained—in English—that they began singing together in 2008 and, fearing homophobic discrimination, at first performed all their concerts in masks. Recently, however, they have begun removing their masks; the ceremonial removal of masks during this concert symbolized the courage it requires to come out, and the audience responded with great fervor to an emotion and life experience they could understand, even while the lyrics of the songs remained opaque.[18] In another example: Sound Circle, a Denver-based a cappella women's ensemble of sixteen singers, presented *Path of Beauty: Singing the Grand Canyon* at the 2012 Festival. While the singers sang, the venue's lights were lowered and photographs taken by Christopher Brown were displayed on a screen. The songs were interspersed with instrumental improvisations performed on a flute and a harp. The song lyrics and the photographs continually evoked a gentle sense of awe at the beauty of the Grand Canyon, so that the thematic program was clear. Other show elements were not included—the singers did not speak or dance—but the artistic director did request that the audience refrain from clapping between songs, in order to preserve the continuous flow that is characteristic of shows. Although in some ways *Path of Beauty* fulfilled the traditional expectations of a choral recital, the inclusion of just a few show elements pushed this event beyond the traditional boundaries of a recital, and Sound Circle clearly recognized and intended this effect, describing the event as a "collaborative performance experience" rather than a concert.

Choralography, Dance, and the Impact of GALA Performances

GALA's innovative tendencies are often evident in the choralography and dance included in performances, and particularly in the combinations of normally unrelated song and dance traditions. Both choralography and dance have become important enough to GALA choruses that the annual leadership conference of September 2011 featured a workshop on the topic by John Jacobson, a renowned music choreographer. Further, some of the largest GALA choruses even have choreographers on staff, although there are other GALA choristers who oppose the addition of movement to choral music concerts. Indeed, GALA insiders often deploy the abbreviation SMQ (Serious Music Queens) to identify singers who want to perform "serious" music (that is, canonical masterworks, or standard repertoire) and who do not want to perform choralography or dance. Choristers who are especially devoted to the Western art music tradition sometimes even seek out GALA choruses that perform choral recitals, in order to avoid the requirement that they perform choralography while singing. I once overheard a singer from a chorus that specializes in the canonical repertoire say rather gratefully, "I'm pretty sure our chorus's constitution has a clause prohibiting choralography."[19] And yet, while many in GALA circles do not appreciate bodily movement combined with choral singing, it is becoming ever more common for GALA choruses to include choralography and dance in their performances.

As is evident from the description of *(Accentuate the) Positive*, the New York City Gay Men's Chorus has made something of specialty of presenting contemporary pop songs with classical ballet dancing; in its 2016 Festival show, for example, choristers sang Radiohead's "Creep" (with lyrics including "You're so fucking special / I wish I was special / But I'm a creep / I'm a weirdo") while three dancers performed a ballet trio. The combination of colloquial, even shocking, language with the serene and disciplined movements of the dancers was unexpectedly moving. On July 3, 2016, the Vancouver Men's Chorus opened its performance with "Nil S'en La," which was described in the Festival program as a "traditional Irish Gaelic folk song." The singing was accompanied by two instruments that most often accompany traditional Irish music, a bodhran (an Irish frame drum) and a fiddle. However, a group of choristers danced at the front of the stage, and their gestures were those of R&B dance movements, featuring fluidly moving arms rather than the rigid straight arms so characteristic of Irish dance.[20] Here again, the combination of song and dance from two different traditions was unexpected, and it worked well, with the energy of the dance movements mirroring the energy of the singing.

GALA choruses do present innovative kinds of movements that extend beyond choralography and dance. At the 2016 Festival, for example, two choristers from the Ensemble Vocal Extravaganza of Montreal, Quebec, accompanied a song with plastic cups, stacking and unstacking them on a table in front of the chorus, creating a rhythmically sophisticated and tightly choreographed percussion line from the simplest of materials.[21] And the Calgary Men's Chorus sang in an aquatic center in May 2011; this performance, titled *Blue*, was a collaboration with synchronized swimmers and a special guest from Cirque du Soleil. However, choralography and dance retain a special place in the imagination of most choristers; as we saw above, GALA insiders often specify the nature of a particular chorus according to whether the singers are expected to perform choralography.

The inclusion of dance can powerfully emphasize the lyrics of a song, either because the movements amplify the message and emotion of the words, or because the movements are incongruous with the vocalized text, conveying a sense of discontinuity. In addition, the inclusion of movement can powerfully reinforce a chorus's communication of the GALA mission, which is to create and promote a more inclusive society (see chapter 6). On July 4, 2016, the Boston Gay Men's Chorus sang Katy Perry's hit song "Firework" with very active choralography; at the song's culmination the choristers left the risers, swarming around the stage while waving long red ribbons in rhythm to the music.[22] This chorus includes a number of older men (evident from their white hair), and all of them participated equally in doing the vigorous movements while continuing to sing in full voice. This performance showed the vitality of people of all ages and contested a pervasive stereotype about the frailty of senior citizens. Similarly, on July 6, 2016, the Gay Men's Chorus of Washington, DC, presented a complete performance of Carl Orff's *Carmina Burana*, a staple of the standard repertoire for symphony orchestras and their associated choirs. The performance featured twelve dancers wearing brightly colored costumes. These dancers included men who were young and conventionally beautiful, but also a dancer with a significant protruding belly, and another who had a white beard.[23] All were featured equally throughout the performance, and the performance's unspoken message was clear: men of all body types and ages are worthy objects of the audience's gaze. The choralography and dance in both performances—"Firework" and *Carmina Burana*—promoted body positivity and contested ageism.

Chorus America, one of the world's largest professional choral music associations, sponsored a study of the impact of choral performances on audiences (Brown et al. 2016). The study's authors surveyed more than fourteen thousand audience members who attended choral performances across the United States, asking them (among many other questions), "What was most memorable to you about the concert?" (55). The most common answer to this question, chosen by 29 percent of the respondents, was not the singing itself but rather "other production elements," including "videos, on-stage interviews, narration, staging, audience participation, lighting, etc." In other words, what audience members remember best—and arguably are most affected by—are the show elements that GALA choruses so ably include in so many of their performances. This finding is good news for GALA leaders, who are always seeking to present performances that fulfill GALA's mission of changing the hearts and minds of concertgoers. By moving beyond the traditions of the choral recital, GALA choruses are creating performances that are memorable to their audiences, and therefore GALA choruses can reasonably hope that audience members will reflect on and ponder the message of the performance after it has concluded.

Of course, GALA's choral recitals can also be memorable and impactful. The perception of any performance is specific to the individual listener. Choral music listeners are accustomed to the conventions of a choral recital and presumably appreciate these; that is one reason why they attend choral music performances. For me, one of the most memorable GALA performances I have ever heard was a stand-and-sing presentation of "It Is Well with My Soul," sung by Illuminati, the small ensemble of the Columbus Gay Men's Chorus, on July 8, 2012.[24] As a Christian, I appreciated hearing a song I have known for many years (a song with a message that affirms my faith), and I remember still the stunningly beautiful interlocking harmonies and full and blended vocal tone created by the singers. I commented to friends later that, upon my hearing that particular performance, it was well with my soul. GALA audience members, we can safely assume, frequently have experiences like mine, in response to both choral recitals and shows.

Creative Performance as an LGBT Specialization

Why is it that GALA choruses, rather than other community choirs, have led the way in creating memorable, innovative choral performances (as GALA insider Dennis Coleman argued, above)? Observers of LGBT life have long noted the tendency for LGBT people, but gay men especially, to pursue careers in performance and in the creative arts. It is a stereotype, but a stereotype based in some realities, that gay men are drawn to careers in acting and that they are overrepresented on the stages of Broadway. They are often professional performers.[25] In addition, they seek out careers requiring personal creativity, such as interior design, hair styling and makeup artistry, and the like. In each of these cases, the work requires the worker to go beyond finding a "right" answer (such as in medical diagnosis) or executing a task in exactly the correct way (such as in automobile repair). In the stereotypically gay endeavors, the workers must perform a role, presenting their own interpretation of it, or create something new and unique for a customer. Scholars argue that there is a logical reason why performativity and creativity have become the specialized domains of gay men—and, as I will argue, their argument applies to LGBT people more broadly.

Gay men begin their lives as young boys in a heteronormative society. Like all people, they become aware of their sexual orientation before or during puberty, but they also simultaneously become aware that their particular sexual orientation is unacceptable to those around them. They must, there-fore, from an early age, perform a role that is not instinctively theirs. Like all those born with male genitalia, they face enormous—if unspoken—pressure to be conventional males, meaning persons who do, or who will one day, desire to have sex with women. (The consequences of doing otherwise, in the homophobic milieu in which they live, can be catastrophic.) As David M. Halperin (2012, 196) notes, gay boys spend their childhoods impersonating straight men, "studying masculinity in order to act it out." And this experi-ence extends to young lesbians and to transgender youth. "Nearly all gay men and lesbians had to 'perform' some version of normative heterosexuality before 'coming out.' Even out queer people often retain a sense that gender and sexuality, including heterosexuality, are performative" (Hughes and Román 1998, 7). LGBT youth become self-taught experts in the performa-tivity of heterosexuality, and then they become interested in the phenome-non of performance more generally. These youth, and eventually adults, therefore commonly participate in the performing arts, such as choral music.

Moreover, this line of thinking argues, LGBT persons' life experiences prepare them not only to perform, but also to create new art. For example, in order to live happy lives as adults, lives that include sex and romance with partners to whom they are attracted, LGBT people must forge social con-nections that they did not see modeled in their heteronormative families while they were growing up. If they wish to live with a committed partner, they must envision a different kind of partnership than the one created by their mothers and fathers (that is, a partnership that involved one cisgender male and one cisgender female), and then figure out how to present that partner to their friends and work colleagues, and so on. In effect, they must create a new reality for themselves. This imperative has a happy consequence because LGBT people become skilled in creating all kinds of new ideas and models, including artistic ones. "One reason that lesbians and gay men often make great artists may be that being gay and creating art both require similar strengths: the ability to create an original world of one's own and a willing-ness to jettison the conventional wisdom in favor of one's own convictions" (Kaiser 1997, 89).

It makes sense, then, that GALA choruses, where gay men and lesbian women are found in great numbers, are loci for innovations in the choral arts. Jean-Louis Bleau, the former artistic director of the Calgary Men's Cho-rus, recalled with gratitude how willing his choristers were to try new perfor-mance practices (interview, June 24, 2016). The chorus was able to do "amaz-ing things," such as collaborate with synchronized swimmers in a performance at a public swimming pool, precisely because almost all its singers are gay men. LGBT choristers are more likely to embrace unprecedented performance practices than are singers in other community choirs, and LGBT artistic directors are more likely to conceive of these than are straight directors. This understanding of LGBT people's relationship to artistic creativity also explains why GALA choruses commission and perform so much new repertoire, in much higher numbers than do other community choirs.

We might even say that the US and Canadian choral music scene owes something of a debt to GALA choruses. As the 2016 Chorus America study showed, and as choral music participants are aware, choirs of all stripes are increasingly adopting the kinds of innovative performance practices premiered by GALA choruses, framing their performances not as choral recitals but as events centered on thematic programs. Choral music audiences appreciate this development because they find the extramusical elements of choral concerts to be memorable and impactful. In short, GALA choruses are at the forefront of innovation in choral music, and this prominence is in large part due to the nonnormative sexual and gender identities of GALA singers and artistic directors.

Conclusion: Why Disidentifying Matters

As we have seen, GALA participants embrace many norms of the community choir tradition, but they are also open to, and usually deeply committed to, transcending those conventions. One prominent way in which they transcend the conventions of the Western choral music tradition is by singing "gay songs" that foreground LGBT perspectives and experiences. Another prominent way in which they go beyond, and even alter, choral music's conventions is by presenting their songs in the context of innovative performances that expand the boundaries of the choral recital. Acknowledging that GALA choristers value and pursue both of these impulses—participating in Western choral music while at the same time transforming it to represent a disempowered group—we can understand their performances as acts of disidentification.

José Esteban Muñoz (1999), the originator of this line of scholarly investigation, argues that disidentification has political implications. When people in minority positions engage in cultural production in order to highlight their own minority perspectives, he writes, they pursue "a strategy that tries to transform a cultural logic from within, always laboring to enact permanent structural change while at the same time valuing the importance of local or everyday struggles of resistance. . . . Disidentification negotiates strategies of resistance within the flux of discourse and power" (12, 19). As GALA choruses have mastered the Western choral music tradition and have become leaders in expanding its boundaries, they have created an important venue for representing the realities and ideals of the LGBT singers in their ranks. They have "transformed a cultural logic from within," an endeavor that has an unmistakable political agenda. In the following chapters, I examine in detail the nature of GALA choruses' political agenda, a central organizing idea that they often refer to as their "mission."

6 • GALA Choruses on a Mission

GALA Choruses' mission statement is "supporting GLBT choruses as we change our world through song" (GALA Choruses n.d.a.), and virtually all member choruses of the umbrella organization have mission statements that refer in some way to changing the world through song. Certain choruses' mission statements mirror this language very closely; for example, the One Voice Mixed Chorus of Saint Paul, Minnesota, declares its mission to be, "Building community and creating social change by raising our voices in song" (One Voice n.d.a.). The social change, or transformation, sought is often specifically identified: the social change that GALA choruses most commonly claim to pursue is greater acceptance for LGBT people in society at large. Generally, GALA insiders seek acceptance that is made manifest in the transformed attitudes of their listeners ("changing hearts and minds") rather than in altered institutional structures, although they certainly value changes in laws (such as permitting same-sex marriage and forbidding discrimination on the basis of sexual orientation or gender identification). Throughout the rest of this book, I will refer to "GALA's social change mission" with this understanding in mind—that the social change GALA choruses actively work toward is a reduction of homophobic beliefs and attitudes, rather than specific legal and policy changes.

GALA choruses' mission statements usually also emphasize excellent music making; they are focused on changing the world through song, rather than through petitions or lobbying of politicians. For example, the Seattle Men's Chorus and the Seattle Women's Chorus jointly endorse the following mission statement: "Our voices transform society through innovative and entertaining programs that build community, illuminate the experiences of LGBTQ people and their allies, expand inclusion, and inspire justice" (Seattle Choruses n.d.). Similarly, the Triad Pride Men's Chorus and the Triad

Pride Women's Chorus of Greensboro, North Carolina, share the following mission statement: "Triad Pride Performing Arts consist of LGBTQ [sic] and their allies, who perform choral music to entertain, enlighten, and enrich while promoting equality and social justice for all people regardless of sexual orientation or gender identity—fostering pride, understanding, and acceptance" (Triad Pride Performing Arts n.d.).[1]

These two common threads—music and social change—can be traced back through the mission statements of some of the most venerable of GALA's member choruses. For example, the ANNA Crusis Women's Choir in Philadelphia, Pennsylvania, identified on the GALA Choruses website as the organization's oldest chorus (GALA Choruses n.d.b.), states succinctly on its website, "Our passion: Musical excellence. Social change" (ANNA Crusis n.d.). And these ideas persist in the mission statements of much more recently founded youth choruses. Diverse City Youth Chorus was founded in Cincinnati, Ohio, in 2014, and its mission statement is: "Diverse City Voices encourages and fosters artistic expression, personal development, and leadership in lesbian, gay, bisexual, transgender, intersex, queer/questioning and allied youth and presents performances that provide an opportunity and space for young people, however they identify, to say 'this is a place where I am accepted for who I am and everything that I bring'" (Diverse City Youth Chorus n.d.).[2]

GALA choruses' commitment to pursuing the social change aspect of their mission is what most strongly distinguishes them from other community choirs. To be clear, community choirs often have mission statements (sometimes called vision statements); indeed many professional and community organizations have mission statements emblazoned on their websites and promotional materials. However, most choirs' mission statements are not as frequently invoked as they are in the GALA milieu. More saliently, most community choirs do not consider themselves to be on some kind of mission to foster social change, even though they endorse wholeheartedly the idea that choirs exist to present musically excellent performances, and often say that they aim to be a caring community for their own singers (Averill 2003, 16). Jim Johnson, a baritone singer in the Quarryland Men's Chorus of Bloomington, Indiana, articulated this point exactly when he said to me, "We [GALA choruses] are mission-driven choruses. . . . Other [community] choruses, their mission is to put on a good Bach performance or whatever. We are distinctly different from those choruses. We're going to have good music, but there's a message behind it" (interview, June 24, 2012). Joe Nadeau, artistic director of the Heartland Men's Chorus in Kansas City, Missouri, echoed this idea: "We're not just a chorus; we don't just get up and sing the

Fauré *Requiem*. . . . We want to make beautiful music *and* we want to make a better society" (interview, February 20, 2011).

Throughout the course of my research, numerous GALA insiders quoted former director of the New York City Gay Men's Chorus Gary Miller's memorable summary of this fundamental idea, that their focus on social change is what makes GALA choruses distinct: "If you want to sing, join a chorus; if you want to change the world, join a gay or lesbian chorus."[3] As John Quillin, artistic director of the Gay Men's Chorus of Charlotte, North Carolina, noted, "I repeat [Gary Miller's] quote constantly, because it is the clearest explanation of what GALA is all about" (interview, March 29, 2011). Charlie Beale, the current artistic director of the New York City Gay Men's Chorus, reiterated that GALA choruses need to prioritize their focus on social change in order to preserve their distinct place in the choral music scene: "We *must* keep the focus on the mission, otherwise [our choruses] will be middle-class glee clubs" (interview, August 16, 2011). Guy Hebert, who sang with the San Francisco Gay Men's Chorus from 1995 to 2000, gave a ringing endorsement of the notion that GALA choruses are, and must be, committed to social change, pointing out that his time with the chorus coincided with the most active period for the AIDS Coalition to Unleash Power (ACT UP), another gay rights organization. "And we're trying to make the same points as ACT UP, but through music. AIDS in a horrible way brought attention to the [false] idea that all homosexuals are pedophiles. But we are people's sons, brothers, fathers. . . . Gay people are musical, we're spiritual, we're not the nonpeople they're trying to say that we are. We're real people, just like you. We are human, we love, we care, we love our children and our nieces and our nephews. . . . If you're regarded as not human, you automatically become an activist, just by expressing your humanity. . . . I am a man, not a disease. This is why we're making music" (interview, May 11, 2014).

Identifying with the Mission

It seems that GALA artistic directors are indeed keeping their singers focused on GALA's social change mission. During interviews with me, numerous singers quoted their own chorus's mission statement, without prompting, and from memory.[4] Others asked for a moment to look up their chorus's mission statement so that they could quote it to me correctly, and still others emailed me the exact wording after our interview, to be sure that this important statement was accurately recorded in my notes. One interviewee from the Dayton Gay Men's Chorus in Dayton, Ohio, even quoted—

again from memory—the mission statements of two other gay men's choruses in his state, those of Cincinnati and Columbus (Fred Poland, interview, June 16, 2011). Brandon Dowdy, a tenor in the Turtle Creek Chorale of Dallas, Texas, explained that he had memorized his chorus's mission statement by remembering "the two e's and two u's: educate, entertain, unite and uplift" (interview, August 11, 2012).[5] Moreover, Dowdy demonstrated a clear understanding of what these ideals mean in practice. As he explained, the Turtle Creek Chorale has performed with evangelical Christian singer Sandi Patty and the US Army Chorus, artists representing communities who have not traditionally been supportive of gay rights. Dowdy argued that performing with such artists is a way of "creating allies. . . . Gay pride is a part of who we are, but it's not all of who we are. That's not the largest part of our mission. If we're going to really do our mission, we have educate, entertain, unite, and uplift the entire community, not just the gay community."

Other singers made it very clear, without quoting their chorus's mission statement exactly, that they identify strongly with their chorus's sense of being on a mission to create social change. To give just a few examples: Robert Frederick and Brian Tombow of the Dayton Gay Men's Chorus explained that the chorus presents most of its performances to "the general public" (interview, August 17, 2011). "The audience needs to get over the hurdle of the gay men, and they do, because they appreciate the sound, and then they realize, 'Hey these are human beings, not oddities,'" said Frederick. Tombow immediately followed up with, "We want people to take us as equals. We want to change attitudes." John Whalen, a tenor in the One Voice Mixed Chorus, told me that his chorus focuses on singing well and on doing social justice work in the community: "The chorus has two agendas, and I'm committed to both" (interview, January 3, 2013). Whalen's commitment is shared by his fellow choristers. In 1999, when One Voice did its first series of outreach performances in local schools, sixty choristers used vacation days from work in order to be available during the school day (Jane Ramseyer-Miller, interview, November 1, 2011).

Derek Smith, a baritone in the Gay Men's Chorus of Washington, DC, began by reciting a list of performances when I asked him why the chorus was important to him: "We sang at the Kennedy Center, at the inauguration [of President Barack Obama in 2013], at the vice president's residence, at the [2016] Festival in front of other GALA choruses. We've done youth outreach . . . all of these things are deeply important to me. It's everything we do to change hearts and minds" (interview, September 2, 2016). Linda Krasienko, an alto in Windsong, Cleveland's Feminist Chorus (in Ohio), said that she trusts her director's decision to program a wide range of repertoire because she believes strongly that the chorus's repertoire "has to appeal to a wide audience. We are performing for the audience. Not for myself, but for the audience" (interview, November 25, 2014).[6]

The GALA Choruses organization employs a variety of strategies to encourage this kind of identification with and support for GALA's social change mission. For example, GALA leaders offer workshops on education and outreach to artistic directors and other insiders who attend the annual managers' and directors' retreat and the annual leadership symposium. Having attended a number of these workshops, I can attest that they constitute forums for fascinating debates about how to best fulfill the mission (more on this topic later). During the 2016 Festival, GALA's focus on the social change mission was on display regularly. That year, each attending GALA chorus was asked to introduce itself using a one-minute video that was screened while the chorus filed onstage. I lost track of how many of these videos included the phrase "changing hearts and minds," as in, "Our chorus's goal is to change hearts and minds in the X region or city." Some choruses referenced the same idea using different wording, but dozens of choruses used exactly this phrase to signal their commitment to the social change mission.

Artistic directors inculcate loyalty to GALA's social change mission among their singers at various times and in various ways. For example, in the Heartland Men's Chorus, new singers receive a presentation about the chorus's mission at the beginning of the year (Joe Nadeau, interview, February 20, 2011). The Triad Pride Men's Chorus has a committee that evaluates every invitation to perform; the committee's mandate is to determine whether the performance opportunity is compatible with the chorus's mission (Woody Faulkner, interview, September 24, 2011). Seattle Women's Chorus rehearsals include dedicated time during which choristers share with the group how audience members, especially their own family members, were affected by previous performances. Anne Bush, the Seattle Women's Chorus singer who told me about this practice, said that "It's really common to hear that someone's mother came [to a concert], and she's really been struggling with all of this, and . . . it's really moving!" (interview, August 1, 2012). Bush provided evidence that this sharing time helps foster a focus on the social change mission among singers; she immediately followed up her previous comment by saying, "Dennis [Coleman, the artistic director] says that we change lives every time we sing, and I agree."

GALA Choruses as "Political" Organizations

GALA singers, conductors, and administrators overwhelmingly agree that GALA choruses are, and must be, mission-driven organizations. Further, they articulate broad agreement on the focus of their social change mission—singing to change the world—both in formal public statements and in remarks made during interviews with me. However, they are less unified in characterizing their social mission as "political" work. Some singers and artistic directors are drawn to participate in their local chorus for precisely this reason, a belief that singing in a chorus is a way of expressing political views, or dissenting from mainstream society, as scholar Kay Kaufman Shelemay (2011, 370) puts it (see chapter 2). Those who are motivated by this process of dissent often use the word *political* without hesitation. For example, Beth Fox of the ANNA Crusis Women's Choir said, "ANNA is a feminist choir. We stand for social change, social justice. It's not just a choir, it's more political than that" (interview, August 15, 2012). Donald Butchko said that singing in the North Coast Men's Chorus of Cleveland, Ohio, "adds a political side effect. It's very empowering" (interview, September 25, 2014). Guy Hebert made the analogy to another well-known political movement by saying that singing with his GALA chorus was a way of "making a statement. . . . It reminded me of Black men in the 1950s holding up signs that read, 'I am a man.' Our message is, We are human, we love, we care, we love our children, our nieces and nephews" (interview, May 11, 2014). Indeed, the political profile of GALA choruses is well enough known that Adam Adler, a choral conductor and music educator in Canada, told me, "I doubt I would ever apply for a GALA job, because I'm not committed to the activist side of the gay rights movement" (interview, July 11, 2014).

Other GALA insiders acknowledged that their choruses constitute political organizations but pointed out that they themselves were not motivated to participate in pursuit of a political agenda. For example, David Mcintyre, who led the Prairie Pride Chorus in Regina, Saskatchewan, said that a number of the choristers were "concerned about equality. . . . They wanted to have a significant impact on how Regina saw the LGBT community" (interview, July 31, 2012). Mcintyre was supportive of these choristers' aspirations, but he stated that this impulse was not his primary motivation: "I'm not a political person, I guess." Matthew Gillespie of the Calgary Men's Chorus described his chorus's "political" work—singing at a World AIDS Day concert, singing at Gay Pride events, and so on—but then said, "I see singing in a choir as singing in a choir, not as singing in a *gay* choir. And I think for a lot of people in the CMC, it's about singing, not about making a political statement" (interview, January 5, 2013). Patrick Holcomb of the North Coast Men's Chorus quoted part of his chorus's mission statement to me but then said that he participates in the group for other reasons: "I don't have a political agenda so much as a personal agenda. Either like it or don't buy a ticket!" (interview, September 14, 2014).

When applied to a GALA chorus, the word *political* is something of a flashpoint, and disagreements about its meaning center on a statement that GALA leaders used to deploy with some frequency. The official iteration of this statement, which appeared on the GALA Choruses website for years, was "Every time a member chorus of GALA Choruses sings, the chorus commits a political act." This statement has been attributed to Stan Hill, former artistic director of both the San Francisco Gay Men's Chorus and the Twin Cities Gay Men's Chorus,[7] and variations on it crop up in conversations, around the internet, and in scholarly publications that are eager to emphasize this aspect of the GALA movement (Avery, Hayes, and Bell 2013, 255; C. Hayes 2016). In 2011, when I began conducting research for this book, the "political act" statement occupied pride of place on the GALA Choruses website, but it has since been removed.

Perhaps the word *political* carried too much baggage for too many GALA insiders. I heard a number of dissenting views about this statement from singers during a GALA workshop held on September 23, 2011. Matt Purcell of the Quarryland Men's Chorus said, "Our group doesn't push the gay agenda per se. I find the GALA 'political act' idea kind of . . . I don't know." Alex Strife of the Choral Project of San Jose, California, followed up: "It's kind of aggressive!" Shari Goettl of Desert Voices in Tucson, Arizona, also implied that the "political act" statement might be inappropriate for GALA today: "We used to say, 'Out, loud and proud.' I think we can get rid of the 'loud' now; we don't need to go back in the closet, but we don't need to blow the closet door off, either." Fascinated by this exchange, I discussed it with others later the same day. Ron Casola, founder of two GALA choruses, frowned when I asked him whether his groups were political, and he answered emphatically, "No, no, no!"[8] Speaking of Voices of the Desert (of Phoenix, Arizona), he explained, "The chorus belongs to the GLBT Chamber of Commerce. If anyone asks us questions about politics, we refer them to the Chamber." When I asked some singers from Harmony: A Colorado Chorale (of Denver) about the "political act" statement during the GALA Festival the following summer, they immediately qualified the statement: "It's a politics of love, understanding, and acceptance."[9]

The individuals I met who were uncomfortable with characterizing chorus initiatives as political acts are not necessarily representative of the majority opinion among GALA insiders. But the organization's decision to remove the "political act" statement from its website was, we can assume, thoughtfully considered. Certainly, the statement—centering on the word *political*—was controversial. In 2008, a newly established mixed chorus in Texas called Resounding Harmony voted to abstain from membership in the GALA organization. As its artistic director told me, Resounding Harmony's members initially imagined that they would join GALA, but "they eventually decided that they disagreed with the 'political act' statement. It's not that they hated gays or GALA, but they had a different mission [that was] definitely *not* political" (Tim Seelig, interview, September 15, 2011).

What are the political acts that GALA choruses may or may not (or, should or should not) commit? Jane Ramseyer-Miller, artistic director of One Voice Mixed Chorus in Saint Paul, equated political work to singing for "people who don't love us," pointing out that her chorus is located in the congressional district that was represented by Republican Michele Bachmann from 2007 to 2015 (interview November 1, 2011). Singing in local public schools, therefore, constituted important political action, and generated significant opposition (see chapter 1). Mike Killen of the Rainbow Harmony Project in Winnipeg, Manitoba, who said frankly that he is "not comfortable with political protest at a choir concert," explained that some choristers wanted the group to raise their fists at the end of a concert (interview, September 23, 2016). Killen was relieved that the gesture was made optional; at the concert approximately half a dozen singers raised their fists while the rest did not, "and nothing more was said of it." Most commonly, however, GALA insiders identified political work as the singing of specific repertoire, especially songs that celebrate LGBT identity. Alyssa Stone of the Lesbian/Gay Chorus of San Francisco gave the example of "Too Straight Polka,"[10] calling it "political choral music," and saying, "I can't imagine the Mormon Tabernacle Choir singing that!" (interview, June 25, 2012). Linda Newlon of Windsong, Cleveland's Feminist Chorus, similarly distinguished between the songs she sings with her Sweet Adelines barbershop ensemble, and the repertoire performed by Windsong: "[Windsong's repertoire] is 'women strong.' It's so different from all the classic love songs we're always singing in Sweet Adelines. It's music with a political message" (interview, December 4, 2014).

The varying opinions on what *political* means and how political GALA choruses should be, I argue, are best understood as divergent perspectives on how GALA choruses ought to pursue their social change mission. Stated another way, GALA insiders have varying understandings about how best to persuade (potentially homophobic) audiences to respect gender and sexual differences.

Fulfilling the Mission

GALA insiders see their choruses as fulfilling their social change mission in a variety of ways. Two of these are discussed at length elsewhere in this book and bear repeating here. First, GALA choruses create social change by creating inclusive communities for their own singers; they provide an accepting and welcoming social group for people who have felt marginalized, usually because of their sexual orientation or gender presentation (see chapter 2). As Tara Napoleone-Clifford, a singer in the Kansas City Women's Chorus, said, "Our mission has a personal effect on our members. It allows singers to be who they are, without any ridicule or finger pointing" (interview, June 30, 2011). Vic Hooper, artistic director of Rainbow Harmony Project, similarly connected the ideas of mission (which he glossed as "mandate") and community: "Our mandate is music first, yes, but it's to develop the community, to take in any gay person who walks off the street and let them sing" (interview, September 9, 2011). Second, GALA choruses' concerts provide a forum for LGBT people to come out, to publicly identify themselves as members of a minority group. (Coming out is a powerful strategy for reducing prejudice against LGBT people, as both GALA insiders and other scholars contend, and as I discuss in chapter 8.)

Often, when GALA insiders talk about fulfilling their social change mission, they use the word *outreach* to describe their past actions and future plans. GALA choruses demonstrate strong intentionality and commitment to their outreach work. The Gateway Men's Chorus of St. Louis, Missouri, for example, recruited a social media marketing expert to its board in order to promote its concerts and maximize the impact of outreach efforts (Al Fischer, interview, January 31, 2012). The Gay Men's Chorus of Charlotte, North Carolina, presented a series of so-called drive-by performances in public spaces such as museums and cafés in order to increase its outreach to the general public (John Quillin, interview, March 29, 2011). The Reveille Men's Chorus of Tucson, Arizona, developed a program of outreach to religious organizations in its city (Octavio Partida, interview, November 7, 2016). Its choristers learned to sing a song called "Grace," which references the Christian hymn "Amazing Grace," and offered to perform this song at religious events. In 2016, they sang it (by invitation) at a Unitarian Universalist church and at a multifaith holiday season event. The GALA organization itself obtained funding to develop a touring version of a show based on Tomie dePaola's 1979 book *Oliver Button Is a Sissy*, which tells of a boy who is teased for disliking sports and other "boy" activities. The funding supported the creation of a four-member cast version of the script, along with recorded choral tracks, a teaching guide, and visual aids to support an anti-bullying lesson. At a conference session titled "Education and Outreach," GALA leaders encouraged artistic directors to take this show to their own choruses for the purpose of concertizing at elementary school assemblies.[11]

This kind of outreach work can be, as GALA insiders acknowledge, fraught with difficulty. Mainstream life in the United States and Canada is still rife with homophobia. Indeed, this reality is why GALA choruses are so committed to their social change mission: they know that it remains necessary to "change the hearts and minds" of many people. John Whalen discovered as much by participating in the Out in the Schools program. "School administrators are scared," he said (interview, January 3, 2013). "There are vocal groups who accuse anyone who speaks about homosexuality of 'having a homosexual agenda.' In rural areas especially, difference and change are frightening." It is for this reason that GALA leaders counsel choruses to "soft-pedal the gay angle" when doing outreach.[12] At the "Education and Outreach" workshop described previously, for example, speakers encouraged artistic directors to offer to present school shows with themes like "The History of the Civil Rights Movement," with the goal of communicating the idea of justice for all, rather than focusing specifically on LGBT people. Artistic directors then discussed the possibility of having choristers introduce themselves by name and profession at the conclusion of a school presentation. Some felt that this action would be an effective form of outreach, "giving the message" that LGBT people are doctors, firefighters, and so on. Others, however, suggested that students be invited to ask questions afterward, rather than being required to listen to the choristers' introductions. The concern underlying this discussion was the continual worry that choruses could become "branded as gay, gay, gay"—and then be prevented from doing outreach work. (See chapter 7 for further discussion of GALA's integrationist approach to social change.)

As a part of their outreach, GALA choruses are increasingly focused on fostering collaborations with other community groups. At another workshop for GALA leaders, artistic directors discussed the possibilities of performing at events hosted by other LGBT organizations, sports teams, branches of the military, other performing arts organizations (such as other community choirs), churches, ethnically identified communities, and Boys & Girls Clubs of America.[13] In a discussion led by Charlie Beale on the following day, Beale advocated the collaborative approach but urged his peers to consider its greater purpose: "Can we be true to our mission and still be responsible to the needs of other constituencies?"[14] In other words, collaborations for the sake of collaborations are not what GALA choruses ought to seek out. Decisions about collaborative performances—like decisions about programming, auditions, and other issues raised in this book—must be made with GALA's social change mission in mind. As I argue throughout this chapter, GALA choruses are profoundly shaped by their commitment to their mission. Their pursuit of this mission is what ultimately distinguishes them from other community choirs.

GALA insiders shared many examples of actions their choruses took to fulfill the social change mission. For example, Willi Zwozdesky told me that he was proud of the "social action" his Vancouver Men's Chorus undertook when it dedicated a concert season to remembering the legal battle fought by the Vancouver-area Little Sister's Book and Art Emporium in 2000 to import "obscene" LGBT products from the United States into Canada for sale in the store (interview, September 5, 2011).[15] Other GALA singers said that their chorus's mission was put into action via performances in "places where people aren't used to hearing [openly] gay people sing" (Eric Aufdengarten, interview, October 25, 2011), or "places that make us uncomfortable" (Fred Fishman, interview, April 25, 2012). These interviewees often referenced singing in small towns, or in bigger population centers where there is no established gay or lesbian chorus. Allen Kimbrough of the Dayton Gay Men's Chorus, for example, told me that he was excited that his chorus fulfilled its mission (in part) by performing at an Episcopal church in Springfield, Ohio, a working-class town approximately thirty miles from the larger city of Dayton (interview, October 2, 2011). Singing in a rural town might indeed make urban choristers uncomfortable, given the recurring "formula story" in which "rural space is backwards and inhospitable to gays and lesbians" (Kazyak 2011, 562). Nevertheless, GALA choruses have been engaging in this particular kind of mission fulfillment since the dawn of their movement. The organization's website points out that the San Francisco Gay Men's Chorus tour of 1981 sparked the founding of new lesbian and gay choruses, and this nucleus of young choruses combined to create the GALA Performing Arts organization (as GALA Choruses was formerly known) later that year (GALA Choruses n.d.b.). Because performing in "uncomfortable" places continues to be important to GALA choruses, in 2011 the managers' and directors' retreat included a workshop on how to introduce a chorus to (what was described as) "a new, unfriendly city."[16]

As is evident from the examples above, when GALA insiders talk about how their chorus pursues or fulfills its social change mission, they often reference concertizing, the act of singing for an audience. Therefore chorus leaders devote much thought to how performances ought to be presented. In GALA circles, ideas about which performance practices are most appropriate are the subject of passionate discussion. At the heart of this discussion is the consensus that performances ought to engage audiences, to convince them of the chorus's message, and to "change hearts and minds." For example, the Twin Cities Gay Men's Chorus features a signature final song in its concerts, and audiences sing along with it; this sing-along part of the concert was introduced, the chorus's artistic director said, to create a sense of connection between the audience and the singers.[17] Other choruses announce that their upcoming concert will feature a sing-along song and post the voice parts online, allowing audience members to practice before attending the concert. Still other choruses invite audience members to become personally involved by texting their choice of encore song to the artistic director during intermission (the song with the most votes is duly performed as an encore). And some GALA choruses require their singers to act as ushers before concerts begin; the idea here is that the singer, while walking an audience member to his or her seat, can begin a conversation and—hopefully—build a sense of connection with that person. Hilariously, the New York City Gay Men's Chorus once performed a show titled *Lavender Air*; choristers offered optional airport security–style body checks at the entrance of the concert venue.[18]

In a study of choral music audiences, Chorus America compared the audiences of three GALA choruses with those of twenty other community choruses in the United States and Canada. The study suggested that GALA choruses are finding success in their attempts to actively engage their audiences: "in general, audiences at programs offered by LGBTQ choruses tend to report higher levels of audience participation [than audiences at concerts offered by other community choirs]" (Brown et al. 2016, 57). "Audience participation" was defined as singing along with the choir, clapping along, dancing or moving along, and talking with a stranger at the concert. These findings imply that the ushering, sing-alongs, and other audience engagement initiatives by GALA choruses are, in fact, encouraging audience members to feel like active participants who are connected in some tangible way to GALA singers.

Some artistic directors believe that presenting a choral recital (defined in chapter 5) is the best way to fulfill their choruses' missions and foster a feeling of connection with their audiences. As one participant at a 2011 GALA workshop put it, "The mission of the group is, we're human beings too, we're just like you. And the mission is best served by having a traditional concert, where everyone feels comfortable clapping."[19] Dennis Coleman, on the other hand, told me that, "in GALA, the chorus is supposed to communicate directly with the audience" (interview, September 24, 2011). Therefore, he argued, choruses should create what he called "theatrical events" (and what I call "shows" in chapter 5), performances in which songs, narrations, dances, and other elements are presented in a "choreographed, constant flow." Coleman and others further argue that GALA's social change mission demands that all songs be sung from memory. As Gary Holt, artistic director of the San Diego Gay Men's Chorus, said, "Having a physical barrier [of the held scores] between us and the audience is an impediment to everything we're trying to convey."[20] However, Vic Hooper contested this point, saying that since "this group [the Rainbow Harmony Project] is all about diversity," he allows singers to hold scores while performing if they so choose, acknowledging before the audience that some people find it easier to memorize music than others (interview, September 9, 2011).

Programming to Fulfill the Mission

Because the message is so important—indeed, at the center of GALA's social change mission—artistic directors also pay careful attention to the lyrics of the songs they conduct. Another word used for deciding which songs to sing, and how to present them in the context of a performance, is *programming*. Artistic directors talked to me at length about their programming choices as they related to GALA's mission. Dennis Coleman put it most succinctly: "The fact that it's a great piece of music is not a good enough reason for me to perform it. I will never program a piece that has any text that contradicts our message, is sexist, or something like that. The text is ulta-important. The text has to be [supportive of the mission], or I won't perform the music" (interview, September 1, 2011).

Carol Sirianni explained that she makes time "at *every* rehearsal" to explain her programming decisions to the singers in the GLASS Youth Choir of Surrey, British Columbia, because she wants to be able to defend her choices as based on something more than her own musical preferences: "Often the reason for my rep choice is educating the audience or communicating our philosophy" (interview, October 9, 2011). Stan Hill believes that it is important to program repertoire "that has enough universality to it that a straight audience can relate to it" (interview, September 24, 2011). Jason Schuler of the Dayton Gay Men's Chorus said, "Because of the DGMC mission, I program Hannukah songs, Kwanzaa songs, spirituals, *and* Christmas carols for our December concert" (interview, September 16, 2010). Schuler noted that this kind of programming diversity communicates the chorus's message, "because the chorus is about inclusion." As Charlie Beale told me, "Music is the means by which you express your values" (interview, August 16,

2011). For Beale, a thoughtful defender of GALA's focus on its social change mission, programming choices must "challenge stereotypes, not reinforce them," and therefore he rejects the idea that gay men's choruses ought to sing exclusively musical theater numbers. Instead, he programs songs in a wide range of styles including jazz, gospel, and heavy metal. What is notable here is that these four artistic directors program rather different songs for their groups to sing—but all make their choices with GALA's social change mission in mind. They seek to convey a message and ultimately to convince their audience to "relate to" or embrace that message.

GALA insiders' focus on reaching out to audience members, to attempting to change their hearts and minds in service of a social change mission, bears a strong resemblance to the priorities and methods of evangelical Christians. Like evangelical church musicians, GALA choruses are focused not only on presenting beautiful music to appreciative listeners, but also on convincing those listeners of their message. In the case of GALA choruses, that message is that LGBT people deserve a full and equal place in society. In evangelical Christianity, the message is different, but the impulse to persuade outsiders is analogous. Said another way, GALA choruses are committed to preaching the gospel of gay rights through their singing. As Charlie Beale said to his fellow GALA artistic directors during a workshop, "If we're singing to the gays, well, we have to keep our core audience. But our mission implies that we are *always* looking out of that, getting outside of our comfort zone, singing to the straight people, the homeless people, the people with AIDS."[21]

This comparison is self-evident to GALA leaders who come from evangelical backgrounds. David Mcintyre described his chorus's evangelical posture: "It reminds me of growing up in an evangelical church. I would describe this as a ministry. . . . The chorus members have a kind of fervor—the same kind of fervor as people in the church. They wanted to spread the good news of being gay. That was a very important part of being in the chorus" (interview, July 31, 2012). Rich Cook, artistic director of MenAlive, the Orange County Gay Men's Chorus (in California), and a former music minister in evangelical circles, put it this way: "Music is a big part of winning souls to Christ in the evangelical movement. And I use a lot of the same principles with the gay chorus: use the music to attract people, to bring them in, don't hit them over the head with the message, but let them enjoy the experience and let the message sink in. Let the process work" (interview, May 14, 2012). Dennis Coleman told me that the skills he learned as a Southern Baptist music minister, "transferred directly to the gay chorus world. I transitioned from one kind of ministry to another. You have to be a charismatic leader and a good public speaker. You have to disciple volunteers and singers. And of course you have to use music evangelistically, to reach people who don't believe the way we do" (interview, September 1, 2011). Coleman regrets that some GALA artistic directors do not share the church background that informs Cook, himself, and others: "Some of them don't have the experience of using music to touch people. . . . Some directors have only had this [academic] training, so they don't understand evangelism." To dedicated artistic directors from religious backgrounds like Coleman, Cook, and Mcintyre, GALA choruses are evangelical organizations, and GALA insiders do well to learn from the evangelical church's methods.

Embodying the Mission: What's in a Name?

One way that GALA choruses fulfill their social change mission is by singing in public while claiming their sexual and gender identities—in other words, by presenting their bodies and singing voices under the banner of LGBT. Janice L. Kinney (2010, 108) made exactly this claim in her study of feminist women's choruses; in her dissertation she identifies four ways in which the singers in these choruses engage in activism. Perhaps unsurprisingly, this section of her work is subtitled "Changing Hearts and Lives." According to Kinney, singers in women's choruses—many of which belong to GALA Choruses—pursue their mission statements in the same way that the men's choruses and mixed choruses do, by "conveying a transformational message" in the lyrics of the songs they sing (111). In addition, they perform in support of fundraisers, diversity celebrations, and the like, and they collect and distribute donations to other nonprofit community organizations (110–15). First on Kinney's list, however—and mentioned first by many of my own interlocutors—is the idea that gay and lesbian choruses pursue their social change mission by performing as self-identified gay men, lesbian women, transgender singers, and their allies. Kinney claims that in being publicly identified as LGBT singers, these choristers embody a "transformational presence" in their communities.

Kinney's argument echoes that of my interlocutors in GALA circles: they affirm over and over that when a GALA chorus performs in public, its choristers fulfill their mission in the very act of performing. As Kinney (2010, 110) puts it, "The mere act of appearing onstage in a group identified as [LGBT] . . . is a political statement." In making this claim, Kinney references the potent idea encapsulated in GALA's "political act" statement. In what follows, I focus on the long-running disagreement about the public identification of GALA choruses as LGBT groups—that is, the "gay name" controversy. As we shall see, GALA leaders and singers have engaged in passionate debates about the names of GALA choruses precisely because the name of a chorus (what it uses to present itself to the general public) is directly tied to the way the chorus pursues the social change mission.

The Stigma of "That One Word"

Willi Zwozdesky recalled that "for the first fifteen years [of the Vancouver Men's Chorus's existence], at every annual general meeting, one member moved that the name be changed to the Vancouver *Gay* Men's Chorus" (interview, September 5, 2011). Paul Johns, a longtime singer in the Seattle Men's Chorus, said, "The fight about 'the *g* word'—which is what we called it—came up about every three years [during the 1980s and 1990s]."[22] For much of GALA's early history, the argument centered on men's choruses and on this question of whether their names should incorporate the word *gay*. This debate has been referenced only once in the sparse scholarly literature about GALA choruses. Julia Balén (2009, 40) summarizes the various positions on this question by saying, "Over the organization's almost thirty years, a [wide] range of strategies have become more or less accepted." But during the time I conducted research with GALA choruses, in the second decade of the twenty-first century, I discovered that the issue was still being debated. The name of a chorus continues to matter because, as queer studies scholar William B. Turner (2000, 199) argues, "the representational codes—the stories and assumptions about identities and their politics—that persons have in their heads have an enormous impact on how these persons respond to political appeals. Consequently, mobilizing persons for political action entails astute management of these representational codes." As Turner acknowledges, potential audience members connect the representational code that is a chorus's name to their own preexisting ideas about LGBT people, and therefore a chorus's name is a crucially important piece of the social change project that all GALA choruses pursue.

The controversy over whether a men's chorus ought to call itself a *gay* men's chorus was mentioned to me in approximately one-third of the interviews I conducted with GALA insiders. It was the subject of a heated discussion at the very first GALA conference I attended, in January 2011. Stan Hill, a leading figure in GALA circles, eventually slammed his hand onto the table and exclaimed, "That war has been fought!" He went on to explain his war analogy by saying that this issue is "the number one cause" of choruses' splitting.[23] The war metaphor is perhaps too strong, but the debate certainly evokes tremendous emotion for GALA insiders. Paul Jones, another GALA artistic director, offered another analogy. He explained that his chorus changed its name from the Sacramento Men's Chorus to the Sacramento *Gay* Men's Chorus in 2008, after twenty years of performing (interview, January 8, 2011). He likened this process to coming out of the closet, another deeply consequential and emotionally laden experience for many LGBT people.

A number of GALA men's chorus insiders explained to me the arguments against using the word *gay* in their chorus names. Eric Aufdengarten of the Heartland Men's Chorus encapsulated the most common argument when he said that many people "put up a wall" when they hear the word (interview, October 25, 2011).[24] Since choruses like the Heartland Men's Chorus aim to sing to audiences of straight (and potentially homophobic) people in order to fulfill their mission, they want to avoid dissuading those people at the outset by using a name that may repel them. Dennis Coleman, one of the most articulate defenders of this argument, used the same metaphor: "It's a hot-button word that simply erects a barrier against the very people we're trying to reach" (interview, September 1, 2011). He argued that the social change that GALA choruses are aiming to create happens in the concert hall, when audiences hear a choir create compelling music and subsequently put that realization together with their knowledge that the singers are gay men. Ultimately, Coleman and his allies hope that homophobic audience members will reconsider, and even change, their thinking about who gay men are and what they do. This transformation in thinking will not happen, of course, if the audience members do not enter the concert hall in the first place. Brandon Dowdy acknowledged that the name of the Turtle Creek Chorale is "a constant topic of conversation" among chorale singers (interview, August 11, 2012). Dowdy said that he personally does not believe the chorus should include *gay* in its name, pointing out that the chorus has "been very successful in reaching the community at large. [Former first lady] Laura Bush was honorary chair of one of our concerts. And we sang with the US Army Chorus! [Our name] is our silent witness as gay men. If we were called the Turtle Creek Gay Men's Chorale, we wouldn't have these opportunities. That one word carries such a stigma." Tim Seelig, the former artistic director of the chorale, made the same argument about the chorale's recordings. "I don't want to shut the door before people even listen," he said (interview, September 15, 2011). Instead, he expects that people will appreciate the beauty of the recording—and later discover, when reading the liner notes, that (most of) the singers are gay men.

Aufdengarten, Coleman, Dowdy, Seelig, and others point out that men's choruses who do not use the word *gay* in their names are not trying to hide the fact that they are gay. Usually, these choruses make reference to this identity on their websites and marketing materials, and it is announced at concerts. They vigorously reject the accusation, leveled by other GALA insiders, that avoiding the word is an act of "taking the chickenshit route" or a reflection of the choristers' "internalized homophobia."[25] Rather, they claim that this choice is pragmatic, that it acknowledges the reality of a world in which many potential choral music listeners still hold deep prejudices against sexual minorities. Furthermore, they point out that the very name can be discouraging to potential singers: there are plenty of closeted gay men who want to meet and sing with other gay men, but who will resist joining a chorus that publicly identifies as gay (Jason Schuler, interview, September 16, 2010). And donors may be reluctant to give to a *gay* men's chorus for fear of receiving receipts contained in envelopes stamped with the chorus's name. In fact, Paul Jones explained that when his chorus changed its name to the Sacramento Gay Men's Chorus, it went through a legal procedure called DBA (doing business as); on paper it remains incorporated as the Sacramento Men's Chorus (interview, January 8, 2011). The chorus took this route specifically so that some of its longtime donors could continue to write checks to the chorus under the old name, one that would not inadvertently "out" the donors to their mail carriers.

The argument against including *gay* in a chorus's name rests on the premise that one three-letter word can be so offensive to potential audience members that it will prevent GALA choruses from fulfilling their mission—that is, prevent them from communicating with the people who would otherwise attend a concert, purchase a recording, or make a donation. Is this premise well founded? GALA singers certainly advance anecdotal evidence to support it. For example, David Greene of the North Coast Men's Chorus told me that he wished the chorus would add the word *gay* to its name (interview, October 10, 2014). However, he pointed out that the chorus was invited to sing at a Martin Luther King Jr. Day celebration on the condition that it be announced by name only, and that choristers not identify themselves as gay in any public remarks during the performance. "Several members of the chorus dropped out because of this; I agreed with them, but I like the chorus too much to quit," he said. And, he acknowledged, the chorus probably would not have been invited to perform in front of a large African American crowd if it had possessed a gay name. It would have been unable to fulfill its mission, which begins, "The North Coast Men's Chorus provides high quality musical entertainment for diverse audiences," because it would not even have been given the opportunity to perform (North Coast Men's Chorus n.d.).

GALA insiders acknowledge that the LGBT identification, or gay name, is so disturbing to some people that they will shut GALA choruses out of opportunities regardless of the choruses' ability to sing. GALA's anecdotal evidence of this phenomenon is buttressed by a landmark study of résumés conducted by Andras Tilcsik (2011, 605), which proved that openly gay men in the United States face significant employment discrimination. Specifically, Tilcsik showed that a résumé bearing a "gay marker" was 40 percent less likely to garner an interview callback from an employer than an identical résumé without the marker. The "gay marker" in this case was a single line stating that the applicant had been elected treasurer of a "gay and lesbian campus organization" (597), work experience that, as Tilcsik points out, should have been valued by the employers to whom he sent the résumés (598). The callback results clearly showed that significant numbers of employers will reject a job candidate simply because they spot the word *gay* or *lesbian* on the candidate's résumé. In the United States in the twenty-first century, references to LGBT identity, and specifically the word *gay*, are still a barrier to entry—and therefore some GALA leaders and choristers say that, in order to pursue their mission, they ought to avoid using a gay name.

GALA Choruses includes a number of choruses that avoid using a gay name but that offer a different rationale for this choice. For example, the president of the board of the Perfect Harmony Men's Chorus in Madison, Wisconsin, told me that the chorus deliberately avoids the word *gay* because it wants to welcome straight men and women (Julio Avila, interview, February 27, 2012). Perfect Harmony has been successful in this project; some straight men sing in the chorus, and some straight women serve on the board. "We do not distinguish ourselves as a gay organization. . . . Being gay is a facet of our life, but it's not how we define ourselves," the board president said. Similarly, Mike Killen said that he appreciated the name of his chorus because "I want Rainbow [Harmony Project] to be a good choir that happens to be gay, rather than a gay choir. Being gay is part of who I am, not *just* who I am" (interview, September 23, 2016).[26] David Mcintyre said that he advocated for his mixed chorus to be named Prairie Pride Chorus because "I didn't want us to think of ourselves as a 'gay choir.' I wanted us to be a choir, to bring all the forces of our humanity to bear to create sound" (interview, July 31, 2012).

People who embrace this philosophy exemplify what scholars call a "post-gay" mindset, in which members of LGBT communities seek to build bridges toward mainstream society, and do so by emphasizing their similarities to straight people (Warner 1999, 61–69). Post-gay advocates also deemphasize sexual orientation as a distinguishing characteristic, thereby again reinforcing the similarity of LGBT and straight people (as Mike Killen said, in reference to how he talks about his chorus, "Why should I have to walk into a room and say, 'I'm Mike, I'm gay'? Straights don't say, 'Hi, I'm heterosexual'" (interview, September 23, 2016). Amin Ghaziani (2011, 119) points out that this "post-gay logic" often manifests itself most clearly in the names of gay organizations: rather than calling themselves gay, lesbian, or queer, they choose words like *pride* or *alliance*, words that mute the difference between gay and straight people (114). Perfect Harmony, Rainbow Harmony Project, Prairie Pride, and other GALA choruses use this post-gay strategy when they name their groups. They come to the same conclusion as the other groups, especially men's choruses, who refuse to use the word *gay* in their names for fear of alienating audiences, but they advance a different rationale for doing so. However, in both cases, their decision about their choir name is tied to their goal to sing in front of, and hopefully persuade, potentially homophobic audiences, and thus to pursue their social change mission.

Advocating for the Gay Name

The argument in favor of using the word *gay* to name a GALA chorus was most eloquently expressed to me by Adam Coatney, who sings tenor in the Dayton Gay Men's Chorus. He pointed out that the chorus's mission statement says that it should be a "gay affirming presence" in the region (interview, August 4, 2011). The act of publicly naming the chorus as gay is thus crucial: "This is a group of men that are openly gay, and they're happy to be together onstage. . . . When men are unafraid, unashamed, proud to say who we are—it's in the title—that rubs off on the audience. That in itself is gay affirming," he said. Chris Raines, a chorister in the Gay Men's Chorus of Charlotte, explained a similar rationale by referring to the Charlotte audience: "We have to be political because we're in a conservative area, so it's important for us to call ourselves 'gay'" (interview, September 23, 2011). Both of these choristers referenced the notion that the name of their chorus was directly bound to its mission or, alternately stated, to its political work. They maintain, along with many other GALA insiders, that in order to accomplish GALA's all-important mission, choruses must publicly identify themselves as LGBT at the outset. Beautiful singing does not lead to the kind of social change that GALA choruses seek if listeners are unaware that the singers identify as members of sexual and gender minority groups.

Those who advocate for using a gay name argue that GALA choruses have to self-identify as LGBT for the simple reason that they want to attract LGBT singers, the natural constituency of the choruses. If the choruses are to be sustainable—to live another day in order to pursue their mission—they must continue to welcome new singers. Also, GALA choristers usually understand their social change mission as a call to create an inclusive society not only in their cities or regions, but also within their own choruses; as I explain in chapter 2, many GALA insiders link the notion of their mission directly to their notion of the chorus community. Therefore, they argue, the LGBT people in the local area must be made aware that the chorus exists especially to welcome them (Fred Poland, interview, June 16, 2011). The underlying premise here is that, if a GALA chorus does not explicitly identify itself as gay or lesbian or LGBT in its name, some people will miss all other indications and remain unaware that the chorus is in fact an LGBT organization. This possibility is quite real, as Anne Bush discovered. Bush sings with the Seattle Women's Chorus, in which, she estimates, lesbian women account for approximately 60 percent of the membership (interview, August 1, 2012). Speaking of the other 40 percent, she said, "It's amazing how many of them don't realize it's a gay organization." During a Seattle Women's Chorus retreat, Bush roomed with a Catholic woman who, when she joined, had not known that the chorus was a GALA chorus—that is, an LGBT-identified chorus. The woman quickly became uncomfortable and eventually quit singing in the chorus. I myself encountered this kind of ignorance in my own profession; in discussing my research with a senior colleague (a long-time college professor of choral music), I mentioned the Turtle Creek Chorale. My colleague was visibly shocked. "Of course I know who they are," he said, "but I didn't realize they were . . . like that."

Sharon Donning, a singer with the West Coast Singers, a mixed chorus in Los Angeles, is a firm believer that GALA choruses ought to signal their LGBT identity with their names. She pointed out that her chorus has "an extended name": "the chorus of the lesbian/gay community of Los Angeles" (interview, April 24, 2012). "I've always thought it [the extended name] really important," Donning said. "There's been a couple of battles over it. One side literally didn't want everybody to know they were gay. They thought the community would look down on the chorus and on them personally, and they thought it would prevent the chorus from getting gigs. Where in reality it had the opposite effect. But I thought, if we're trying to serve the gay and lesbian community, we have to let them know that we are a gay and lesbian chorus. We wanted to let gays and lesbians know that they had options if they wanted to join a chorus."

Beyond attracting LGBT singers to their ranks, supporters of the gay name claim that GALA choruses have a moral imperative to "be out," or to come out, as the Sacramento Gay Men's Chorus did (Jane Ramseyer-Miller, interview, November 1, 2011). In order to be a "transformational presence" in their communities, choruses must claim their sexual orientations and gender identities in their very names. They must do so not only to avoid the possibility of misunderstanding, but more importantly, to fulfill their work of concertizing intentionally as LGBT singers (and not merely as singers). GALA choristers are singing to change the world, not singing for the joy of singing—and they cannot affect the perception their audiences have of LGBT people unless those audiences know that the performers identify as LGBT. Guy Hebert explained the importance of names for the San Francisco Gay Men's Chorus by pointing out that issues of life and death can be at stake when LGBT people decide to self-identify as such. Hebert participated in the chorus shortly after the invention of protease inhibitors (in the late 1980s). Gay men were still dying of AIDS in great numbers at that time, and Hebert recalled singing with small ensembles of the chorus at the bedsides of AIDS victims in San Francisco hospitals. "We were losing people left and right. It was like making music while the Titanic sinks. There was a war going on around us! And that's why we had to have gay in our name. You *had* to be out, otherwise no one would even mention this.... Harvey Milk knew the importance of being out: [it is tantamount to saying that] normal people are gay, not just the people you're arresting [for sodomy, etc.] So it was a *statement* to have gay in the chorus name" (interview, May 11, 2014).

Continuing Debates

In GALA circles, the question of chorus names—and especially of whether a men's chorus ought to be called a gay men's chorus—continues to provoke strong feelings among insiders. Dennis Coleman went as far as to say that "there is a subtle undercurrent of discrimination [against choruses like his own Seattle Men's Chorus that do not use the word *gay*] that has rankled me for years" (interview, September 1, 2011). And Tim Seelig, artistic director of the Turtle Creek Chorale, said that he and Coleman had "endured a lot of abuse from our own people" over this issue (interview, September 15, 2011). Carol Sirianni told me that in 2010 her mixed youth chorus changed its name from the punctuated G.L.A.S.S. (meaning Gay, Lesbian, and Supportive Singers) to the word GLASS, removing the periods. Sirianni explained the change using post-gay logic: "Taking the periods away takes away the implication that each letter represents a separate word. Now it's just one word, GLASS, like bird or tree. There's no intention to hurt anybody or exclude anybody; it's a feeling of moving past that." She continued, "You would not believe the ruckus this raised!" adding that the minister of the United Church where the group rehearsed came close to closing his church's doors to the choir (interview, October 9, 2011). Sirianni explained that the minister, a liberal supporter of LGBT rights, "perceived [the name change] as going back into the closet, as walking away from our identity."

The names (and name changes) of GALA choruses continue to be debated and were a hot topic at the 2016 GALA Festival.[27] At one of the Festival's open table sessions, a board member of the New York City Gay Men's Chorus shared that his chorus considered replacing the *gay* in its name with *queer*.[28] He shook his head, remembering the intensity of arguments ("Oh my god! So we had to wait on that"). The crux of recent debates focuses on whether GALA choruses ought to acknowledge in their names the wide spectrum of choristers who sing with them, or, conversely, whether they ought to maintain the names they have worked so hard to establish. The New York City Gay Men's Chorus is a case in point: as explained in chapter 1, the chorus fought a legal battle in order to perform at American Choral Directors Association (ACDA) events as a gay men's chorus, rather than as a men's chorus as the ACDA preferred. Longtime participants, especially, therefore have a strong attachment to the current name of the group. Their unwillingness to change the name is likely also linked to their distaste for the word *queer*, a word associated with the gay liberationist wing of the gay rights movement, the wing to which most GALA choristers do not belong (see chapter 7).

Other choruses have resolved the debate in favor of changing their names. The chorus formerly known as Aria: Windy City Women's Ensemble (from Chicago, Illinois) changed its name in 2014 to the Windy City Treble Quire. As a singer in the chorus explained to me, the word *women* came to be understood as limiting.[29] The chorus today includes singers with a variety of gender identities, not only cisgender women, who sing in the soprano and alto ranges featured in the group's repertoire. As the Windy City Treble Quire seeks to embody its mission statement—"to inspire change, celebrate diversity, and honor the dignity of the LGBTQ+ community"—it has chosen a name that references the diversity of its choristers (Windy City Sings n.d.a.).

Conclusion

GALA insiders largely demonstrate pride in and commitment to their choruses' social change mission, although they have differing—and sometimes conflicting—notions about how that mission ought to be pursued. At the same time, some individuals articulate thoughtful critiques of their movement's commitment to its social change mission. For example, an artistic director at a GALA conference in 2011 expressed concern about his fellow artistic directors' consistent focus on programming what some called "message pieces." Choristers are spending an inappropriate amount of time learning these message pieces (songs with lyrics that in some way support the social change mission), he said, and are neglecting to learn the "staples" of the choral repertoire, and thereby failing to grow as singers: "To ignore the staples of the repertoire is to shortcut the education of the choir. Choruses that are so focused on mission that they don't sing staples is like a seventh grader never reading *A Tale of Two Cities*."[30] Fred Fishman, a former singer in two different GALA choruses, argued that "the mission needs to change over time because needs change. Just to get onstage and say we're gay men singing together, by the 1990s, that had been done for a long time.... And if choruses are doing just that today, they're not really doing their job. We should always be questioning what we're doing" (interview, April 25, 2012).

One of the most urgent questions that arises stems from the cause-and-effect link between the two parts of the GALA mission: GALA insiders claim that by making music, they create social change, by which they mean that they diminish homophobia among their listeners. Jane Ramseyer-Miller, a thought leader in the GALA organization, revealed the challenge inherent in this assertion when I asked her directly about how music creates social change. "It may seem clichéd," Ramseyer-Miller responded, "but music stirs hearts and bodies. It can move people's hearts.... I'm not sure how to make that happen, but it is something I'm thinking a lot about" (interview, November 1, 2011). Charlie Beale echoed her concern, voicing the question that underlies the next section of this book: "I believe that choruses ought to live up to their mission statements. This is of course difficult.... There's an element of self-congratulation in some GALA choruses. I know from broad experience that people go to Broadway shows, cry, get up the next day, and aren't really changed. So I want the movement to be rigorous about this. How do we know that we're changing the world through song? How can we verify that people's lives have changed?" (interview, August 16, 2011). In the final two chapters of this book, I investigate how exactly GALA choruses' pursuit of their mission can lead to changed hearts and minds.

7 • GALA Choruses as Part of the Gay Rights Movement

On July 2, 2016, the Columbus Gay Men's Chorus of Columbus, Ohio, presented its show at the 2016 GALA Festival. A highly innovative and technically skilled presentation, titled *Finding Oz*, this show was scheduled as a Coffee Concert, meaning that there were no other competing Festival performances occurring at the same time. The event was therefore well attended. One portion of the show was called "Defying Gravity"; it consisted of a video montage of images of choristers, along with brief subtitles describing the choristers' accomplishments. Examples included: "Became an uncle," "Opened an LGBT bookstore," and "First in family to graduate from college." The audience—other GALA singers who were in attendance at the Festival—responded audibly with much louder applause to two images in particular: "Got married in front of family," and "Graduated from the Air Force Academy." In this chapter I argue that this incident demonstrated GALA choristers' commitment to integrationist politics, which are often understood—or rather oversimplified—as advocating for same-sex marriage and military service by LGBT soldiers. This brief but unmistakable show of support for integrationist goals revealed the political orientation of GALA choruses and exemplified how we can best understand these choruses in the aggregate, as belonging to a social movement with a distinct commitment.

GALA insiders often talk about GALA choruses and their musicking as a "movement." As we saw in chapter 6, this movement is both musical and social; it aims to perform music, and it does so in the service of a social change mission. GALA participants acknowledge that their endeavors are intended to reach beyond entertaining audiences; their work, they often say, is political in nature. In this chapter I analyze this facet of GALA Choruses more deeply, by looking at the organization through the lens of social movement theory. I argue that GALA Choruses is most accurately characterized as part of the integrationist wing of the gay rights movement. Further, I argue that concertizing can and should be understood as the preeminent collective action engaged in by its member choruses: singing in public is their preferred "tactic," as social movement theorists describe it.

The literature on social movements is substantial and growing. Leading voices have argued that all social movements are worth studying because they represent an important exception to the human status quo: "The forces that discourage a sense of agency among ordinary citizens in most societies are overwhelming" (Gamson 1995, 95). "Our own commitment to our daily lives and the demands of our everyday roles and relationships, and our notion of what is possible (given the invisible but powerful structures of social life), all act to ensure that the default position of any activity—such as enjoying music—is to preserve the status quo. Hence it takes special effort and circumstances for any activity to be truly oppositional, in form as well as in ostensible content" (Rosenthal and Flacks 2012, 18). To challenge traditional gender and sexual mores, as the gay rights movement has done, is an attention-worthy endeavor for precisely this reason. In the early 1990s, John D'Emilio (1992, 236), a historian of the gay rights movement, was able to lament that "the gay and lesbian movement is appallingly understudied." This situation has, thankfully, changed, but the most common scholarly focus is court cases and legal challenges; scholars have been interested in how the gay rights movement provoked changes in laws, rather than in how it affected attitudes (Faderman 2015; Rayside 2008; Vaid 1995, 179–80). Although some GALA choruses have performed at rallies in support of same-sex marriage laws, or in protest against discriminatory policies, their purpose is rather different. As we have already seen, they seek not so much to foster change in societal structures or institutions, but rather to "change the hearts and minds" of their listeners, and they aim to enact this change through singing.

Social movement scholarship frequently examines the tactics, or collective actions, engaged in by protestors. The traditional repertoire of tactics used by modern social movements dates back to the French Revolution and includes boycotts, petitions, strikes, street marches and demonstrations, the hanging of public figures in effigy, and so on (Tarrow 1994, 33, 40–45). Scholars have argued that music performance can be, and often is, a tactic employed to good effect by social movements (Rosenthal and Flacks 2012). Ron Eyerman and Andrew Jamison (1998, 43) devote an entire book to exploring how social movements use songs and other cultural artifacts as "tools for protest and the formation of collective identity." Eyerman and Jamison explain that the singing of "We Shall Not Be Moved" during a lunch counter sit-in, for example, was an important social action conducted by civil rights activists during the 1960s, and that actions like this one reinforced the activists' "commitment to a common cause" and helped them "articulate meaning and identity" (162). They describe a musical performance by social movement members as an "exemplary action," which they define as "a form of communicative action" presented in front of an audience (172). Exemplary actions aim to communicate "a vision of what the world could be like . . . this vision is expressed through the form or content of the action and is an end or good in itself" (172).

Eyerman and Jamison's exemplary actions are what other social movement scholars call tactics. Feminist scholars Leila J. Rupp and Verta Taylor (2003, 217) argue that the field needs to broaden its conception "of social movement tactics or collective action repertoires [to] allow us to understand how and when the distinctive cultural forms, practices and institutions created by subordinated groups are, in fact, being used for political purposes." This chapter responds to Rupp and Taylor by analyzing the choral concert as a social movement tactic. Concertizing by GALA choruses constitutes a way for LGBT people to contest the heteronormative cultural codes that still prevail in the United States and Canada. And yet, at the same time, GALA choruses generally embrace homonormativity (see chapter 4); they thus favor an integrationist approach. "Changing the world through song"—GALA's oft-quoted mission statement—is a cogent summary of their social movement commitment. GALA choruses are consistently focused on creating a world that is fully welcoming to LGBT people. They perform for a political purpose, and they seek to change the world by singing, a tactic that emphasizes their "normality" and that provides a nonthreatening way to advocate for their goals.

Understanding Social Movements

Scholars of social movements have offered several complementary definitions of what constitutes a social movement (Darnovsky, Epstein, and Flacks 1995, vii; Jasper 1997, 5). Sidney G. Tarrow (1994, 33), a leading social movement theorist, summarizes social movements as "sustained interactions between aggrieved social actors and allies, and opponents and public authorities." He argues that a social movement is not just any group engaged in collective action—such as a rioting mob—but rather a group that 1) mounts a "collective challenge" to "elites, authorities, other groups, or cultural codes"; 2) has a "common purpose" that motivates its actions; 3) has a sense of "solidarity," meaning a shared identity; and 4) pursues "sustaining collective action" that "mobilize[s] people through social networks and around identifiable symbols" (4). Although discourse about "our movement" is commonplace in GALA circles, none of my interlocutors ever specifically referred to GALA as a *social movement*. As we can see, however, the GALA Choruses organization and its actions conform to Tarrow's definition.

First, by identifying as LGBT, GALA choruses mount a challenge to heteronormative society, whose norms are powerfully present in the US and Canadian choral music scene. As we saw in chapter 1, GALA choruses have even pursued legal action in order to be publicly recognized not just as choirs, but as gay and lesbian choirs. Second, GALA choruses have a common purpose, which they articulate in their mission statements (in line with the parent organization's "changing our world through song"). Artistic directors work hard to foster a sense of loyalty to the GALA mission, and singers eagerly assent to this purpose, as we saw in chapter 6. Third, singers in GALA choruses have a powerful sense that they belong to a family-like community (see chapter 2), and they spend significant money and time every four years attending the GALA Festival, which reinforces their sense of solidarity with the thousands of other GALA singers (see chapter 1). Fourth, each chorus engages in persistent collective actions in the form of public concerts; most choruses perform at least three times per calendar year, and many perform dozens of times. It is this fourth aspect of their work as social movement actors that is the focus of this chapter.

The research on social movements has produced many insights that apply to all social movements, and that can be usefully applied here. For example, social movements are generally structured in one of two ways; either they are "social capital rich," and characterized by the presence of many local chapters and face-to-face interactions between members, or they are "social capital poor" (Putnam 2000, 154). The GALA organization is one facet of the gay rights movement that is rich in social capital, with its hundreds of local choruses that meet together at least once per week. All social movements are in some sense identity movements, writes Mary Bernstein (1997), and they pursue strategies that either celebrate or suppress their differences from mainstream society. Movements that have "strong organizational infrastructures that have fostered a shared identity"—like the GALA organization—tend to "emphasize sameness rather than difference" (540). Further, such movements tend to use a strategy Bernstein calls "identity for education," which "challenges the dominant culture's perception of the minority or is used strategically to gain legitimacy by playing on uncontroversial themes" (537).

Singing beautiful music, chosen to appeal to a broad audience, in order to be perceived as legitimate—or as some GALA insiders call it, "normal"—is exactly what GALA choruses do, year in and year out. As we will see, this activity is strategic, drawing from an understanding that singing choral music is a "nonthreatening" way to promote their cause.

One important finding of social movement scholars is that every social movement is marked by an internal divide, reflecting fundamentally different opinions on how the movement should achieve its goals (Tarrow 1994, 91). The animal rights movement is a well-known case: on one side are organizations like Animal Liberation Front (ALF), which raids and sets fire to laboratories where animals are used in research experiments. On the other side are groups like People for the Ethical Treatment of Animals (PETA), which promotes veganism and encourages supporters to avoid wearing leather or fur. Both wings of the animal rights movement focus on the same broad goal (to create a world where animals are never intentionally harmed by humans), but they embrace different approaches toward this goal, and they have divergent beliefs about which tactics will ultimately be most productive.

Political scientist David Rayside (2008, 10, 11) explains that the two groups within a social movement are first, "those who seek transformation of, and resist acquiescence to, existing social, economic, and political institutions"; and second, "those more willing to imagine an accommodation to such institutions, providing that advances in the movement's political agenda can be secured within them." Why does this division persist across various social movements? James M. Jasper (1997, 237) argues that movement participants are primarily divided according to their preference for certain tactics; movement tactics are selected by participants according to their "taste." Taste, as it is understood by Jasper, is not a shallow or fleeting aspect of one's personality, but rather a set of consistent preferences developed over many years, resulting from one's accumulated life experiences (what Pierre Bourdieu called "habitus") (238). Movement tactics, furthermore, "are important routines, emotionally and morally salient in these people's lives," and therefore movement members do not want to participate in tactics that are not to their taste (237). Some supporters of the gay rights movement, for example, prefer to engage in street protests (kiss-ins and the like), while others prefer to negotiate legal settlements behind closed doors. All of them are working toward the same broadly defined result, but their choice of tactics is very different. As I explain below, the divide between the two approaches in the gay rights movement has been much discussed, and scholars have tended to valorize one approach over the other.

The Integrationist and Liberationist Divide

GALA Choruses and its member choruses represent the second of Rayside's two groups; they seek to be accommodated within society as it exists now. The leaders and the rank-and-file choristers in GALA Choruses support the notion that LGBT people ought to be integrated into social structures such as military service, marriage, and of course, choral singing. Their position is usually described by scholars as assimilationist and normalizing—terms that, as I will explain, carry a pejorative connotation.[1] Further, these scholars usually contrast the integrationist wing of the LGBT rights movement with an opposing wing that is variously called radical (Balén 2009, 33), progressive (Chasin 2000, 22), confrontationist (Herrell 1992, 233), or distinctive (Ghaziani 2011, 103). The difference between these two positions has been called "the 'suits versus queers' divide" (Lochhead 1996, 56) and "a war between the Suits and the Streets" (Faderman 2015, 265), referencing the idea that integrationists (the "suits") desire to be integrated into the business world and into mainstream middle-class society more broadly. Following Urvashi Vaid (1995) and Neil Miller (2006), among others, I will call the contrasting wing of the LGBT rights movement—that to which GALA Choruses does *not* belong—the liberationist wing. Gay liberationists, as they are often called, seek not to assimilate into existing societal structures, but rather to create new, more liberatory structures. They see the US (and Canadian) militaries and two-partner (heteronormative) marriage, in particular, as oppressive institutions that LGBT people, and their straight allies, ought to reject. Furthermore, gay liberationists favor using publicly disruptive tactics, such as street protests, in pursuit of their goals.

The differences between the integrationist and liberationist approaches in the LGBT rights movement have been the subject of much discussion. Indeed, as Vaid (1995, 37) writes, "Gay and lesbian history could be read as the saga of the conflict between these two compatible but divergent goals." Historians of the American gay rights movement trace the origin of the conflict to the 1950s, and to the founding of the Mattachine Society. Harry Hay, one of the founders of the Mattachine Society and a towering figure in the history of gay rights, was a Communist and a protoliberationist, as were most of the other founding members. This early group of leaders was ousted from the Mattachine Society, and the group subsequently articulated different strategies for reaching its goal of equality for gay men and lesbian women. The new Mattachine leaders "rejected the notion of gays and lesbians as a minority group, stressing that homosexuals are really no different than heterosexuals" (Miller 2006, 306). As Marilyn Reiger, one of the second generation of Mattachine leaders who replaced Hay and his cohort, said, "We know we are the same . . . no different than anyone else. Our only difference is an unimportant one to the heterosexual society, unless we make it important" (qtd. in D'Emilio 1992, 43). Hay scorned his successors, saying that they were interested in being "middle class" and "respectable" (Faderman 2015, 73), and scholars have generally agreed with him (D'Emilio 1983, 81; Miller 2006, 321). The gay liberationists of today see themselves as the descendants of Harry Hay, and they have a strong disdain for gay rights activists whose message is that LGBT people are worthy of equal respect and equal rights because they are fundamentally the same as middle-class heterosexual people, or, "normal."

Liberationists allege that integrationists have "repudiated the [gay rights movement's] best histories of insight and activism" (Warner 1999, 25), and that ultimately the integrationist project is "really hopeless" (Bronski 1984, 212) because it "cannot deliver genuine freedom or full equality" (Vaid 1995, 3). Some critics go even further, equating integrationists with "soft" racists who tolerate and cooperate with racism (Walters 2001, 16), and with American imperialism (Puar 2007, 4, 9). These liberationists claim that gay men and lesbian women who seek integration are "complicit with a heterosexual power structure that is fundamentally indifferent or inimical to them" (Jagose 1996, 115), and that integrationists seek to maintain this power structure for selfish reasons, in service of their own economic interests (Bernstein-Sycamore 2012, 1; Bersani 1995, 66–67; Taylor 2012, 174).

Integrationists refute such arguments, although the integrationist perspective is not nearly so well represented in scholarly writings. Integrationists maintain that they are indeed pursuing social progress, and that their achievement of "normalcy," or similarity to heterosexuals, is in fact a way of fighting for expanded LGBT rights. David Link (1996, 277) explains: "[People] respond to what is in front of them, to what they can see and feel. They are not interested in how lesbians and gay men are different from them—that much is obvious. They want to know about the common ground. Lives become connected not through difference but through similarity. Connected lives become interesting because of difference, but they do not initially connect at that level." Link goes on to argue that "straight-acting" gay men are much more disconcerting to homophobes than are stereotypical flamboyant gay men because the straight-acting men violate the stereotype, and thus the assumptions, perpetuated by straight society.

Harry Hay's—and later liberationists'—contention that integrationists value their middle-class status more than their commitment to justice is obliquely confirmed by Bruce Bawer (1993, 35), one of the loudest voices for integration: "Many homosexuals were raised in conventional middle-class homes in conventional middle-class neighborhoods, and they want to spend their lives in similar homes and neighborhoods, and they don't see why being gay should prevent them from doing so." At least one scholarly study has affirmed this argument: Frederick R. Lynch (1992, 180) studied a group of middle-class suburban gay men between 1982 and 1985 and found that their top priorities were job/career/income and home ownership; their sexual lives were a comparatively lower priority. "The middle-class suburban settings in which most respondents were raised, lived, or wanted to live, strongly reinforced devotion to work, home ownership/maintenance, and continued interaction with heterosexual coworkers, relatives, and friends" (183). Many expressed liberal political views but were not interested in joining political groups. Lynch was particularly interested in investigating these men's involvement in gay civic organizations—he found that it was low—and noted, "While many respected the gay liberation groups for having won legal rights and limited social acceptance, the suburbanites were put off by the style of gay lib spokespersons" (185).

GALA Choruses as an Integrationist Organization

As we saw in chapters 3 and 4, GALA Choruses is dominated by middle-class White people, and the organization reflects those people's middle-class values. As supporters of gay liberation would therefore suspect, GALA choristers by and large prefer the integrationist style of politicking, and the organization as a whole evinces a consistent integrationist ethos (a claim that I make based on the dominant patterns of thought and behavior that I observed).

However, as in any human society, within GALA circles there are people whose perspective differs from that of the majority. Not all GALA choristers would characterize themselves as integrationists. I met some of these outliers while conducting my research. One was Neka Zimmerman, a twenty-five-year-old tenor in the Rochester Gay Men's Chorus. Zimmerman clearly understood himself as distinct from the "mostly forty-plus" singers in his chorus (interview, December 19, 2016). He shared with me that he does not have close friends in the chorus and does not spend much time with his fellow choristers outside rehearsals. "I really appreciate being around older queer people," Zimmerman said. "I would never have met the other choristers in my regular queer circles. I don't actually listen to music often! But I think it's important to seek out connections with other generations. It's cool to be part of something like [the Rochester Gay Men's Chorus], and I think I have something to contribute because I'm trans, and younger, and an activist, and an anticapitalist. I have a perspective that our mostly White, mostly cis[gender], mostly middle-aged singers don't share." Another GALA singer who sees herself as differing from GALA's integrationist norm is Shannon Wyss, who sang with Bread and Roses Feminist Singers (in the Washington, DC, area) from 1995 to 2008. Wyss told me that, having attended the GALA Festival three times, "I noticed that GALA people are generally much more assimilationist than me. Well, this was my perception at the time. Most people [at the Festival] were middle-aged, White, cisgender, monosexual people. In DC, I hang out with a lot of activists and trans people. They are mostly well educated and radical" (interview, May 23, 2012).

Both Zimmerman and Wyss had many positive things to say about their involvement in GALA choruses, and they are quoted on other topics in other parts of this book. However, both stood out as exceptional in a few ways. Of the ninety-seven GALA insiders I interviewed, they were two of only five people to use the word *queer* to describe themselves. In terms of the way Zimmerman and Wyss positioned themselves in the larger gay rights movement, both said that they were "activists" and contrasted their own profiles with the "assimilationists" who constitute the majority population in GALA choruses. As scholar Michael Warner (1999, 71, 74) points out, most rank-and-file members of the LGBTQ community do not use labels like assimilationist or separatist, but most are vividly aware that there is a "fault line" in the gay rights movement, and that the people falling on either side of the line are increasingly inhabiting "two different worlds." GALA choruses are part of the integrationist world, what Warner calls the "normalizing" wing of the movement (52).

In the broadest sense, GALA choruses belong to a longer tradition of community choirs working for social change by promoting their singers as acceptable members of the American mainstream. For example, scholars have compared GALA choruses to the Mormon Tabernacle Choir, which calmed the fears of many Americans, who historically viewed the Mormon religion "with tremendous skepticism and trepidation" (Avery, Hayes, and Bell 2013, 258). Christmas-themed television programs broadcast during the 1960s and 1970s featured the Mormon Tabernacle Choir so that viewers began to associate Mormonism with "the very holiday that meant peace and joy," ultimately learning "tolerance of [the Mormons'] unique brand of Christianity."

GALA insiders often talk about their work for social change—that is, their work to "change hearts and minds" about LGBT people—by describing what that work is *not*. They claim, rather commonly, that GALA choruses are not threatening. For example, Eric Helmuth, a composer, accompanist, and singer for various GALA choruses, said, "GALA choruses have this disarming ability. Our mission is changing hearts and minds through song. You just can't be threatened by a group of men, or women, singing about who they love. It's very positive, it's very affirming" (interview, August 10, 2012).[2] Likewise, Susan Avery, Casey Hayes, and Cindy Bell (2013) use the word *nonthreatening* twice in reference to GALA choruses, in a rather short section of a book chapter about community choirs.

When GALA representatives say that their singing is nonthreatening, they are implicitly or explicitly contrasting their public actions with the kinds of street protests favored by gay liberationists. And so they explain that "we want to make beautiful music *and* we want to make a better society. But we don't want to be involved with strong, confrontational activism like marching with signs" (Joe Nadeau, interview, February 20, 2011). Linda Krasienko, who sings with Windsong, Cleveland's Feminist Chorus, and who volunteers with the North Coast Men's Chorus in the same Ohio city, said that her GALA involvement is "a way to be supportive without standing on a corner and waving a flag" (interview, November 25, 2014). Her colleague in the North Coast Men's Chorus Bryan Fetty said of his participation in the group, "I will never be a flag-waving activist, but this is a way of being a non 'in-your-face' kind of activist. It's a very subtle way of doing it, through music" (interview, October 9, 2014). Fetty went on to give an example of the kind of "subtle" political work that his chorus undertakes: "Our chorus sang at a church last week. I might be the first *out* gay person [that the church parishioners] have ever talked to. And it was presented in a nonthreatening manner. If I had been there waving a flag and pressing pamphlets on them, they might have walked on by. But singing is not a confrontational way of being in front of someone. Music removed that barrier. It made it easier for them [the parishioners] to want to carry on a conversation with the guys." Woody Faulkner, artistic director of Triad Pride Men's Chorus in Greensboro, North Carolina, summed up this integrationist approach to creating social change by saying, "'Political' doesn't necessarily mean activist. You can be passively political. And that's how GALA choruses are political. . . . We draw more flies with honey than with vinegar. If you come across too militant, you make the news but you don't make too many friends" (interview, September 23, 2011).

GALA insiders acknowledge that theirs is a political organization (see chapter 6), but they contrast their style of politicking with that of liberationists.[3] This tendency was especially apparent when some of my interlocutors referenced the AIDS Coalition to Unleash Power (ACT UP), a well-known gay liberationist organization. ACT UP was especially active in large cities in the 1980s and 1990s, and it engaged in attention-grabbing street protests. Eric Sawyer (2002, 90), a member of ACT UP, points out that ACT UP prioritized "street theater, witty chants, slick graphics and sound bites," and that its members tried to include in every street protest some action that would result in members being arrested. These provocative actions were strategic; ACT UP members aimed to be arrested because they believed that being arrested increased the chance that their protest would be covered by the news media. Peter Criswell of the New York City Gay Men's Chorus described his political work with this chorus by contrasting it to ACT UP's street protests: "I'm not really an ACT UP kind of guy, so singing in the chorus was my way of being political. It was less radical" (interview, January 8, 2013). Gary Miller, who was the longtime artistic director of the same chorus, is an ardent supporter of the idea that GALA choruses ought to fulfill the "political part" of their mission, and he noted that audience members too can demonstrate their political loyalties by attending GALA concerts: "[Attending a concert] is an easy way, a safe way, to look at and support gay people. You don't have to listen to ACT UP people shouting at you" (interview, June 27, 2014). Brian Tombow of the Dayton Gay Men's Chorus in Dayton, Ohio, is a former member of ACT UP. He characterized what ACT UP did as "militant gay activism" (interview, August 17, 2011). He agreed that the chorus is like ACT UP in one way—"it's a political project; we're trying to change society's perception of us"—but, he clarified, "it's not militant."

GALA insiders also contrast their own public performances with the Gay Pride Parade (or at least, with stereotypical understandings of this parade). Alexandra Chasin (2000, 210) argues that these parades are "perhaps the most symbolically weighty kind of event that the lesbian and gay community has engaged in," and as such, they constitute a reference point for many LGBT people when they enter into discussions of public activism.[4] For some GALA insiders, the Pride Parade is a good example of what GALA choruses are not. Miguel Felipe, former artistic director of the Maine Gay Men's Chorus, said that his chorus's concertizing was a way of influencing hearts and minds because, "When you see two hundred men doing something cooperative, those are the moments when people say, 'Huh, there's more to gay men than Pride Parades and illicit sex'" (interview, July 31, 2013). Rich Cook, artistic director of MenAlive, the Orange County Gay Men's Chorus (in California), emphasized that the image his chorus presents to the public is definitely "not the image of gay men in their underwear, like in the Gay Pride Parade" (interview, May 14, 2012).

Both Felipe and Cook—and other GALA insiders I interviewed—made haste to say that they support the notion of Gay Pride Parades; and in fact, some GALA choruses have even marched in local Pride Parades (Woody Faulkner, interview, September 23, 2011). However, they are deeply concerned that the stereotypical representation of the parades makes the idea of sexual difference a hard sell in Middle America or the Midwest. Indeed, anti-gay groups have strategically used photographs of Gay Pride Parade marchers, particularly images of people wearing only small amounts of clothing, to argue that LGBT people in general are a threat to mainstream values (Faderman 2015, 351). Alex Strife, a singer in the Choral Project of San Jose, California, told me that he is very opposed to Pride Parades specifically because the way these marches are presented in mainstream media is ultimately detrimental to what GALA choruses are trying to do: "I feel that we as a community get so hung up on being gay, but you change people's minds with what you do, not by showing your gayness."[5]

When GALA insiders describe the political work of their choruses in positive terms—describing what it *is*, rather than what it is not—they use language favored by integrationists (and despised by liberationists). Eric Aufdengarten, a singer in the Heartland Men's Chorus of Kansas City, Missouri, said that the work his chorus does is "a quiet activism that allows me to come out to friends in a way that is not threatening to them" (interview, October 25, 2011). Donald Butchko contrasted his GALA chorus, the North Coast Men's Chorus, with other LGBT advocacy organizations by saying, "the chorus is a little more passive" (interview, September 25, 2014). Alyssa Stone explained the goal of singing "political choral music": "You want to offend people just enough so they're talking about it when they leave, but not enough so they won't come back! You have to strike a balance. They [the members of the Lesbian/Gay Chorus of San Francisco] want people to think, not to be offended. Because that's the way to change things, to get people to look at things in a different light" (interview, June 25, 2012).[6]

Commonly, GALA singers and artistic directors talk about the power of their social change work by invoking the word *normal*—the very word that gay liberationists find so distasteful and even lob as an insult against "normalizers," meaning integrationists. Here are a few examples: "The chorus has a slow but cumulative effect on the public: we are normal people, we have the same wants and needs as everyone else, and we deserve respect" (Adam Coatney, interview, August 4, 2011). "The chorus is a way of families and loved ones seeing a face of the gay community that is: 'Hey, they're normal, they're like me'" (Rich Cook, interview, May 4, 2012). "I really believe that change occurs in audiences when they come to a concert and see the normalcy. . . .

The image that most people have of gay people is the undressed people in the gay parade. When you come to a [GALA chorus] concert, you see teachers, plumbers, neighbors" (Dennis Coleman, interview, September 1, 2011). As other scholars have repeatedly found, the invocation of normalcy is common to middle-class LGBT people who believe that verbalizing how normal they are is an important way to foster acceptance of LGBT people in mainstream society (Gamson 2005, 10; McQueeny 2009, 159). GALA's leaders and singers by and large concur with this strategy; individual choruses and GALA Choruses as a whole reveal that the organization values and prioritizes a White, American, middle-class understanding of normalcy.

GALA's integrationist ethos is revealed not only in what singers and conductors say, but also in what they do onstage. As we saw at the beginning of this chapter, GALA choruses often present—and applaud—performances that honor the two best-known political commitments of integrationism: military service and same-sex marriage. Andrew Sullivan, one of the most widely known integrationists, argued in his 1995 book *Virtually Normal* that the best political moves gay men and lesbian women could make would be to participate in large numbers in monogamous marriage and in military service (173). Acceptance into these two institutions—marriage and the military—has, for many people in the years since, become shorthand for integrationist politics (Warner 1999, 52). Chapter 4 of this book expands on GALA's celebration of same-sex marriage; here I turn to GALA's valorization of the inclusion of LGBT people in military service.

GALA's affirmation of "normal" middle-class American values is most vividly seen in performances that evoke and celebrate the American military. During Dennis Coleman's final season as artistic director of the Seattle Women's Chorus, he directed a show focused on the women who worked making munitions during World War II. The singing, speaking, acting, and costuming in this show all celebrated the Rosie the Riveters who supplied the American war effort. The 2016 GALA Festival presentation of this show received unqualified support, a sustained standing ovation, from fellow GALA singers in the audience.[7] In 2012, the Gateway Men's Chorus of St. Louis, Missouri, performed a song titled "Here's Where I Stand."[8] The chorus's artistic director, Al Fischer, told me that he and his chorus were glad that one of their singers performed the song standing in his dress blues (a military uniform). Fischer explained that the chorus sang the song "with a sense of celebration" in the wake of the September 2011 repeal of the ban on gay men and lesbian women serving openly in the US military (interview, January 31, 2012). The Turtle Creek Chorale of Dallas, Texas, highlights on its website, "Two performances with the U.S. Army Chorus and Former First

Lady Laura Bush serving as honorary chair for the event" (Turtle Creek Chorale n.d.). The chorale's artistic director for these 2009 performances stated (during a meeting of GALA artistic directors) that the chorale "conceded many demands" in order to organize this joint concert; he was gratified to report that the chorale now has a photo showing the choristers onstage with twenty-eight US soldiers.[9]

GALA's commitment to the integrationist approach to gay rights is further revealed in what specific choruses, or the GALA organization itself, sometimes choose *not* to do. In the spirit of being nonconfrontational, choruses have sometimes declined to perform at places and times where they believe an LGBT presence might cause offense. For example, the Vancouver Men's Chorus has been "cautious about not trying to perform where we won't be welcome, like in a Catholic Church," said the chorus's long-term artistic director Willi Zwozdesky (interview, September 5, 2011). One of the founders of the Dayton Gay Men's Chorus felt compelled to double-check after the chorus's artistic director arranged for the chorus to perform at a statewide Boys Choir event. "The organizer I contacted said that she couldn't be sure that the other choirs [at the event] would accept" the presence of adult gay men, Fred Poland reported. "So I said, 'No problem, we'll withdraw.' There was only one [Dayton Gay Men's Chorus] member who had a problem with this, and he was a gay libertarian" (interview, June 16, 2011). In addition, choruses sometimes downplay suggestions of sexual and/or gender difference—such as male effeminacy—even while they are performing, in order to avoid offending audience members. This practice is sometimes glossed as declining to appear "too gay."[10] Eric Unhold of the North Coast Men's Chorus said that his chorus regularly debates how songs should be presented, especially when they include dancing: "I've heard plenty of times comments like, 'Let's scale it back, it's too much, it's too campy.' Some members have even chosen not to sing at certain concerts because they feel it's too gay" (interview, October 13, 2014). Robert Frederick of the Dayton Gay Men's Chorus pointed out that the chorus performs its Christmas concert each year in a church, and it is important not to "offend" the audience (interview, August 17, 2011). He elaborated that a singer once showed up for the Christmas concert wearing high-heeled shoes: "He was making it too gay. The dress code was immediately changed, so that could never happen again. And [the artistic director] regularly reminds us not to wear too much jewelry."

The GALA organization actively discourages the kind of tactics associated with gay liberationists. GALA's leaders made their position very clear during the 2016 GALA Festival, which was held in Denver, Colorado, at the same time and in the same city as the Western Conservative Summit, a meeting of Republican and Christian conservative political operatives. Some choristers proposed to mount a street protest outside of the Western Conservative Summit venue and began trying to organize the protest on Facebook. The possibility was shut down by the GALA leadership. At one of the Festival's open table sessions, three participants lamented this turn of events, saying it was "a betrayal of the GALA mission," but their view was decidedly in the minority.[11] My own view is that the three people who made these complaints failed to understand that while GALA Choruses is part of a social movement, it espouses a specifically integrationist style of advancing social change. As social movement scholar James M. Jasper (1997, 242) points out, "actions and the choice of tactics send all sorts of signals; they tell an outsider as much about a group as its explicit arguments do." Presenting concerts in a wide variety of venues at the heart of straight society is strongly encouraged by the GALA leadership, but public protests against a specific right-wing group is not the kind of tactic they are willing to endorse.

GALA's Favored Tactic: The Choral Music Concert

As we saw above, social movements are marked by their commitment to collective actions, also called tactics. The choice of actions, or tactics, differs according to the taste of the members in opposing wings of various social movements. GALA Choruses' preferred collective action, and the one choruses engage in hundreds of times each year, is the choral concert. GALA choristers are by and large gay integrationists, and they believe that singing beautifully in public is a nonthreatening way to convince straight society to integrate LGBT persons into existing social institutions.

Anthropologist Don Handelman's (1998) theory of public events is helpful in understanding how a performance—like a GALA concert—can be an effective tactic. Handelman defines public events as organized "formalizations of space, time and behavior" that follow a script that is more or less the same each time the event takes place (11). GALA chorus concerts are certainly public events in this sense; audiences can predict what will happen, at least in broad outline, because community choirs almost always present their work in the same way. Some GALA choruses enact a literal script when they perform (Charlie Beale, interview, August 16, 2011), but in the larger sense, they all fulfill the same set of expectations: at a choral concert, the choir stands in front, facing the listeners, who sit quietly and demonstrate their support and approval by clapping. Although (as I argued in chapter 5) many

GALA shows demonstrate a high degree of innovation in their performance practices, all GALA concerts are formalized, scripted public events as Handelman understands them.

Handelman (1998, 11–12) argues that public events are always functional; they *do* something to their participants, both to the actors and to the audience members. A public event such as a choral concert can be an event that presents, an event that re-presents, or an event that models. A choral concert that "presents the lived-in-world" is intended to be a statement, a reflection of the current situation, and as such it contains "no program of controlled transformation"; it is not a strategy for creating social change (41, 46). Concerts performed by the majority of community choirs fall into this category of events that present; these choirs sing what artistic directors call the "standard repertoire," and they sing it in the standard way. The intent of such concerts is to reaffirm the greatness of the Western choral music tradition rather than to change hearts and minds.

By contrast, a choral concert that re-presents offers "propositions and counter-propositions, within itself, about the nature of . . . realities" (Handelman 1998, 49). In doing so, it raises doubts about the legitimacy of the current social order. GALA performances are often very effective events that re-present. During such performances, GALA singers offer a number of propositions that challenge heteronormativity: they publicly proclaim themselves to be members of sexual and gender minorities (often in the very name of their chorus); they affirm the goodness of same-sex love; and, at times, they explicitly question the authority of dominant institutions, re-presenting these institutions as illegitimate insofar as they betray their own rhetoric by discriminating against LGBT people.

Some GALA performances, for example, challenge the proposition that schools are places that welcome children and provide a social good. "Pushed Down the Stairs," from the oft-performed *Naked Man* by Robert Seeley, vividly describes the physical and emotional violence suffered by a schoolboy at the hands of his classmates ("Guess who got hated the most? The little fag"). Similarly, the words during the first minute and a half of "Taunts," from *Watershed Stories* by Canadian composer David Mcintyre, are not sung, but rather hissed, spoken, and shouted, as the pianist pounds out hugely dissonant chords and the choristers restate the insults LGBT children routinely hear at school ("You disgusting pervert!"). Other GALA shows reiterate this point, highlighting the vicious bullying LGBT (and overweight and other "different") children are subjected to in a place where they must spend at least thirty hours each week; examples include *Oliver Button Is a Sissy*, inspired by Tomie dePaola's 1979 book of the same name, and *Finding Oz*, the Columbus Gay Men's Chorus show of spring 2016.

GALA choruses also sometimes sing songs that challenge the tenets of the Christian faith, the dominant religion of the United States and Canada. When the Dayton Gay Men's Chorus sings, for example, "I Saw Daddy Kissing Santa Claus," it effectively re-presents received notions about a central figure in one of the most important holiday narratives in Christianity. Christmas and family togetherness are important, they imply, and Santa Claus is a beloved figure—but he might be gay. More importantly, your own father might be gay. Similarly, when the North Coast Men's Chorus performs "Every Sperm Is Sacred," a send-up of the Catholic Church's teaching about birth control, it ups the satire factor by adding a preamble. During this portion, a chorister dressed as a priest (wearing a clerical collar) reads recent statements by church leaders condemning homosexuality as a sin and a disorder, proclaiming the text with great solemnity and using exaggerated pronunciation. The preamble connects the church's antigay teaching to its anti–birth control teaching, portraying each as ridiculous; the addition of costumed dancers playing nuns, monks, von Trapp children, and a bishop helps to make the performance more satirical, as the dancers demonstrate irrational joy over words that vilify the sexual practices of the majority of people, both gay and straight. When audiences attend a GALA concert that re-presents, they hear lyrics that challenge dominant notions about foundational US and Canadian institutions, lyrics that present a different way to think about these institutions—and by extension, a different way to think about LGBT people.

Finally, many GALA concerts are events that model, which, according to Handelman (1998, 28), are events that "index or preview a hypothetical future condition that will be brought into being, and provide procedures that will actualize this act of imagination." A concert that models always has the goal to effect some change in the participants, to "transform" both singers and listeners (27, 31). A GALA concert almost always is—or almost always aims to be—an event that models. And the hypothetical future it models is a future in which LGBT people are fully accepted by heteronormative society, and are able to exercise all of the rights and freedoms that straight people enjoy. This kind of modeling is evident in many of GALA's commissioned "gay songs" that are composed of lyrics taken from the statements of choristers themselves (see chapter 5). Works like *Naked Man*, which features stories gathered from singers in the San Francisco Gay Men's Chorus, model a world in which LGBT people can voice their own truths and have their stories heard and respected. Perhaps the preeminent example of a song that models is the much-performed "Everything Possible." This song is a lullaby written by Fred Small and arranged by Vancouver Men's Chorus director Willi Zwozdesky. The narrator of "Everything Possible" is a loving parent, affirming to their child that, in the future, everything will be possible for the child. "You can be anyone you want to be / You can love whomever you will," the song proclaims; "Some women love women, some men love men / Some raise children, some never do / You can dream all the day, never reaching the end / Of everything possible for you."

The transformational power of "Everything Possible" rests on the fact that it allows LGBT singers to affirm, in public, that in the future every good outcome will be open to people who love others of the same gender. Perhaps even more significantly, the lyrics assume that in this future world, parents love their children unconditionally and celebrate their children's same-sex relationships. Singing about this "possible" world—which many interlocutors told me was deeply meaningful to them—offers choristers a way to articulate their hope for a different and more loving future, and offers the listeners a way to envision it. In Handelman's (1998, 28) terms, this performance that models allows everyone involved to "preview a hypothetical future condition." In other words, the performance is an effective social movement tactic. For Eyerman and Jamison (1998, 172), the performance is an "exemplary action" that expresses "a vision of what the world could be like." GALA choristers, for their part, say that singing "Everything Possible" is a way to change hearts and minds. Handelman (1998, 40) argues strongly for the efficacy of events that model: "Short of transforming the premises of social and cosmological order, there is no more radical action that a people can take than to set up intentional simulations of their worlds: systemic models whose instructions are to act upon and to change the ordering of these worlds in comprehensive and consequential ways."

Conclusion

Participants in GALA choruses are best understood as integrationists, agents in the gay rights movement who hope to achieve greater integration for LGBT people in society, especially within enduring institutions like marriage and the military. Furthermore, they believe that the best way to achieve these goals is by changing the hearts and minds of the public at large, gently persuading listeners through nonconfrontational songs that a different, more inclusive, world is indeed possible. Scholars of social movements affirm this belief, arguing that modeling a different world through public performance is a powerful way to persuade audiences to think differently.

GALA insiders articulate a fairly consistent rationale to explain how their concertizing contributes to social change. They point out that they sing as often as possible for audiences composed of their own families, friends, and work colleagues, as well as choral music lovers in their region—that is, people who come from the same US/Canadian middle-class background as the singers. And, given that these audience members (like the choristers) grew up in a heteronormative society that discriminates both legally and socially against LGBT people, at least some of them may distrust or dislike the very notion of same-sex love. GALA choristers understand this situation. They aim to undermine the fear of the Other implicit in homophobia by emphasizing their own "normalcy," that is, their similarity to their audience members. During interview after interview, I heard GALA insiders talk about their audiences as being on a journey away from fear and toward understanding.[12] They explained that singing beautiful music, and singing it well, is an effective way to undermine such fears and to move listeners toward greater acceptance of LGBT people and the notion of equal rights.

The question for scholars is: is this proposition true? In other words, does hearing a GALA chorus sing actually affect the attitudes of listeners, especially those who are homophobic? Rob Rosenthal and Richard Flacks (2012, 154), in their study of music and social movements, affirm possibilities articulated by other social movement scholars: "By saying things out loud in public, musicking can confer an aura of reality and legitimacy on previously suppressed ways of thinking." However, they avoid explicitly arguing that hearing songs can cause people to change their minds or to become supporters of a social movement. As we saw at the conclusion of chapter 6, GALA leaders themselves debate whether their concertizing actually leads to changed hearts and minds. I engage in this debate in the following chapter.

8 • Social Change

Assessing GALA Choruses' Central Claim

It is difficult, perhaps impossible, to assess whether a social movement has accomplished its goals; trying to define the "success" of social movements "has always bedeviled students of protest" (Jasper 1997, 295). Take, for example, the movement to abolish nuclear weapons: the movement has built a broad awareness of the danger of such weapons, and ongoing advocacy no doubt contributed to the willingness of various national governments to sign the Treaty on the Non-Proliferation of Nuclear Weapons, which dates from 1970. However, as of 2020, some countries that possess nuclear weapons have refused to sign the treaty, and the leader of North Korea openly threatened to use such weapons in 2017. Has the movement to abolish nuclear weapons succeeded? It is hard to say.

Similarly, it is difficult to state with absolute confidence that hearts and minds are changing regarding sexual and gender norms, and that this change, if it is occurring, can be attributed to the gay rights movement and organizations within that movement such as GALA Choruses. Robert D. Putnam (2000, 352) points to the fact that numerous broad-based surveys of public attitudes in the United States show that "without a doubt America in the 1990s was a more tolerant place than America in the 1950s or even the 1970s ... the increase in tolerance in recent decades has been stark and broad." Putnam argues that a powerful generational shift is underway, and that younger people are much more likely to express tolerance of racial integration, feminism, and civil liberties for LGBT people: "The increasing tolerance of the last several decades is almost entirely due to the replacement of less tolerant people born in the first half of the twentieth century by more tolerant [baby] boomers and

[Generation] X'ers" (357). David Rayside (2008, 46) confirms that the dramatic decrease in disapproval of homosexuality among the American public during the 1990s was mirrored by an even bigger drop in disapproval in Canada. However, in 2016 the United States elected a president who expressed contempt for all kinds of civil liberties during his campaign, and whose administration "amassed a striking record of anti-LGBT actions in its first year in office" (Cahill, Geffen, and Wang 2018, 3). While some gay rights activists, including some GALA choristers, celebrate changes in the law—especially the legalization of same-sex marriage—as definitive proof that their efforts are succeeding, the advent of the Trump administration showed that laws can quite easily be repealed, or at least credibly challenged by the highest powers in the land. Changes in the attitudes of average members of the public, such as audience members at choral music concerts, are even more ambiguous and more resistant to easy testing.

In this chapter I explore GALA insiders' belief that they are accomplishing their social change mission. As we saw in chapter 6, this mission ("changing our world through song") focuses on transforming the attitudes of (potentially) homophobic listeners, rather than effecting structural change in governments, public institutions, or private organizations. This chapter delineates GALA choristers' powerful, though anecdotal, evidence of the changed hearts and minds that their music making produces. I subsequently discuss the results of an experiment that I conducted to measure the level of homophobia expressed by university students both before and after attending a GALA chorus concert. Finally, I argue that we can assert with confidence that GALA concerts further social change because they provide a venue for choristers to come out, one social action that has been repeatedly shown to be effective in shifting individual and societal attitudes about LGBT people.

Widespread Belief in Social Change

GALA singers and artistic directors are united in their belief that their concertizing contributes to progressive social change, meaning that it helps foster more strongly positive attitudes toward LGBT people among the public at large. They point to various forms of evidence in support of this belief, as we shall see, and they are in general agreement that however this social change may be made manifest, it can be attributed to performances by GALA choruses. They express this belief with confidence. For example, David Hodgkins, artistic director of Coro Allegro in Boston, Massachusetts, said, "There are a lot of people across the country who appreciate music and who have been convinced, by attending GALA concerts, that these [singers] are real people, with real feelings, and that they deserve equal rights" (interview, April 9, 2014). In speaking about the broader societal shift toward greater acceptance for LGBT people, Jean-Louis Bleau, former artistic director of the Calgary Men's Chorus, said, "The choral movement has been an integral part of that change, and it continues to be about [that change]" (interview, May 31, 2016). Fred Poland, a founding singer in the Dayton Gay Men's Chorus (in Ohio), agrees with prominent GALA leaders, like those just quoted, who articulate this belief frequently: "With every concert, someone somewhere's heart is changed" (interview, June 16, 2011). And in one of many similar examples, a promotional video for Out Loud: The Colorado Springs Men's Chorus, screened at the 2016 GALA Festival, featured choristers explaining that their concerts "showcase gay people in a positive light," and that in so doing, "we've touched a lot more lives than we even know."[1] Julia Balén (2009, 40), one of the only scholars who has written at length about LGBT choruses, affirms this widespread belief by writing that choruses "create social change" by performing in many places.

GALA participants provide many concrete—but anecdotal—forms of evidence for their claim that their singing creates more positive attitudes toward LGBT people among listeners. They often point to audience reactions that they themselves have observed as evidence that their singing impacts the emotions of listeners—and by implication, causes those listeners to feel and think differently. For example, Danielle Lynette of Harmony: A Colorado Chorale explained that her father was "moved to open acceptance of trans people" as a result of hearing the chorale sing; she saw him hugging a transgender singer from the chorale after a concert.[2] Tara Napoleone-Clifford of the Kansas City Women's Chorus (in Missouri) told me that she "definitely believes" that music moves people: "You can see audience members crying sometimes [at her chorus's concerts]" (interview, June 30, 2011).[3] Composer Roger Bourland pointed out that during the inaugural presentations of his work *Hidden Legacies*, commissioned by the Gay Men's Chorus of Los Angeles, audience members wept so much that for subsequent performances, choruses hired grief counselors to staff the doors: "The piece really resonated with people; it really, really touched lives" (interview, December 10, 2012).

Even more than tears, audience members' statements are important to GALA insiders because these provide tangible evidence that individual attitudes have changed. For example, Rich Cook, artistic director of MenAlive, the Orange County Gay Men's Chorus, asserted, "I *know* that audience members have been changed by performances" (interview, May 14, 2012).

Cook then told the story of a singer in the chorus who invited his father, a Mormon elder, to a MenAlive concert. The following evening, the son and his father went to dinner. The Mormon elder told his son, "Because I saw you [perform] I've been changed for good," quoting from a song the chorus had sung at the concert. Chris Raines, a singer in the Gay Men's Chorus of Charlotte, North Carolina, recalled, "Audience members have said to us, 'You guys sound so wonderful, I just wish you weren't gay.' This shows that the music touched them and came into conflict with their deeply held values."[4]

GALA participants also proffer other kinds of concrete evidence as proof that their singing fosters social change, evidenced by actions taken by decision-makers in straight society. John Whalen, a tenor in One Voice Mixed Chorus of Saint Paul, Minnesota, said thoughtfully, "I *trust* that our choir is making a difference. But I can also point to results. For example, areas where One Voice has performed had a higher percentage of No votes [against proposed legislation banning same-sex marriage in Minnesota]. And also students [at public schools where One Voice has performed] have told us that we're making an impact. When we started out, we had to use a shoehorn to get into schools! But now we are swamped with invitations, and we often get invited back. . . . Also, some of the students who heard us at school later joined One Voice" (interview, January 3, 2013). Other interlocutors echoed Whalen in arguing that invitations extended by non-LGBT organizations are evidence that the choruses are effectively advocating for greater inclusion of LGBT people in mainstream society. For example, Vic Hooper, artistic director of the Rainbow Harmony Project in Winnipeg, Manitoba, told me that his chorus has won prizes at the Winnipeg Music Festival, and that in 2011, the Winnipeg Symphony Orchestra invited the chorus to sing the choral part in a pop music concert: "This speaks volumes about how far we have come, about how much more accepted gays are in society" (interview, September 9, 2011). Joe Buches, artistic director of the Philadelphia Gay Men's Chorus in Pennsylvania, shared that in 2012 he made a presentation about GALA repertoire at a regional American Choral Directors Association (ACDA) conference; he underlined that the newly elected president of the ACDA herself introduced his presentation and told him later that she is interested in having more GALA choruses perform at national ACDA conventions (interview, March 27, 2012). Buches's story is particularly significant because of the contentious history between GALA Choruses and the ACDA (see chapter 1).

Outsiders, at times, affirm that GALA chorus performances affect listeners' emotions and therefore hold the possibility of "changing hearts and minds." For example, Karen Hauge (2012) reviewed the show *When I Knew* by the Heartland Men's Chorus of Kansas City, Missouri, writing that it was "touching" and "hugely powerful." She confessed to weeping as she listened ("Tears and sniffles abounded for me") and concluded that the Heartland Men's Chorus has a "lasting positive impact" on Kansas City. Similarly, John Culhane (2017) wrote that while listening to the Philadelphia Gay Men's Chorus, "I found myself fighting back tears." Culhane mused about the impact of the chorus's singing on his two young daughters, and he hoped that "hearing the soaring voices of the gay chorus" would one day "encourage them in actions that improve others' lives and prospects."

Social Change Begins at Home

One manifestation of social change that is especially valued by GALA insiders is the attitudinal change they see in themselves, their fellow choristers, or both. Their reflections about this phenomenon are a good reminder that homophobia is not just the province of straight people; LGBT people too can be intolerant of others and can experience internalized homophobia. Therefore, sometimes social change needs to begin at home. Drew Kotchan of the Calgary Men's Chorus told me that by participating in the chorus he has "widened his appreciation for all types of people" (interview, May 31, 2016). Specifically, he said, "I used to be annoyed by really 'swish' men, but as a result of being in the chorus, I now just appreciate men like that for who they are. And I now feel guilty about how I used to feel revulsion toward butch lesbians. Participating in the chorus has made me more relaxed in general, especially with my younger brother who is gay and much more campy than I. That used to turn me off, but now I'm totally into it!" Kotchan spoke extensively about becoming "braver" about claiming his own gay identity, an emotion echoed by Tom Fortuna of the North Coast Men's Chorus of Cleveland, Ohio. Fortuna talked about singing with the chorus at Gay Pride events and at the Gay Games of 2014: "What a feeling! I just felt so overwhelmed to be a part of this and not be ashamed of who I was. It was just phenomenal" (interview, October 16, 2014). Fortuna followed this statement by sharing a story about his growing ability to speak out against homophobia: "I mentioned the North Coast Men's Chorus to [a work colleague]. He said to me, 'It's a fag chorus,' and I calmly said, 'No, it's a gay chorus.' And I'm healthy today." This kind of transformation in rank-and-file choristers is part of what inspires GALA leaders. Jane Hoffman, a former national board member of GALA Choruses, summarized the sentiments of many by saying, "I've seen people just come alive, with the music and the community, and just being free and being yourself—choruses are liberating!" (interview, March 1, 2012). John Quillin, the artistic director of the very busy Gay Men's Chorus of Charlotte, North Carolina (see chapter 2 for more on the chorus's demanding schedule), explained that he does all the management and musical direction for the chorus as a volunteer: "I continue to be involved because I see the change. People really are changed by participating in chorus! A number of our chorus members have come out [to their parents] by inviting their parents to a concert. In some cases, our concerts are the only gay events families will attend" (interview, March 29, 2011).

GALA choristers are especially grateful for the changed attitudes they see among their own family members and friends, people who in many cases had previously demonstrated no support for the notion of LGBT rights. Bryan Fetty of the North Coast Men's Chorus said, "The impact we can have on audience members, that's very cool to me" (interview, October 9, 2014). He explained that his own family members—people to whom Fetty "was not totally out" some years ago—are now "ardent supporters" of the chorus. Furthermore, they bring friends to the chorus's concerts; Fetty estimated that an average of thirty people from the small Ohio town where he grew up now attend each performance. Eric Aufdengarten, who sang with the Heartland Men's Chorus, told me that he worked at the state attorney's office in Kansas. "The Kansas government is a fairly conservative place," he said (interview, October 25, 2011). Eric invited the work colleagues from his carpool to an upcoming chorus concert, rather nervously. Later that day, a colleague stopped by his desk to say that he had purchased a ticket. Eric asked, "Do you know what the Heartland Men's Chorus is?" and the colleague said, "Well, I saw the website, so I do now!" Eric was heartened to see that this man, along with others and their girlfriends, came to the concert, and that the group subsequently attended numerous other concerts and fundraisers. Their financial contributions to the chorus are tangible evidence that these conservative government employees now support the singers in the Heartland Men's Chorus—that is, they support gay men in their community.

GALA circles abound with stories about parents, especially, demonstrating their love and public support for GALA choristers, and some of these stories are quite emotionally laden. Charlie Beale, artistic director of the New York City Gay Men's Chorus, recalled with a smile that when he came out to his family, at age nineteen, his mother was "the most freaked out" (interview, August 16, 2011). "We never really talked about my life as a gay man," he said, "but I heard from my sister that my mother now brags to her friends. She says that her son is doing pioneering work with gay choruses, changing the world through song!" Adam Coatney, a first tenor in the Dayton Gay Men's Chorus, said that his parents were "very squeamish" when he came out at age seventeen, but that they are now proud of him: "And I think the choir is a part of that. They're proud of what I'm doing with the choir—and they donate every year" (interview, August 4, 2011). Eric Unhold, a tenor in the North Coast Men's Chorus, asserted that "people are *moved*" by the chorus's singing, and that "some audience members can be radically affected by a particular song. For example, I played the main character in a show called *Tales of the City*. My character writes a coming out letter to his parents.[5] So I was nervous about how my parents were going to react; it was their first time ever attending a GALA concert. Anyway, it was meant to be! They just happened to sit next to another couple whose son was just coming out, and who was [also] in the chorus. And their conversation helped both couples to be more accepting. Because of that concert, my relationship with my parents changed. I could tell from their [previous] reactions to anything to do with their son being gay. It was an important part of their journey" (interview, October 13, 2014).

One of the most emotionally charged stories about a parent's changed attitude comes from Derek Smith, a baritone in the Gay Men's Chorus of Washington, DC (interview, September 2, 2016). Smith began by telling me that when he came out to his mother, "she was rediscovering Jesus after twenty years of being Buddhist. So she was *not* supportive. She started sending me brochures for conversion therapy summer camps.[6] In 2008, I called to tell her that I had been diagnosed with HIV. She said, 'Well, I can't say I'm surprised.' I hung up on her. . . . In the spring of 2016, my parents came to [the Gay Men's Chorus of Washington's performance of] *Carmina Burana*." Weeping, Smith continued, "My mother came to my concert—this is what this chorus means to me. After the concert, my mother threw her arms around me and told me she was proud of me. And this was the woman who was condemning me to hell!" The second part of the same concert included the Christian hymn "Nearer My God to Thee." While singing this hymn, Smith said, he could see his mother from his spot on the stage. "I could see my mother wiping tears from her eyes, and I just about lost it, as you can imagine. Afterward, I could see her standing, cheering, and whistling. I was in tears. It meant everything to me." In fact, both of his parents, plus an aunt, attended that concert, and Smith said that he observed all of them cheering. After the concert, they each hugged Smith and told him that they loved him. Reiterating why the chorus is important to him, Smith said that he is glad to participate in all of the concerts his chorus presents: "It's everything we do to change hearts and minds, like my mother's."

Celebrating Social Change

GALA leaders emphasize the social change they are creating—the greater tolerance for LGBT people that they are fostering among choral music audiences—in various ways. For example, the Columbus Gay Men's Chorus website maintained for some years a page called "Lives Changed through CGMC," which featured letters received from community members. One Voice Mixed Chorus has a "Community Impact" page that documents the chorus's extensive outreach work, especially concerts and workshops in public schools (One Voice n.d.b.). The Heartland Men's Chorus created an entire show, narrated by internationally syndicated columnist Dan Savage, called *When I Knew*, which features voice-overs from family members of the choristers explaining when they came to realize that they could love and support their gay father or brother. On occasion, GALA choruses even present evidence of the impact their concertizing is making in published media reports; for example, on January 30, 2014, Rapid Growth Media published an article about the West Michigan Gay Men's Chorus (Mullen 2014). The article includes a story about a gay man and his father who were reconciled after years of estrangement when, by chance, the father heard the son perform with the chorus.

The GALA Choruses organization encourages the dissemination of these kinds of stories, buttressing its theme that concertizing by GALA choruses contributes to progressive social change by transforming the attitudes of audience members. For example, GALA's August/September 2017 newsletter included a section titled "Raising Our Voice: Choruses Sing Out for Justice and Equality" (email to author, August 31, 2017). This section mentioned thirteen different local choruses, valorizing each for fostering social justice through singing. (One sample: "Allegrezza's spring concert was 'Turn the World Around'—music as the catalyst for personal transformation and the vehicle for social change.") The section concluded with a request that recipients of the newsletter "tell us how your chorus is raising its voice in your community." GALA's artistic directors do respond to such requests, and their stories are highlighted on the GALA Choruses website. On July 1, 2017, Thea Kano, the artistic director of the Gay Men's Chorus of Washington, DC, contributed a blog post about the chorus's recent tour of southern American states. Referencing her post's title ("Moving the Needle with Love") in her conclusion, Kano wrote: "The Southern Equality Tour may be the most significant thing GMCW has ever done. We sang to empower and encourage those already doing the hard work in those southern states. We returned home reenergized to continue that work, standing up to the equality needle, tapping it—always with love—with our voices raised high. Because someone always needs to hear us."

The Burning Question: How Is Social Change Effected?

In chapter 7, I analyzed GALA's concertizing as a social movement tactic, a tactic that—social movement scholars argue—is effective in offering counterpropositions about the current social order and in presenting a model of a future, transformed world. But do such counterpropositions and models in fact change the thinking (the hearts and minds) of those who listen to them, especially listeners who are homophobic? Do they "move the needle," as Thea Kano would have it? My formulation of this question, as it relates to GALA Choruses, is new, but it belongs to a larger area of scholarly inquiry that has long been engaged in asking how members of a majority population come to respect as equals the members of a formerly despised minority. What mechanisms effectively reduce prejudice? In particular, how can we reduce the stigma that still attaches to LGBT people in the United States and Canada?

Social scientists and psychologists answer the question by referring to the contact hypothesis: "The *contact hypothesis* holds that under certain conditions, contact between members of a majority and a minority social group can result in decreased bias of the former, the in-group, toward the latter, the out-group" (Simon 1998, 74). The contact thesis was first tested in cases of racial prejudice (Overby and Barth 2002, 434). L. Marvin Overby and Jay Barth (2002, 453) subsequently showed in a large-scale study that the contact thesis is demonstrably true in reference to homophobia. They reported that "exposure to gays and lesbians has tolerating effects," meaning that respondents who reported a higher percentage of gay people living in their own neighborhoods also reported feeling more positively toward LGBT people in general. To summarize, "The powerful potential of contact for reducing homonegativism among heterosexuals has been demonstrated. For example, research . . . demonstrates that two contact variables—having positive interpersonal experiences with homosexuals and having homosexual acquaintances or friends—are strongly correlated with positive attitudes toward lesbians and gays" (Simon 1998, 74–75). Scholars have arrived at a consensus: "People with contact experiences consistently held more favorable attitudes than those without contact, even when other background variables are taken into account" (Herek 1994, 219).

When GALA choristers say that their concertizing changes hearts and minds, they are echoing the contact hypothesis. According to this argument, contact between homophobic people and LGBT people—specifically, the contact between an LGBT chorus and an audience during a concert performance—leads to the reduction of stigma against LGBT people. Listeners at a GALA concert virtually always hear a well-prepared, excellent choral music performance (see chapter 1). They also have positive interpersonal experiences with the choristers: not only do the audience members hear the chorus sing, they often have brief conversations with singers while being escorted to their seats, or during after-concert receptions. In other words, the audience members have contact with people who proclaim themselves—in the words of their songs and even in the names of their choruses—to be lesbian, gay, bisexual, or transgender. And it is incidents of contact such as these that are (believed to be) profoundly influential in changing homophobic attitudes.

Scholars remain interested in testing the contact hypothesis; in fact, the question of whether brief contact with a self-identified gay or lesbian person could reduce homophobic attitudes was at the center of the biggest academic scandal of recent years. In December 2014, Michael LaCour and Donald Green published an article in the eminent journal *Science* titled "When Contact Changes Minds." The article recounted an experiment supposedly overseen by the authors, in which canvassers went door-to-door in Los Angeles, holding twenty-minute-long conversations with residents on the subject of same-sex marriage. The authors claimed that the experiment showed that "both gay and straight canvassers produced large effects [that is, convinced residents to express support for same-sex marriage] but only gay canvassers' effects persisted in 3-month, 6-month and 9-month follow-ups" (1366). These findings were widely reported in mass media, and gay rights supporters rejoiced: here was proof that brief contact with LGBT people does indeed reduce homophobia! If only it were true. Sadly, the article was retracted the following year, after other scholars showed convincingly that the experiment had never taken place, and that the data was faked (Broockman, Kalla, and Aronow 2015). Donald Green, a tenured professor at Columbia University, lost a large research grant; and Michael LaCour, whose academic career was just beginning, was denied the assistant professorship previously offered to him by Princeton University. The silver lining to this academic cloud appeared in 2016 when two of the original critics of the Green and LaCour article, David Broockman and Joshua Kalla, published the results of their own study, again in the journal *Science*. Broockman and Kalla found that a mere ten-minute conversation with a canvasser did, in fact, reduce transphobic attitudes (prejudice against transgender people), but they carefully noted that this change in attitude did not depend on whether the canvasser identified themselves as either transgender or cisgender.

Leila J. Rupp and Verta Taylor (2003) studied drag performances at a gay bar in Key West, Florida, in what is one of the most empirically robust studies of contact via a musical performance. The authors go beyond simply asserting that such performances lead to social change and actually assess whether and how drag performances affected the way audience members think. Rupp and Taylor explain that "the vast majority of the girls' [drag queens'] numbers appropriate dominant gender and sexual categories and practices, neither embracing nor rejecting them, but instead using the fact that femininity and heterosexuality are being performed by gay men to make something quite different. They do this in a variety of ways, sometimes commenting directly on sexuality and gender, sometimes challenging their apparent femaleness with their actual maleness, sometimes arousing erotic responses that do not fit into the categories of heterosexuality or homosexuality, thus confusing or exploding those categories" (124). During a drag show, as the authors point out, straight men are often savagely mocked (191); a drag performance is a rare situation when straight people are portrayed as weird and exceptional (207).

Rupp and Taylor (2003, 190) solicited audience members' responses to these performances, conducting focus groups with a total of forty audience members. They describe the spectrum of audience reactions they observed, acknowledging that "the impact [of a drag show] is ambiguous" (146). However, they report that "almost ninety percent" of the focus group members commented on how the show challenged the categories of male and female and/or gay and straight (201). Rupp and Taylor conclude that "the diverse individuals who flock to the 801 [Cabaret, the performance venue] come away with an experience that makes it a little less possible to think in a simple way about gender and sexuality" (189), an outcome that they characterize as "profoundly political" (202). They continue: "Cultural forms such as drag performances are political and . . . the fact that they are cast as entertainment may make them especially effective in reaching people and changing the ways they think" (209–10). However, Key West is an LGBT travel destination, as Rupp and Taylor acknowledge, and 70 percent of their focus group members identified as GLBT (189). These focus group members therefore may not be representative of the American population at large, in that LGBT-identified people are more likely to have prior life experiences that force them to think deeply about categories of gender and sexuality. Indeed, Rupp and Taylor's respondents may have been primed to note how the show challenged the categories of male and female, and gay and straight.

Inspired by reading the work of the psychologists and social scientists cited above, I decided to empirically test the claim that GALA choruses effect social change by influencing the attitudes of their listeners. The ethnographic findings derived from my interviews with GALA choristers (detailed earlier in this chapter) are compelling—so compelling that they deserve to be tested as rigorously as possible. In what follows I describe an experiment I conducted with the aim of answering the question of whether GALA choruses change hearts and minds when they sing. The results, as I argue below, may be of interest to GALA's leaders; I trust that they will also inform readers more deeply about the central theme of the series to which this book belongs. The next section draws from the terminology, and outlines the methodology, of a typical quantitative study; such studies are not commonly used by scholars in my field of ethnomusicology. I therefore offer this summary of my experiment with the additional intent of expanding my own field of scholarship.

Testing GALA's Central Claim: Does Listening to a GALA Chorus Change Attitudes?

Psychologist Gregory Herek has spent his career analyzing attitudes that heterosexual Americans have toward gay and lesbian people. Herek (1994, 208) created the ATLG (Attitudes toward Lesbians and Gays) Scale, which encompassed a list of twenty statements (e.g., "Lesbians just can't fit into our society") and Likert-scale responses (i.e., responses ranging from "strongly disagree" to "strongly agree"). By administering the ATLG Scale to various groups, including students at six different universities, he found it to be a reliable tool for "assessing heterosexuals' attitudes" (215). Herek urged other scholars to use the ATLG Scale to further this line of research (223), noting that its statements could be reworded or replaced over time, as needed (225). Following Herek's invitation, I created a list of twenty-nine items that incorporated five of Herek's ATLG statements about gay men. Along with so-called distractor items like "Musicians performing religious music should not receive government funding," and "I prefer instrumental music to vocal (singing) music," my questionnaire asked respondents to agree or disagree with the following ATLG items:

Item 1: Just as in other species, male homosexuality is a natural expression
of sexuality in human men.

Item 2: Male homosexuality is a perversion.

Item 3: Sex between two men is just plain wrong.

Item 4: Being gay is merely a different kind of lifestyle that should not be
condemned.

Item 5: I think gay men are disgusting.

I administered the questionnaire to a group of university students and
then took those same students to a concert presented by the Dayton Gay
Men's Chorus in December 2016. In the days after the concert, the students
filled out the same questionnaire. Each student who completed the three
components of the experiment received a twenty-dollar payment as well as
free entry to the concert (tickets for which cost twenty dollars). My goal was
to see whether the students' answers to the five ATLG questions changed in
any significant way after they attended a concert presented by a GALA chorus. I sought to find out whether the students demonstrated less antipathy
toward gay men after having heard a group of them sing for over an hour, and
thus ascertain whether listening to a typical GALA chorus provoked a
change in their attitudes.

The circumstances of the experiment provide important context for
understanding its results. First, the group of attendees I recruited constituted
a sample of convenience, as it is sometimes called. I asked university students
to participate in the experiment because they are legal adults and because I
can contact them easily, given that I am a faculty member at their institution.
It is an open secret that many findings in psychology, music cognition, and
other fields are based on surveys of university students; the published reports
make broad claims about tendencies among people at large, but the truth is
that the subjects of many of the experiments come from this one group that
is not necessarily representative of society more broadly. My experiment,
therefore, is part of a long and not especially illustrious tradition. Second, the
number of students who eventually completed all three components of my
study was smaller than I had hoped; the final total number of respondents
was thirty-one (N = 31). The concert we attended occurs every year during
the first weekend of December, which is also the time when university students are busiest with end-of-semester assignments and tests. Unfortunately,
the other two concerts on the annual calendar of the Dayton Gay Men's
Chorus take place when our university is not in session, and therefore even
fewer students would have been available had I tried to conduct the experiment at another time.

With that said, I had some reason to hope that this experiment would be helpfully suggestive in answering my question. First, my sample consisted of the kind of people GALA choruses most hope to reach, members of mainstream, middle-class, US and Canadian society who may harbor homophobic ideas. GALA leaders are well aware that their concerts can consist of "singing to the choir" because their audiences are heavily populated by members of the LGBT community. In fact, their belief that a significant portion of their audience consists of people who already support them and their mission was confirmed by a recent large-scale study. Chorus America compared GALA choruses' audiences to audiences of other community choirs and found that GALA concerts are twice as likely to attract people who identify themselves as "friend of singer"; in addition, GALA concerts are less likely than other community choir concerts to attract listeners who say they have "no relationship" to anyone in the choir (Brown et al. 2016, 23). While GALA singers and artistic directors deeply appreciate their dedicated supporters, especially the gay men and lesbian women of their cities, they remain focused on their mission of "changing hearts and minds." They therefore aim to sing to those whose hearts and minds need to be changed. The group of university students who participated in my experiment were at least potentially such listeners.

Second, the participants in the experiment were students at a private Catholic university. Many of the students come from Catholic families, and expressions of Catholic faith are common on our campus. Mass is celebrated multiple times per day, for example, and students often mention their church or parachurch involvement during class discussions. Because the Catholic Church still condemns persons with homosexual inclinations as "objectively disordered" (Holy See n.d.), it was reasonable to believe that some significant percentage of the students at my university—represented randomly in my sample—would hold anti-LGBT views (Holy See n.d.). In other words, by recruiting students from a Catholic institution, I was recruiting participants whose attitudes might be of the sort that GALA choruses seek to change through song.

Third, the concert that the students attended, shortly after they first expressed their opinions on the questionnaire, occurred just four weeks after the election of Donald Trump to the presidency of the United States. The county where our university is located—Montgomery County in Ohio—is a bellwether county, meaning that the divide among county voters in presidential elections reliably reflects the national electorate. In 2016, county voters chose the Republican Donald Trump by a slim majority (48.4 percent voted for Trump, and 47.1 percent chose the Democratic candidate, Hillary Clinton) (Politico 2016). The vote revealed a right-wing, populist turn in the

local electorate, which had chosen Democrat Barack Obama in the two previous elections. In the weeks leading up to the election, students demonstrated their voting intentions by posting signs in their dorm windows, wearing campaign T-shirts, and so on. Though I made no systematic attempt to
count this kind of evidence, I was fascinated to see how much visible support
Donald Trump received on my campus. Like many self-identified progres-
sives, I had assumed that Trump would be an unacceptable choice for educated cosmopolitans, and that voting for Clinton was a foregone conclusion
for voters on my—indeed on any—university campus. The election of
Trump, and the willingness of my students to publicly proclaim their support for him, revealed that significant numbers of them were willing to
endorse a candidate who repeatedly made misogynistic and racist
statements.

Nadine Hubbs (2014, 6) has argued that expressing pro-gay sentiments
has become part and parcel of middle-class American identity in the
twenty-first century. Signifying support for LGBT people, if not causes,
has become a way for White middle-class Americans to distinguish themselves from lower-class "rednecks," the regressive White people who are
still—supposedly—openly homophobic. Hubbs goes on to make a more
intricate argument about White middle-class disdain for country music,
the music that presumably represents the antigay rednecks. But her first
assertion is what concerns us here: White middle-class people have undergone a sea change in this regard during the past twenty years. In such circles, and especially among those who hold university degrees, it is now
unacceptable to say that LGBT people should not be hired for certain jobs,
should not be allowed to marry each other, and so on. Therefore, I worried
that asking White university students (who constituted the large majority
of my sample) about homophobic statements would be a nonstarter. On
the other hand, many of them had voted for Donald Trump, whose candi-
dacy was predicated on returning the country to some mythical past in
which White heteronormativity reigned supreme. If students at my university did indeed hold anti-LGBT views, they would be most likely to express
them in the weeks shortly after a representative of those views had tri-
umphed in the polls.

Results of the Experiment

Fifty-four students completed the first survey and attended the Dayton Gay
Men's Chorus concert. However, only thirty-five of them completed the

second survey, and only thirty-one of those provided usable data. Of these thirty-one, fourteen identified themselves as male, and seventeen as female. In terms of religious commitments, twenty-three identified themselves as Catholic, four as agnostic, one as atheist, and three as "other." As for their political leanings, twelve stated that they were moderates, ten liberal, five conservative, three independent, and one progressive. Twenty-nine participants claimed to be heterosexual or straight, one was asexual, and one was bisexual. The participants rated their agreement on twenty-nine statements, or items; only responses to the five ATLG items included in the survey are analyzed below. Participants responded to each statement by selecting one of five options (strongly agree, agree, neither agree nor disagree, disagree, or strongly disagree). For the purpose of statistical analysis, statements were converted to numbers using the following scale: strongly agree was equal to 5, agree to 4, neither agree nor disagree to 3, disagree to 2, and strongly disagree to 1.

In general, a comparison of these participants' ratings, as recorded on the questionnaire both before and after attending the concert, showed little or no change in their attitudes toward gay men. This finding was confirmed by a number of statistical tests. First, I conducted a paired t-test to examine how participants' raw scores (ratings of agreement/disagreement with Herek's five ATLG items) changed after attending the concert. For this test, I calculated the average rating for each item at each stage (i.e., for each item I calculated two average ratings, one from before the concert and one from after it). I then conducted an item-by-item comparison of these ratings from before and after the concert in order to determine whether the group demonstrated any significant shift in its collective tendency to agree or disagree with the ATLG items. There were no significant differences between the participants' attitudes before and after hearing a group of gay men sing, and, in fact, the averages revealed that the participants had strongly positive attitudes toward gay men before they attended the concert. For example, the most common answer to item 1 ("Just as in other species, male homosexuality is a natural expression of sexuality in human men"), on both sets of questionnaires, was "strongly agree." For item 2 ("Male homosexuality is a perversion"), the average rating before the concert was 1.90 with a relatively low standard deviation (SD) of 1.14, and the average rating afterward was 1.61 (SD = 0.99), showing that at both times the group as a whole strongly disagreed with that statement. This pattern persisted for items 3, 4, and 5. Because the participants had such marked pro-gay attitudes before the experiment began, there was not much room for a demonstration of increased approval of gay men and of male homosexuality in their average ratings after the concert.

In order to normalize individual participants' ratings in relation to each item's average rating, I then converted each participant's survey ratings to z-scores. Z scores let us see how much any individual result deviates from a mean (an average), and they can be positive, negative, or zero in value, indicating, respectively, that an individual's response was higher, lower, or equal in value to the mean response.[7] The z-scores for each participant's before and after surveys were calculated separately. Paired t-tests of z-scores for all thirty-one participants showed no significant differences in the ratings before and after the concert for items 1, 3, 4, and 5. However, the results of this test on item 2 proved an exception: the mean z-score rating on this item ("Male homosexuality is a perversion") changed significantly after the concert. The mean z-score rating before the concert was -1.049 (SD = 0.741), and after was -1.366 (SD = 0.661); in other words, the average rating tended toward disagreeing more strongly with the statement after the concert. This difference was highly statistically significant ($p = 0.0067$).

I then ran one-way ANOVAs, or analyses of variance, to determine the effect of religion and politics on participants' ratings for each item. As a statistical method, ANOVA is useful for comparing results across multiple factors, allowing us to hypothesize about these factors' effect on the results. For example, we might hypothesize that religion was a factor in how respondents answered the questions. ANOVA allows us to test such hypotheses by comparing the mean for, say, Catholic and non-Catholic respondents; a large variance in mean would indicate that religion was indeed a factor. If a large variance is found, additional tests such as paired t-tests must be conducted to determine the reason for the variance; ANOVAs simply reveal that a factor had an effect, not what that effect was. Four religious groups were identified; the number of Catholic participants was much larger than the number in any other religious group. ANOVA testing found no significant effect of religion on participants' ratings for any ATLG items; that is, participants' commitment to Catholicism, or to some other religious belief, did not seem to influence their ratings. However, one-way ANOVA testing on the influence of political perspectives on ATLG ratings did show a significant effect of politics on answers to item 3 ("Sex between two men is just plain wrong"). Based on this finding, I ran a paired t-test for each political group, comparing ratings before and after the concert for all five ATLG questions. Here again, the general pattern continued: the various political groups who participated in the study demonstrated largely positive attitudes toward gay men and male homosexuality in their ratings, and their ratings did not change significantly after the Dayton Gay Men's Chorus concert. Self-identified conservatives, for example, demonstrated no significant change in their answers for items 1, 2, 3, and 4. However, their results for item 5 ("I think gay men are disgusting") were intriguing: their average z-score rating was -0.557 before the concert, and -1.168 after it, demonstrating a statistically significant change (p = 0.044). This finding indicates that conservatives agreed less with the "disgusting" statement after the concert. Furthermore, political moderates demonstrated a statistically significant change (p = 0.035) in their ratings on item 2 ("Male homosexuality is a perversion") before and after the concert. Moderates' mean z-score rating on this item before the concert was -0.12, and after the concert it was -1.60, meaning that they moved significantly toward disagreeing with the "perversion" statement after attending the concert.

The small numbers of people in each political group in my experiment—five conservatives and twelve moderates—mean that we cannot draw any large conclusions about conservative- or moderate-minded people in general. However, GALA insiders could rightly choose to interpret the results of the z-score comparisons as validation of their success in "changing hearts and minds." Both conservative and moderate students, responding to a questionnaire at a moment when political conservatism was in the ascendant, provided evidence that they nevertheless viewed gay men generally positively. In addition, they viewed gay men even more positively—disagreeing more strongly with negative statements about male homosexuality—after attending a concert performed by a GALA chorus. It is possible that attending the concert made these individuals reconsider their ideas about gay men and male homosexuality even in the midst of a charged political climate. Moreover, the change in conservatives' and moderates' ratings appears to be what provoked the overall statistical shift on item 2, the highly significant change toward more profound group disagreement with the statement "male homosexuality is a perversion." In this limited experiment, the data suggests that audience members shifted slightly toward a more strongly pro-LGBT attitude subsequent to attending a GALA performance.

Students who participated in the study were invited to share written comments on the experience after completing the questionnaire for the second time. Overall, the comments were strongly positive, stating that the students found the concert "enjoyable" and "fun," and thought that the singers were "talented" and demonstrated "great showmanship." Nine students wrote that they appreciated the opportunity to participate in the experiment, and that they would like to attend future concerts presented by the Dayton Gay Men's Chorus. The comments of participant number 28 summarized the appeal of this GALA chorus's integrationist approach (see chapter 7): "I really enjoyed the choir, I thought they were funny and very talented! I loved that they incorporated a song for Military Service members and anyone else that wouldn't make it home for Christmas. I would definitely see them again!"

No comments gave any evidence that participants had consciously changed their attitudes toward LGBT people as a result of attending the concert, although clearly the event raised some basic awareness: "The concert was pretty interesting. I didn't know the gay men's chorus was a thing so this project taught me that" (participant number 16). One student explained directly that "I don't think going to this concert changed my opinions on the questions in the survey. I answered all questions pretty much the exact same" (participant number 24). Comments from two participants showed just how intractable religiously-based objections to homosexuality can be. "I thought the chorus that we attended was interesting, but it did not change my perspective at all about homosexuality. My stance is from a religious viewpoint and I disagree with the practice of homosexuality. However this does not change how I would treat someone who is gay. I enjoyed the singing, but was somewhat uncomfortable with the flamboyance of the singers" (participant number 19). Similarly, participant number 11 wrote, "I thought the DGMC was very talented and their music sounded very well executed. However, since I believe homosexuality is a sin, them openly being proud of a sin seemed very wrong to me. I think people need to realize that most Catholics, as myself, view homosexuality as a sin and immoral but we don't condemn people because of their sin. Also, this is America and we are all free to believe and do what we want so the government should not be interfering in our private lives telling certain people what they can and cannot do based on beliefs/actions."

In sum, most of the students' written comments mirrored the patterns revealed by their responses to the questionnaires. As a group they showed remarkably positive attitudes toward gay men and male homosexuality. Perhaps because of this initial level of acceptance, there was little change in their attitudes after attending a gay men's chorus concert. A statistically significant shift in the amount of disagreement with antigay statements did emerge, but this shift was not reflected in any written comments. Indeed, some students explicitly denied changing their attitudes despite having enjoyed the concert. One inference that can be drawn is that if a GALA chorus concert does succeed in slightly influencing listeners' views, the listeners do not necessarily become consciously aware of their own changed attitudes.

Fostering Social Change by Coming Out

So far in this chapter we have seen that GALA choristers argue that their concertizing creates social change by transforming the attitudes of audience members, although they offer only anecdotal evidence for this claim. Further, my own experiment suggested that GALA insiders are correct in their belief, but its small sample size limits any definitive claims I might make. In this final section of the chapter, I take the most optimistic view, arguing that participation in a GALA chorus is often part of a chorister's, and sometimes an artistic director's, coming out process. By coming out, individuals foster increased tolerance for LGBT people. GALA ensembles, therefore, are agents for progressive social change, just as they claim to be.

Coming out has been the subject of much academic study. As A. C. Liang (1997, 291) notes, "there is no central definition of coming out." However, we know that the common understanding of coming out changed dramatically during the course of the twentieth century (Murray 2010, 180). Before the Stonewall riots of 1969, being "out" was equivalent to what we would call "closeted" today: at that time, coming out meant going to gay bars and revealing one's sexual orientation only to a few others who also attended gay bars (Weston 1991, 44). Gilbert Herdt's (1992a, 29) definition is one that most of my GALA interlocutors would agree with: coming out "refers to a single act whereby someone declares his or her identity as 'homosexual' or 'gay' or 'lesbian' to family, friends, or coworkers who assumed the person to be 'straight' or 'heterosexual.' The declaration may occur in public, private, or secret contexts, and its emphasis is on a single attribute: being 'homosexual.'" As helpful as this definition is, it neglects the reality that many researchers have observed, which is that coming out is not a single act, but a process. Psychologists have neatly categorized this process into various stages (Lynch 1992, 171).

Liang (1997, 219) explains that any instance of coming out includes at least one of three components. First, individuals must come out to themselves, acknowledging to themselves that they are gay or lesbian. Second, they must also speak of this fact to others; individuals often find it necessary to come out to others dozens of times, to various people, in their lives. Indeed, making this declaration of one's homosexuality must be accomplished so many times in an adult's life that the author of a 2014 study says that we should conceptualize coming out not as a process, but rather as a "career" (Guittar 2014, 124–25). Finally, coming out includes participation in a series of acts that are self-designated as lesbian or gay acts (Liang 1997, 291). Among these acts are the rehearsals, concerts, and social gatherings of a GALA chorus.

There are some critiques of coming out, and particularly of how it has become centrally important to both homosexual and heterosexual people's understanding of what it means to be gay. Frank Browning (1998, 105) points out that many gay men, in particular, "cherish and [are] aroused by the curtains of secrecy that surround sex," and that coming out effectively destroys this erotic secrecy. However, the large majority of gay and queer writers from across the political spectrum claim, and ethnographic studies show, that coming out is supremely important in LGBT life today. Bruce Bawer (1993, 241) says it is "a vital act"; Gilbert Herdt and Andrew Boxer (1992, 14) say it is "the most significant developmental event" in the life of an LGBT person); Donald Boisvert (2000, 41) echoes Herdt and Boxer, calling coming out "arguably the most significant moment in a gay man's life" and "a moment of intense spiritual revelation." Kath Weston (1991, 43), in a groundbreaking study of gay and lesbian families, wrote that "aside from AIDS, no other topic encountered during my fieldwork generated an emotional response comparable to coming out to blood (or adoptive) relatives."

GALA's leaders and singers agree with this sentiment, and they demonstrate their valuing of the coming out process by singing a variety of songs about it, some humorous and some deeply moving. One of the most humorous is the contrafactum "Coming Out On Christmas," the lyrics of which are quoted in chapter 5 of this book. Another coming out song that has been performed repeatedly is "Michael's Letter to Mama," composed by David Maddux, with lyrics by Armistead Maupin. The words express the love and trepidation of an adult man telling his parents that "your own child is homosexual." A 2014 presentation of this song from the Philadelphia Gay Men's Chorus is archived on YouTube. This video shows one of the innovative performance practices that GALA choruses increasingly deploy: photos of choristers with their own mothers and fathers were projected on a screen behind the singers, reinforcing the idea that LGBT children can have ongoing loving relationships with their parents after they come out (Saitschenko 2014).

Coming Out and Coming In to a GALA Chorus

For many GALA insiders, becoming involved with GALA in some way has been an important part of their coming out process. It seems to be a common experience for GALA singers, and to a lesser extent, GALA artistic directors. Drew Kotchan referenced the classic metaphor of the closet when he said that joining the Calgary Men's Chorus "helped usher me out" (interview, May 31, 2016). As David Mcintyre, composer and artistic director of the Prairie Pride Chorus in Regina, Saskatchewan, summarized it, "Getting involved in GALA, that's part of my coming out story" (interview, July 31, 2012). Marvin E. Latimer's (2008, 30) study of singers in the Heartland Men's Chorus of Kansas City, Missouri, emphasizes the same point: "Participation in this chorus apparently . . . facilitates the coming out process by affording these choristers a safe environment where they are free to explore their identity, in a positive and affirming way, through a kinship with other like-minded people."

Among those GALA insiders who say that becoming involved with a GALA chorus provided a way for them to come out, we can identify three different points in their "careers" that these participants come out. These three points, or moments in time, correspond with the three essential components of coming out identified by Liang (1997, 291). First, in rare cases, coming out to oneself coincides with participating in a GALA chorus. Eric Helmuth, who at various times has worked as a composer, accompanist, and singer in Boston-based GALA choruses, recalls a specific evening in the early 1990s when, he said, he "understood that what I had always longed for was right, not sinful, not dirty . . . that was the moment when I truly realized what it meant to come out" (interview, August 10, 2012). This moment occurred on the very night that Eric stayed up late to compose a song titled "Finally Here," which has since become an anthem for GALA choruses.

Second, and more commonly, singers begin singing with a local gay-identified chorus as a way to make a public declaration about their own sexual identity. Drew Kotchan explained it this way: "Even though I'm not all out, all over, joining the choir was how I came out. Because people know that most of the guys in the Calgary Men's Chorus are gay, so they'll assume it anyway" (interview, July 27, 2013). Gianluca Ragazzini, in talking about joining Tone Cluster, a GALA chorus in Ottawa, Ontario, said: "It was the time in my life when I was ready to come out completely, and performing with the choir (after rehearsing for months) was the trigger" (interview, March 5, 2012). Tom Fortuna said that "The reason I came out to my kids was the chorus." Fortuna's impetus to tell his grown son and daughter that the North Coast Men's Chorus in Cleveland, Ohio, was actually a gay organization, and that he himself was gay, was that the chorus was going to be featured in the local newspaper the next day; he says that he and his children are now "closer than close" (interview, October 16, 2014).

GALA artistic directors also find that taking a job with a GALA chorus is, in effect, making a public statement about their sexual identity. Ben Riggs, the artistic director of the Twin Cities Gay Men's Chorus in Minneapolis, Minnesota, said, "It's liberating. I'm the only person at the American Choral Directors' Association convention who, when I introduce myself and say the name of the chorus, I out myself" (interview, August 15, 2013). Regina Carlow, the former director of the Lesbian and Gay Chorus of Washington, DC, expressed gratitude for this possibility; she explained that she was an "out lesbian" beginning at the age of nineteen, but that she had trouble saying this truth aloud. "I learned to say the word lesbian because of that chorus. . . . it was so powerful for me to be able to say 'I am the director of the Lesbian and Gay Chorus of Washington.' The chorus allowed me to come out and say who I am" (interview, September 15, 2012).

Third, some GALA singers join their local chorus shortly after they first come out, as a way to affiliate themselves with other LGBT people. For example, Anne Bush told me that soon after she came out, she joined the Seattle Women's Chorus in order to "connect with the gay community" (interview, August 1, 2012). Eric Unhold said that he joined the North Coast Men's Chorus at age twenty-five, "when I was just coming out. . . . I wanted to have a positive, uplifting, supportive way to meet other gay people" (interview, October 13, 2014). And this pattern is one reason, I suspect, that the name of a GALA chorus can be such a contentious issue (as I explain in more detail in chapter 6). Choristers at various stages of the coming out process value the plausible deniability of a nongay name like Cincinnati Men's Chorus or Tone Cluster; they can affiliate themselves with a group of LGBT people and yet not be completely out when they speak about their chorus participation. Others rejoice in the opportunity to publicly claim their homosexual identity, and therefore they want to talk about their "gay" or "lesbian" chorus. Suffice it to say, to be affiliated with a so-named gay or lesbian chorus is to be fully out when one speaks of it. And this explains why, in 2006, when the Sacramento Men's Chorus changed its name to the Sacramento *Gay* Men's Chorus, the change was characterized by the artistic director and the member handbook as "coming out of the closet" (Paul Jones, interview, January 7, 2011; also member handbook for 2011–12).

The Significance of Coming Out

Theorists explain that the act of coming out is deeply consequential because it challenges the hearers of the coming out statement to think differently (Bawer 1993, 240; Browning 1998, 204). Eve Kosofsky-Sedgwick (1990, 81–82) points out that when a person self-identifies as homosexual, their interactions with their own family members may become strained, as their relatives may feel that their own reputations have been damaged. Furthermore, the open secret that has been so comfortably ignored in a newly out person's other relationships must now become explicit, and the larger system of patriarchy—based on conventional understandings of what it means to be a man or a woman—is subverted by the declaration of same-sex attraction.

Coming out forces hearers to think differently about themselves, their past actions, and the society in which they live.

Coming out, then, implicates not only the LGBT people who come out, but also all people who witness their coming out. The witnesses may react negatively or positively to the forced change in their own thinking; however, the empirical research to date shows that reactions are most often positive. Coming out is, in effect, a way of forging contact between an LGBT person and their straight interlocutor. As we saw earlier in this chapter, the contact hypothesis has been tested repeatedly, and scholars have found that contact with an LGBT person reliably reduces homophobia among straight people. As L. Marvin Overby and Jay Barth (2002, 434) put it, the verification of the contact hypothesis makes coming out an ever more urgent necessity: "As gay men and lesbians become more candid about their sexual orientation and interact more openly with heterosexuals, the collective public affective attitude toward homosexuals should become more positive and support for greater civil rights should increase" (456).

GALA choristers agree with these scholarly findings; they celebrate the fact that participation in a GALA chorus provides choristers a way to come out. These choristers understand that by coming out—by naming themselves as LGBT during their concert performances—they create contact with audience members and thereby foster positive attitudes toward LGBT people more generally. Coming out by performing with a GALA chorus is, as singers commonly claim, an important way of pursuing their social change mission. And most crucially, performing with a GALA chorus allows LGBT singers to come out in a group setting, among other people. Allen Kimbrough of the Dayton Gay Men's Chorus was a mental health professional with a good understanding of human psychology. He explained: "The reason that people are able to come out publicly or assume a gay public identity when singing in the chorus is because they are doing it in a group; few people would ever stand onstage alone and say 'I am gay' to their community. In a group there is safety and unity, a sense of doing this with your brothers" (interview, January 7, 2011).

Social scientists, too, underline the importance of a group context. One of the most powerful critiques of the contact hypothesis is that contact with an individual may indeed promote tolerance of that specific individual, but that this changed attitude is not generalizable; respect and love for one particular gay person does not always translate into support for all LGBT people and the notion of gay rights (Simon 1998, 75). Arlene Stein's (2001, 107–28) illuminating ethnography of a small town in Oregon reveals this problem: evangelical Christians there usually made positive comments about the one or two gay men or lesbian women whom they knew personally, but they maintained an anti–gay rights stance all the same. Therefore, the social science research concludes that "contact with homosexuals may work best in reducing prejudice when heterosexuals interact with *multiple* lesbians and gay men" (Simon 1998, 77, emphasis added). GALA choruses provide exactly this opportunity: they allow audience members to see and hear dozens, even hundreds, of men or women proclaiming their LGBT identity at the same time. All of the choristers sing their coming out songs together, expressing the same message at the same moment. The audience is confronted with the reality that LGBT people are not scattered, deviant individuals, but rather participants in a large and unified group.

Conclusion

GALA choruses are vehicles through which singers come out, making a declaration of LGBT identity and thereby challenging the thinking of potentially homophobic audience members. In joining a GALA chorus, choristers publicly link themselves to an organization that is broadly understood to be populated by LGBT people, and—in many cases—is actually named lesbian or gay. And while singing repertoire with lyrics that describe same-sex love, they make contact with their listeners; as Angela Simon (1998, 74) would have it, through these performances GALA choristers create "positive interpersonal experiences" with choral music audiences. GALA singers and leaders work hard to create aesthetically pleasing and artistically excellent concert performances (as we saw in chapters 1 and 5). They do so specifically because they are concerned with presenting an appealing image of LGBT people to those who hear them sing. By coming out, via joining a local chorus, and then by creating this positive contact, GALA choristers foster positive attitudes toward LGBT people among the general population; as they would say, they "change the world through song."

Notes

Introduction

1. LGBT refers to lesbian, gay, bisexual, and transgender people. The Gay and Lesbian Association of Choruses (GALA Choruses) has member choruses in other countries, but the large majority of them are in Canada and the United States. The interlocutors cited in this book are participants in choruses located in these two countries.

2. Field notes, January 7, 2011.

3. Field notes, January 28, 2018.

4. Field notes, February 5, 2018.

5. Field notes, September 23, 2011.

Chapter 1

1. A cutoff is a moment in a song when all singers stop singing, following the conductor's gesture.

2. Field notes, November 15, 2010.

3. Field notes, October 25, 2010.

4. Jason Schuler, interview, September 16, 2010; Tara Napoleone-Clifford, interview, June 30, 2011; Alyssa Stone, interview, June 25, 2012; Cory Barrett, interview, December 12, 2016.

5. Field notes, January 7, 2011.

6. Field notes, September 24, 2011.

7. Field notes, January 7, 2011.

8. See also Janice L. Kinney (2010, 96–98) on excessive talking during women's chorus rehearsals, and the division of singers into groups of "talkers" and "ssshers."

9. Field notes, May 31, 2016.

10. Field notes, January 7, 2011.

11. Field notes, January 8, 2011.

12. Field notes, January 7, 2011.

13. My contention here directly contradicts that of Paul Attinello (1994, 330). Conducting his study in the early 1990s, Attinello found that gay men's chorus singers were generally "very negative" about the idea of having a straight artistic director, and he theo-

rized that these gay men did not want to have a straight "master." Straight artistic directors represented, in Attinello's view, the straight world that openly gay men contest. GALA choruses today hire straight conductors, both men and women, as a matter of routine. It seems, however, that the majority of GALA's artistic leaders still identify as gay or lesbian.

14. According to its website, the Sister Singers Network "is a cooperative web of feminist choruses and ensembles, composers, arrangers, and individual singers working together to support and enrich the women's choral movement" (Sister Singers Network n.d.).

15. Field notes, January 7, 2011. The LGBA is an international group of concert and marching bands; see Lesbian and Gay Band Association (n.d.).

16. Musicianship in this context means the ability to sing music notated in Western staff notation. It is sometimes also called sight-singing or sight-reading music.

17. For an incomplete listing and analysis of works commissioned by GALA, see Coyle (2006) and Mensel (2007).

18. For a rare published statement about the "quality of performance" of gay men's choruses, see Trame (1993, 27).

19. For example, Miguel Felipe of the Maine Gay Men's Chorus voiced this opinion (interview, July 31, 2013).

20. See, for example, Triangle Gay Men's Chorus (n.d.), Turtle Creek Chorale (n.d.), and Vox Femina Los Angeles (n.d.).

21. I heard references to these events from numerous other people interviewed for this book. See also New York City Gay Men's Chorus (n.d.).

22. Field notes, January 7, 2011.

23. Field notes, January 7, 2011.

24. These individuals include Miguel Felipe (interview, July 31, 2013), Ron Casola (interview, September 23, 2011), and Ben Riggs (interview, August 15, 2013).

25. These events were reported by David Hodgkins (interview, April 9, 2014), Eric Helmuth (interview, August 10, 2012), and Fred Poland (interview, June 16, 2011).

26. Field notes, July 12, 2012; John Quillin, interview, January 7, 2011.

27. Field notes, January 7, 2011; Stan Hill, interview, September 24, 2011.

28. Similar concerns were voiced by Carol Sirianni (interview, October 9, 2011) and Adam Adler (interview, July 11, 2014).

29. For example, after nineteen years of service, David Mcintyre was asked to resign from his position at the Canadian Bible College when he revealed that he was gay. "That was a momentous time for me," he recalled soberly (interview, July 31, 2012).

30. Field notes, November 15, 2010.

31. Tim Seelig, interview, September 15, 2011; Eve Campbell, interview, January 7, 2011. A lively discussion concerning this incident was conducted on the ACDA listserv in 1996. Here the varying attitudes of ACDA members were clearly demonstrated: one message compared gay choruses to Satanists, but others roundly condemned the First Baptist Church for discriminating against the Turtle Creek Chorale and the Dallas Women's Chorus.

32. Field notes, July 9, 2012.

33. Field notes, July 7, 2012.

34. Field notes, July 2, 2016.

35. Field notes, July 10, 2012.

36. Yelton Rhodes was founded by a composer quoted in this book, Roger Bourland. In 1992, after writing a piece called *Hidden Legacies* on commission for the Gay Men's Chorus of Los Angeles, Bourland went around the United States hearing various GALA choruses perform this work. It was during this tour that Bourland recognized the need for a publisher of "gay and lesbian music" (interview, December 10, 2012).

37. Field notes, January 8, 2011.

38. Ben Riggs, one of the 2012 Festival organizers, recalled the discussion I heard in 2011; he said that the idea of adjudication was only raised as a "somewhat controversial possibility." Clearly the idea was abandoned (interview, August 15, 2013).

39. Field notes, January 8, 2011.

40. Field notes, July 9, 2012.

41. Field notes, July 11, 2012.

42. People who identified themselves as differencz, Rick Aiello, and JR Russ all uploaded video of the event to YouTube; for one video see Aiello (2012).

43. Field notes, July 7, 2012.

Chapter 2

1. Field notes, September 23, 2011.

2. Steve Milloy described the fees as small (interview, July 16, 2011); Diane Benjamin indicated that services were unpaid (interview, February 10, 2012).

3. Matthew Gillespie, who sings tenor in the Calgary Men's Chorus, also volunteers as the secretary and the casino (fundraiser) committee chair for the chorus and said that this work is also motivating for him: "I enjoy organizing. I like making things smoother and easier for other people. It's a bit of a rush for me" (interview, January 5, 2013).

4. This view was voiced by, for example, Kaeden Kass (interview, February 9, 2017), Anne Bush (interview, August 1, 2012), Mikal Rasheed (interview, February 9, 2017), and Tara Napoleone-Clifford (interview, June 30, 2011).

5. This view was voiced by, for example, Derek Smith (interview, September 2, 2016), David Mcintyre (interview, July 31, 2012), Neka Zimmerman (interview, December 19, 2016), and Alyssa Stone (interview, June 25, 2012).

6. Similar sentiments were voiced by Steven Hankle (interview, July 5, 2018), Jeannie Holton (interview, January 15, 2013), and Beth Fox (interview, August 15, 2012).

7. Other women who voiced this sentiment included Jeannie Holton (interview, January 15, 2013) and Shannon Wyss (interview, May 23, 2012).

8. In *Far from the Tree*, Andrew Solomon (2012, 2) points out that we often understand identities to be transmitted from parent to child, from one generation to the next. Ethnicity, language, and religion constitute "significant bases for identity" that are "vertically transmitted," as Solomon puts it, using a descriptor and examples that are reminiscent of Shelemay's idea of descent. Solomon contrasts vertical identities with horizontal identities—that is, identities that are acquired from a peer group. He specifies: "Being gay is a horizontal identity; most gay kids are born to straight parents, and while their sexuality is not determined by their peers, they learn gay identity by observing and participating in a sub-culture outside the family."

9. Reverb, the community outreach and engagement group of Reveille Men's Chorus, debuted in 2015.

10. Joe Nadeau, interview, February 20, 2011; Kaeden Kass, interview, February 9, 2016.

11. In Christopher Carrington's (1999, 112) study of "lesbigay" families, he found that lesbian and gay people alike engaged in "kinwork" with their friends and acquaintances in order to create their families. Kinwork included sharing holiday meals, providing care when others are ill, visiting patients at the hospital, loaning money, and accompanying others during emotionally difficult times, such as taking a pet to a veterinarian.

12. Field notes, July 6, 2016. Interviewees also used terms related to family, including sisterhood (e.g., Katie Eadie, interview, August 10, 2016) and brotherhood (e.g., Brandon Dowdy, interview, August 11, 2012).

13. Interlocutors who voiced this sentiment included Linda Krasienko (interview, November 25, 2014) and Diane Benjamin (interview, February 10, 2012).

14. Field notes, September 24, 2011.

15. Field notes, September 24, 2011.

16. Field notes, July 10, 2012.

17. Field notes, July 7, 2012.

18. Field notes, July 11, 2012.

19. Seelig conveyed this position in an interview (September 15, 2011).

20. Field notes, July 8, 2012 (Rainbow Women's Chorus); July 10, 2012 (ANNA Crusis); and August 13, 2014 (Windsong).

21. Field notes, July 10, 2012.

22. Field notes, July 10, 2012.

23. Interlocutors who mentioned such a committee included Manny Agon (interview, January 17, 2013), Brendon Dowdy (interview, August 11, 2012), and Derek Smith (interview, September 2, 2016).

24. Field notes, July 2, 2016.

Chapter 3

1. Chorus America highlighted the importance of Mozart's *Requiem* in a study that it conducted into choral music audiences. Surveying the audience at a performance of *Requiem*, the researchers found that 80 percent of respondents attended in order to "revisit a familiar work" (Brown et al. 2016, 26). Clearly, this work in particular has the power to draw an audience.

2. Steve Milloy, one of GALA's few African American artistic directors, recalled that the membership of the Cincinnati Men's Chorus was approximately 50 percent men of color in the early 2000s. This percentage has since dropped and would have been an exception at the time (interview, July 16, 2011).

3. Answers for five singers were not captured in my interview notes. After 2012, I made a concerted effort to contact women, people of color, and transgender singers because they were so underrepresented in my sample at that point. Therefore they may have inadvertently become overrepresented in my interview sample.

4. Tim Seelig also touched on this story (interview, September 15, 2011).

5. I emailed the current artistic director of Columbus Gay Men's Chorus, and the chorus's general email address, to ask whether the chorus has an archived copy of their 1992 Festival program so that I could confirm Benjamin's account. I did not receive a

response. There are a number of songs that speak about Christopher Columbus's voyage. The song with lyrics that most closely correspond to Diane Benjamin's recollection is Lou Monte's "Mr. Columbus, Turn the Ship Around."

6. This view was voiced by, for example, Aditya Adiredja (interview, December 20, 2016; field notes, July 3, 2016) and Maria-Elena Grant (interview, October 29, 2011).

7. Linda Krasienko voiced a similar sentiment (interview, November 25, 2014).

8. Field notes, July 3, 2016. For younger people in the United States, the perception that one cannot embrace both a non-White ethnic identity and an LGBT identity may be changing: a 2012 Gallup poll shows that "nonwhite individuals are more likely [than White individuals] to identify as LGBT" (Gates and Newport 2012).

9. As we have seen throughout this book, "women's chorus" is code for a community choir in which a large proportion of the singers are lesbians; similarly, "women's music" is code for lesbian music.

10. Douglas Harrison (2012, 137) reveals that White Christian gay men also have a religiously-affiliated musical scene in which they can and do participate while keeping their same-sex desires "an open secret"—that is, southern gospel music. In fact, Harrison contends that gay men are essential to the southern gospel music industry: "The most culturally fundamentalist sacred music in evangelicalism could hardly be said to exist without queers and their contributions as fans, songwriters, performers, producers, players and industry executives" (140).

11. One such statement of concern is archived online: "In 2012. . . . I attended my first GALA Festival, the gathering of gay and lesbian choirs from all over the country that meets every 4 years, and discovered, much to my dismay, that there was not a transgender presence anywhere at the 5 day event. Among the 54 choirs that performed, there wasn't a single trans chorus, in the evening production 'celebrating GALA's LGBT history' there was no mention of transgender people, and, although there was a Festival Men's Chorus, Women's Chorus, and Mixed Chorus, there was no Festival Trans Chorus. I ended up setting up a table with a homemade sign outside Boettcher Concert Hall to gather trans folks attending the Festival and determined that in 2016 the erasure of trans singers would not happen again" (Bullington n.d.).

12. The 2016 Festival organizers had difficulty adhering to their own recommended use of language: the concert program titled one concert block "Women's Voices Rising" rather than referring to SSAA (soprano-soprano-alto-alto) choruses or treble choruses.

13. I was honored to be invited to attend the People of Color Gathering even though I identify as White.

14. "Glory" was composed by African American composers John Legend, Common, and Rhymefest.

15. The Gullah, or Gullah Geechee, are an African American ethnic group descended from enslaved people who inhabited the barrier islands of Georgia and the Carolinas. Although this workshop ultimately failed to communicate much about Gullah culture, its inclusion in the Festival program was a clear nod to Black American identities and cultural achievements.

16. Field notes, September 24, 2011. This wording (i.e., "ethnic") is common in the White-dominated choral music scene; the American Choral Directors Association, one of the most influential professional associations of choral conductors, uses "ethnic and multicultural" as the designation for one kind of choral repertoire. This designation is an excellent example of a marked term. The unmarked choral repertoire (all that is not "eth-

nic and multicultural") is presumed to be normal/natural/standard, drawing "no attention to its invisibly privileged status" (Chandler 2017, 112). In the United States and
Canada, the choral music repertoire— and conductors' perceptions of it—replicates the
hierarchy more broadly present in society. Choral music that is associated with White
people is normative, whereas "ethnic" music is exceptional and a deviation from the
norm.

17. National Public Radio reported on the flurry of new transgender choruses on May
21, 2016 (Janovy 2016).

18. Writing about transgender choruses affiliated with GALA Choruses, Sam Bullington identifies a chorus called TransVoices, which was located in Minneapolis, Minnesota, and was—according to Bullington—the second-ever transgender choir on the
planet" (Bullington n.d.).

19. Field notes, July 4, 2016.

20. Words used to describe people who identify with a gender other than the one
assigned to them at birth have quickly evolved in the twenty-first century. I use *transgender* here because it was the word I heard most often during my research. However, one of
my interlocutors referred to herself as a "transsexual woman," and others used *trans*, as in,
"I'm trans." David Valentine's 2007 ethnographic study of three different groups of people who in earlier days might have been called transvestites (men who dress as women on
certain occasions) explains that the members of these groups usually called themselves
gay, cross-dressers, and drag queens. In fact, although Valentine himself titled his book
Imagining Transgender, and by implication included all his informants in this category,
he carefully notes that the informants themselves generally rejected this term, and that
transgender was a word used mostly by activists and social workers (75). In this book, I use
transgender when quoting others who used this word, and when referring to interlocutors who described to me how they transitioned from one gender to another in
adulthood.

21. Field notes, July 4, 2016.

22. Field notes, September 24, 2011.

23. Field notes, July 3, 2016.

24. For centuries in Europe, only men and boys performed onstage, so female roles in
operas—for example—were sung by boy sopranos or by castrati, adult men who had been
castrated before their voices changed. The connection of soprano and alto ranges with
women singers is a social construct of relatively recent vintage; this idea has been broadly
accepted for only (approximately) 250 years.

25. The practice of requiring stereotypically male and female uniforms is common
throughout the choral scene in the United States and Canada. One extreme example is
the female uniforms required by Sweet Adelines ensembles, which are all-women groups
in the barbershop tradition. Camille Newlon, who sings in both a GALA chorus and a
Sweet Adelines chorus, explained that her Sweet Adelines group requires not only specific outerwear but also all-in-one undergarments, specific brands of black pantyhose,
and heavy makeup that is subject to a "makeup check" before performances (interview,
December 4, 2014). By contrast, the uniform requirement Newlon faces in Windsong,
Cleveland's Feminist Chorus, is minimal: singers must wear all-black clothing and a colored scarf.

26. Field notes, July 6, 2016.

27. Joshua Palkki (2017, 28) notes, in relation to transgender high school students who

are interested in choral singing, "If a student is told that they *must* sing a voice part that triggers gender dysphoria, they will likely leave choral music—potentially forever." He understands, as I do, that the connection between voice part and one's gender is deeply important to singers, and artistic directors ignore this connection at their, and their profession's, peril.

28. Field notes, July 5, 2016.

29. Field notes, July 4, 2016.

30. This performance can be viewed on YouTube; see GMCCharlotte 2011.

Chapter 4

1. In chapter 8, I describe a scientific experiment in which other students, also from the University of Dayton, reacted to a Christmas-themed performance by the Dayton Gay Men's Chorus. In that case, five (out of thirty-one) students expressed similar sentiments; for example, one wrote, "I actually liked it a lot and I didn't even know they were a gay men's choir until after [the concert]."

2. *Raise Our Voice* was composed by Michael Djupstrom, with lyrics by Chip Alfred.

3. Field notes, July 11, 2012.

4. For example, Wendy Moy voiced a similar observation (interview, July 4, 2016).

5. Field notes, July 2, 2016; July 6, 2016.

6. Field notes, July 5, 2016.

7. Similar sentiments were voiced by, for example, Hugh Gabrielson (interview, August 22, 2016) and Henry Chau (interview, December 13, 2016).

8. Field notes, July 11, 2012.

9. Fred Poland voiced a similar sentiment (interview, June 16, 2011).

10. Grant's comment ignores the fact that Black sacred music is also performed by university, school, and other community choirs, although it does originate in, and is still strongly associated with, African American churches in the United States.

11. Field notes, September 24, 2011.

12. Field notes, January 7, 2011.

13. Field notes, July 3, 2016. Likewise, local media reported on dissent in the Turtle Creek Chorale ranks before the *Inspiration and Hope* concert (*Dallas Voice* 2013).

14. The analogy here is based on the belief that African American spirituals were sung to convey messages to people escaping slavery via the Underground Railroad, and that gay men and lesbians have developed their own languages, or versions of languages, to talk among themselves. In other words, both developed cultural artifacts that facilitated "secretive in-group communication" (Kulick 2000, 249). Both of these widespread beliefs have been contested by scholars; see Kulick 2000, and Kelley 2008.

Chapter 5

1. This song was composed for the 1996 musical *When Pigs Fly*, in which it was titled "A Patriotic Finale." Music is by Dick Gallagher and lyrics are by Mark Waldrop.

2. One artistic director who used this term in our conversation was Ben Riggs, who has served as artistic director of both the Twin Cities Gay Men's Chorus in Minneapolis,

Minnesota, and the Denver Gay Men's Chorus in Denver, Colorado (interview, August 15, 2013).

3. My experience affirms Barbara Bradby's (1993, 170, 152) argument that for listeners, it matters who is singing: "At an imaginary level, the identity of the performer is indeed important . . . meanings are not simply inherent in musical or song texts, but . . . are produced socially in interaction."

4. "Ya Got Me" is from the 1944 musical *On the Town*, with music by Leonard Bernstein and words by Betty Comden and Adolph Green. This performance can be viewed online; see GMCLA.org 2009.

5. This song was a contrafactum of "I Saw Mommy Kissing Santa Claus" by Tommie Connor.

6. "I Want a Girl (Just Like the Girl That Married Dear Old Dad)" was composed by Harry von Tilzer, with lyrics by William Dillon.

7. Such views were voiced to me by, for example, Carol Sirianni (interview, October 9, 2011) and Roger Bourland (interview, December 10, 2012).

8. "GALA-friendly" is a term I heard used by numerous GALA artistic directors. It refers to composers who are known to be open to arranging or composing for GALA choruses and thus more inclined to accept proposals for commissions.

9. Field notes, July 3, 2016.

10. Field notes July 2, 2016.

11. Field notes, July 8, 2012.

12. "Sure on This Shining Night" has music by Samuel Barber and words by James Agee.

13. *Spring Awakening* has music by Duncan Sheik and lyrics by Steven Sater.

14. "Falling Slowly" has music and words by Glen Hansard and Markéta Irglová; this song won the Academy Award for Best Original Song of 2007.

15. Field notes, July 10, 2012.

16. The title of the show from the Portland Gay Men's Chorus is a clear nod to Benjamin Britten's 1945 orchestral composition *The Young Person's Guide to the Orchestra*. In making this reference, the chorus professes its commitment to the Western art music tradition and reveals its assumption that its middle-class American audience also appreciates that tradition.

17. Field notes, July 10, 2012.

18. Field notes, July 3, 2016.

19. Field notes, January 8, 2011.

20. Field notes, July 3, 2016.

21. Field notes, July 3, 2016.

22. Field notes, July 4, 2016.

23. Field notes, July 6, 2016.

24. Field notes, July 8, 2012.

25. See Tiemayer (2013) for a history of the concentration of gay men in another career, that of flight attendant.

Chapter 6

1. I emphasize here the common threads among GALA choruses' mission statements. Julia Balén (2009, 33) focuses on the differences: "Chorus missions articulate

visions and goals around sexual and gender norms that range from assimilationist to radical."

2. Rarely, choruses' mission statements include only one, or emphasize only one, of the two usual elements. For example, the mission statement of Sound Circle in Boulder, Colorado, says, "The women of Sound Circle, an a cappella women's vocal ensemble, have come together to experience the deep joy of making music together and to share that joy with our audiences" (Sound Circle Sings n.d.). The Kansas City Women's Chorus in Kansas City, Missouri, on the other hand, has the following mission statement: "The Kansas City Women's Chorus is a catalyst for change, pushing ourselves and our audiences beyond what is thought possible. Simply singing is not enough" (Kansas City Women's Chorus n.d.).

3. Interestingly, Gary Miller himself did not recite this aphorism when I interviewed him.

4. Singers who did so included, for example, Aditya Adiredja (interview, December 20, 2016), Adam Coatney (interview, August 4, 2011), and Neka Zimmerman (interview, December 19, 2016).

5. The mission statement of the Turtle Creek Chorale has since been expanded (Turtle Creek Chorale n.d.).

6. Of the fifty-six singers I interviewed, only one seemed not to identify with her chorus's mission to create social change. Nancy Bell, a soprano in The Quire of Iowa City, Iowa, said, "Our main purpose is to sing and have fun." When I questioned this assertion, Bell acknowledged that The Quire does have a mission statement but that she was unsure of the wording, and then she amended her first statement: "Well, that's *my* main purpose, to sing and have fun. But there are members who want The Quire to stand for social justice" (interview, November 18, 2016).

7. Ben Riggs, artistic director of the Twin Cities Gay Men's Chorus, attributed this statement to Stan Hill when he relayed it to me (interview, August 15, 2013).

8. Field notes, September 23, 2011.

9. Field notes, July 10, 2012.

10. The "Too Straight Polka" is based on "Too Fat Polka," by Ross MacLean and Arthur Richardson; the version performed by members of the San Francisco Gay Men's Chorus has new words by Paul Saccone and is arranged by Deke Sharon.

11. Field notes, January 7, 2011.

12. Field notes, January 7, 2011.

13. Field notes, September 23, 2011.

14. Field notes, September 24, 2011.

15. For a summary of the legal battle involving the Little Sisters Book and Art Emporium, see Women's Legal Education and Action Fund (n.d.).

16. Field notes, January 7, 2011.

17. Field notes, January 7, 2011.

18. Field notes, January 7, 2011.

19. Field notes, January 7, 2011.

20. Field notes, January 7, 2011.

21. Field notes, September 24, 2011.

22. Field notes, July 4, 2016.

23. Field notes, January 7, 2011.

24. Woody Faulkner voiced a similar view (interview September 23, 2011); and see also Bawer (1993, 99).

25. These sorts of accusations were discussed, for example, by Willi Zwozdesky (interview, September 5, 2011), Dennis Coleman (interview, September 1, 2011), and Sue Fink (interview, March 12, 2012).

26. Vic Hooper voiced a similar sentiment about the same chorus (interview, September 9, 2011).

27. Field notes, July 3, 2016.

28. Field notes, July 5, 2016.

29. Field notes, July 4, 2016.

30. Field notes, January 8, 2011.

Chapter 7

1. Some scholars use terms other than assimilationist; these terms include mainstreaming (Vaid 1995) and liberal (Chasin 2000, 22).

2. Eric Aufdengarten voiced a similar sentiment (interview, October 25, 2011).

3. Interlocutors who spoke along these lines included Allen Kimbrough (interview, October 2, 2011), Fred Fishman (interview, April 25, 2012) and Tara Napoleone-Clifford (interview, June 30, 2011).

4. Indeed, Richard K. Herrell (1992, 243) found that watchers and marchers in the Chicago Gay Pride Parade expressed sharply opposing opinions "about what the parade should be."

5. Field notes, September 23, 2011.

6. In another example of integrationist discourse, a participant in a GALA workshop quoted Bruce Bawer, the bogeyman of the liberationist wing of the gay rights movement. Referencing Bawer's 1993 book *A Place at the Table*, the man said, "We wanted a seat at the table. Now we're at the table and we need to decide what we're going to do with all this food" (field notes, September 23, 2011).

7. Field notes, July 3, 2016.

8. "Here's Where I Stand" was composed by Michael Gore and Lynn Ahrens and was included in the 2003 movie musical *Camp*.

9. Field notes, January 7, 2011.

10. Field notes, September 23, 2011.

11. Field notes, July 5, 2016.

12. This view was voiced, for example, by David Mcintyre (interview, July 31, 2012) and Charlie Beale (interview, August 16, 2011).

Chapter 8

1. This video can be viewed online in the footage of Out Loud's performance from the 2016 GALA Festival; see Tims 2016.

2. Field notes, July 10, 2012.

3. Shari Goettl of Desert Voices in Tucson, Arizona, voiced a similar sentiment (interview, August 14, 2013).

4. Field notes, September 23, 2011.

5. The show was based on texts from Armistead Maupin's series of novels by the same

title. The song in which Unhold's character writes a letter is called "Michael's Letter to Mama," and it was composed by David Maddux; the lyrics are taken from Maupin's work. This song is often performed by GALA's men's choruses.

6. Conversion therapy is a discredited form of psychiatric treatment that aims to change a person's sexual orientation from gay or lesbian to heterosexual.

7. A z-score is calculated by taking a single person's numerical response for an item, subtracting from it the mean response for that same item, and dividing the result by the standard deviation. For example, on item 2, the z-score for someone who chose "strongly disagree" before attending the concert would be calculated by subtracting the mean answer (1.90) from the respondent's answer (1.00) and then dividing the result (-0.90) by the standard deviation for that answer (1.14), for a z-score of -0.79. Because this score is relatively close to 0, we know that the respondent's answer was close to that of the group as a whole. A respondent who had answered "strongly agree," in contrast, would have a z-score for this question of 2.72.

Bibliography

Adler, Adam. 2012. "Male Choral Singing in Canada: A Waning Culture." In Harrison, Welch, and Adler 2012b, 45–63.

Ahlquist, Karen, ed. 2006a. *Chorus and Community*. Urbana: University of Illinois Press.

Ahlquist, Karen. 2006b. Introduction to Ahlquist 2006a, 1–15.

Ahlquist, Karen. 2006c. "Men and Women of the Chorus: Music, Governance, and Social Models in Nineteenth-Century German-Speaking Europe." In Ahlquist 2006a, 265–92.

Aiello, Rick. 2012. "We Are the Rising Sun—GALA 2012." Uploaded July 13, 2012. You Tube video, 2:06. https://www.youtube.com/watch?v=MFyPqds2-MA

Almaguer, Tomás. 1993. "Chicano Men: A Cartography of Homosexual Identity and Behavior." In *Lesbian and Gay Studies Reader*, edited by Henry Abelove, Michèle Aina Barale, and David M. Halperin, 255–73. New York: Routledge.

American Choral Directors Association. 2016. "Audition Guidelines for Performance at National Conferences." https://acda.org/Editor/assets/Conferences/Application_guidelines2017.pdf

American Choral Directors Association. n.d. "Men's/TTBB Choirs." Accessed August 22, 2019. https://acda.org/ACDA/Repertoire_and_Resources/Repertoire_Specific/Men_s_Choir.aspx

ANNA Crusis. n.d. "About ANNA." Accessed October 17, 2019. https://annacrusis.org/about-anna/

Attinello, Paul. 1994. "Authority and Freedom: Toward a Sociology of Gay Choruses." In *Queering the Pitch: The New Gay and Lesbian Musicology*, edited by P. Brett, E. Wood, and G. Thomas, 315–46. New York: Routledge.

Averill, Gage. 2003. *Four Parts, No Waiting: A Social History of American Barbershop Harmony*. New York: Oxford University Press.

Avery, Susan, Casey Hayes, and Cindy Bell. 2013. "Community Choirs: Expressions of Identity through Vocal Performance." In *Community Music Today*, edited by Kari K. Veblen, Stephen J. Messenger, Marissa Silverman, and David J. Elliott, 249–60. Lanham, MD: Rowman and Littlefield.

Babuscio, Jack. 1993. "Camp and the Gay Sensibility." In Bergman 1993, 19–38.

Balén, Julia. 2009. "Erotics, Agency, and Social Movement: Communities of Sexuality and Musicality in LGBT Choruses." In *The Queer Community: Continuing the Struggle for Social Justice*, edited by Richard G. Johnson, 29–46. San Diego, CA: Birkdale.

Balén, Julia. 2017. *A Queerly Joyful Noise: Choral Musicking for Social Justice*. New Brunswick, NJ: Rutgers University Press.

Bargreen, Miranda. 2001. "Seattle Men's Chorus Jingles Its Bells." *Seattle Times*, December 7, 2001. http://community.seattletimes.nwsource.com/archive/?date=2001120 7&slug=mens07

Barrett, Donald C., and Lance M. Pollack. 2005. "Whose Gay Community? Social Class, Sexual Self-Expression and Community Involvement." *Sociological Quarterly* 46 (3): 437–56.

Barton, Bernadette. 2012. *Pray the Gay Away: The Extraordinary Lives of Bible Belt Gays*. New York: New York University Press.

Barz, Greg. 2006. "We Are from Different Ethnic Groups, but We Live Here as One Family." In Ahlquist 2006a, 19–44.

Bawer, Bruce. 1993. *A Place at the Table: The Gay Individual in American Society*. New York: Simon and Schuster.

Bawer, Bruce, ed. 1996. *Beyond Queer: Challenging Gay Left Orthodoxy*. New York: Free Press.

Bell, Cindy L. 2004. "Update on Community Choirs and Singing in the United States." *International Journal of Research in Choral Singing* 2 (1): 39–52.

Bell, Cindy L. 2008. "Toward a Definition of a Community Choir." *International Journal of Community Music* 1 (2): 229–41.

Bergman, David, ed. 1993. *Camp Grounds: Style and Homosexuality*. Amherst: University of Massachusetts Press.

Bernstein, Mary. 1997. "Celebration and Suppression: The Strategic Uses of Identity by the Lesbian and Gay Movement." *American Journal of Sociology* 103 (3): 531–65.

Bernstein-Sycamore, Matilda. 2012. Introduction to *Why Are Faggots So Afraid of Faggots? Flaming Challenges to Masculinity, Objectification, and the Desire to Conform*, edited by Matilda Bernstein-Sycamore, 1–4. Baltimore, MD: AK Press.

Bersani, Leo. 1995. *Homos*. Cambridge, MA: Harvard University Press.

Bithell, Caroline. 2014. *A Different Voice, A Different Song: Reclaiming Community through the Natural Voice and World Song*. New York: Oxford University Press.

Boisvert, Donald. 2000. *Out on Holy Ground: Meditations on Gay Men's Spirituality*. Cleveland, OH: Pilgrim Press.

Bradby, Barbara. 1993. "Lesbians and Popular Music: Does It Matter Who Is Singing?" In *Outwrite: Lesbianism and Popular Culture*, edited by Gabriele Griffin, 148–71. Boulder, CO: Pluto Press.

Bronski, Michael. 1984. *Culture Clash: The Making of Gay Sensibility*. Boston: South End Press.

Broockman, David, and Joshua Kalla. 2016. "Durably Reducing Transphobia: A Field Experiment in Door-to-Door Canvassing." *Science* 352 (6282): 220–24.

Broockman, David, Joshua Kalla, and Peter Aronow. 2015. "Irregularities in LaCour (2014)." http://stanford.edu/~dbroock/broockman_kalla_aronow_lg_irregularities.pdf

Brown, Alan, Sean Fenton, Kyle Marinshaw, Rebecca Ratzkin, Jason Tran, and Mitch Menchaca. 2016. *Assessing the Audience Impact of Choral Music Concerts*. San Francisco, CA: WolfBrown.

Browning, Frank. 1993. *The Culture of Desire: Paradox and Perversity in Gay Lives Today*. New York: Crown.

Browning, Frank. 1998. *A Queer Geography: Journeys toward a Sexual Self*. Rev. ed. New York: Noonday Press.

Brown-Saracino, Japonica. 2011. "From the Lesbian Ghetto to Ambient Community: The Perceived Costs and Benefits of Integration for Community." *Social Problems* 58 (3): 361–88.

Bullington, Sam. n.d. "Phoenix, Colorado's Transgender Community Choir." *Snake Medicine: A Fresh Perspective.* Accessed January 30, 2019. https://sambullington.org/trans-choir/

Bulow, George J. 2004. *A History of Baroque Music.* Bloomington: Indiana University Press.

Butler, Judith. 1999. *Gender Trouble: Feminism and the Subversion of Identity.* 2nd ed. London: Routledge.

Cahill, Sean, Sophia Geffen, and Tim Wang. 2018. *One Year In, Trump Administration Amasses Striking Anti-LGBT Record.* Boston: Fenway Institute. https://fenway-health.org/wp-content/uploads/The-Fenway-Institute-Trump-Pence-Administration-One-Year-Report.pdf

Cantù, Lionel. 2011. "Entre Hombres/Between Men: Latino Masculinities and Homosexuality." In *Gay Latino Studies: A Critical Reader,* edited by Michael Hames-García and Ernesto Javier Martinez, 147–67. Durham, NC: Duke University Press.

Carbado, Devon. 2013. "Colorblind Intersectionality." *Signs: Journal of Women in Culture and Society* 38 (4): 811–45.

Carrington, Christopher. 1999. *No Place Like Home: Relationship and Family Life among Lesbians and Gay Men.* Chicago: University of Chicago Press.

Chandler, Daniel. 2017. *Semiotics: The Basics.* 3rd ed. London: Routledge.

Chasin, Alexandra. 2000. *Selling Out: The Gay and Lesbian Movement Goes to Market.* New York: St. Martin's Press.

Chauncey, George. 1994. *Gay New York: Gender, Urban Culture and Making of the Gay Male World, 1890–1940.* New York: Basic Books.

Cho, Sumi, Kimberlé Williams Crenshaw, and Leslie McCall. 2013. "Toward a Field of Intersectionality Studies: Theory, Applications, and Praxis." *Signs: Journal of Women in Culture and Society* 38 (4): 785–810.

Choral Journal. 1990. "Letters to the Editor." 31 (1): 4–6; and 31 (3): 5–8.

Chorus America. 2003. *America's Performing Art: A Study of Choruses, Choral Singers, and Their Impact.* https://www.chorusamerica.org/advocacy-research/americas-performing-art

Cincinnati Men's Chorus. n.d. "Concert History." Accessed November 13, 2019. https://www.cincinnatimenschorus.org/cmc-concert-history/

Cohen, Cathy J. 2001. "Punks, Bulldaggers and Welfare Queens: The Radical Potential of Queer Politics?" In *Sexual Identities, Queer Politics,* edited by Mark Blasius, 200–227. Princeton, NJ: Princeton University Press.

Columbus Gay Men's Chorus. n.d. "Illuminati—CGMC's Powerful Sacred Music Ensemble." Accessed September 5, 2019. https://columbusgaymenschorus.com/illuminati/

Constantine-Simms, Delroy, ed. 2000a. *The Greatest Taboo: Homosexuality in Black Communities.* Los Angeles: Alyson Books.

Constantine-Simms, Delroy. 2000b. "Is Homosexuality the Greatest Taboo?" In Constantine-Simms 2000a, 76–87.

Cooper, Evan. 2003. "Decoding *Will and Grace*: Mass Audience Reception of a Popular Network Situation Comedy." *Sociological Perspectives* 46 (4): 513–33.

Cox, Daniel, Juhem Navarro-Rivera, and Robert P. Jones. 2013. *Race, Religion, and Political Affiliation of Americans' Core Social Networks*. Washington, DC: Public Religion Research Institute. https://www.prri.org/research/poll-race religion-politics-americans-social-networks/

Coyle, Patrick O. 2006. "Significant Male Voice Repertory Commissioned by American Gay Men's Choruses." PhD diss., University of Cincinnati.

Culhane, John. 2017. "A Christmas Connection with Gay Culture Thanks to a Gay Men's Chorus." *Slate* (blogs), December 22, 2017. http://www.slate.com/blogs/outward/2017/12/22/how_the_philadelphia_gay_men_s_chorus_reconnected_me_to_gay_culture.html

Cusick, Suzanne G. 1999. "On Musical Performances of Gender and Sex." In *Audible Traces: Gender, Identity and Music*, edited by Elaine Barkin and Lydia Hamessley, 25–48. Zurich: Carciofolio Verlagshaus.

Dallas Voice. 2013. "Turtle Creek Chorale Defends Concert with Tea-Bagging Singer Sandi Patty." June 14, 2013. https://dallasvoice.com/turtle-creek-chorale/

Darnovsky, Marcy, Barbara Epstein, and Richard Flacks. 1995. Introduction to *Cultural Politics and Social Movements*, edited by Marcy Darnovsky, Barbara Epstein, and Richard Flacks, vii–xxiii. Philadelphia, PA: Temple University Press.

Davies, Peter. 2012. "The Male Voice Choir in the United Kingdom." In Harrison, Welch, and Adler 2012b, 325–35.

Dayton Contemporary Dance Company. n.d. "The Mission." Accessed October 29, 2019. https://www.dcdc.org/about

D'Emilio, John. 1983. *Sexual Politics, Sexual Communities: The Making of a Homosexual Minority in the United States, 1940–1970*. Chicago: University of Chicago Press.

D'Emilio, John. 1992. *Making Trouble: Essays on Gay History, Politics, and the University*. New York: Routledge.

DeVenny, David P. 1999. *Varied Carols: A Survey of American Choral Literature*. Westport, CT: Greenwood Press.

Diverse City Youth Chorus. n.d. "About." Accessed October 17, 2019. https://www.facebook.com/pg/diversecityyouthchorus/about/

Duchan, Joshua S. 2012. *Powerful Voices: The Musical and Social World of Collegiate A Cappella*. Ann Arbor: University of Michigan Press.

Duggan, Lisa. 1995. "The Discipline Problem: Queer Theory Meets Lesbian and Gay History." In *Sex Wars: Sexual Dissent and Political Culture*, edited by Lisa Duggan and and Nan D. Hunter, 194–206. New York: Routledge.

Durkheim, Émile. (1915) 1965. *The Elementary Forms of the Religious Life*. Translated by Joseph Ward Swain. New York: Free Press.

Durrant, Colin. 2012. "Male Singing in the University Choir Context." In Harrison, Welch, and Adler 2012b, 109–21.

Engelhardt, Jeffers. 2015. *Singing the Right Way: Orthodox Christians and Secular Enchantment in Estonia*. New York: Oxford University Press.

Eyerman, Ron, and Andrew Jamison. 1998. *Music and Social Movements: Mobilizing Traditions in the Twentieth Century*. Cambridge: Cambridge University Press.

Faderman, Lillian. 2015. *The Gay Revolution: The Story of the Struggle*. New York: Simon and Schuster.

Faiman-Silva, Sandra. 2004. *The Courage to Connect: Sexuality, Citizenship and Community in Provincetown*. Urbana: University of Illinois Press.

Faulkner, Robert. 2012. "Icelandic Men, Male Voice Choirs and Masculine Identity." In Harrison, Welch, and Adler 2012b, 215–31.

Faulkner, Robert, and Jane Davidson. 2006. "Men in Chorus: Collaboration and Competition in Homo-Social Vocal Behaviour." *Psychology of Music* 34 (2): 219–37.

Fenlon, Iain. 2010. *Music and Culture in Late Renaissance Italy.* Oxford: Oxford University Press.

Foreman, Lewis. 2000. "David Conte: Elegy for Matthew." Classical Music on the Web: Seen and Heard, October 2000. http://www.musicweb-international.com/SandH/2000/oct00/conte.htm

Freer, Patrick K. 2012. "From Boys to Men: Male Choral Singing in the United States." In Harrison, Welch, and Adler 2012b, 13–25.

GALA Choruses. 2012. Festival Program. https://galachoruses.org/documents/events/festival2012/GALA_Program2012_Program.pdf

GALA Choruses. n.d.a. "Home." Accessed October 17, 2019. https://galachoruses.org/

GALA Choruses. n.d.b. "History." Accessed August 22, 2019. https://galachoruses.org/about/history

Gamson, Joshua. 2005. "The Intersection of Gay Street and Straight Street: Shopping, Social Class and the New Gay Visibility." *Social Thought and Research* 26 (1/2): 3–18.

Gamson, William A. 1995. "Constructing Social Protest." In *Social Movements and Culture*, edited by Hank Johns*ton and Bert Klandermans, 85–106. Minneapolis: University of Minnesota Press.

Gates, Gary J., and Frank Newport. 2012. *Special Report: 3.4% of U.S. Adults Self-Identify as LGBT.* Gallup. https://news.gallup.com/poll/158066/special-report-adults-identify-lgbt.aspx

Ghaziani, Amin. 2011. "Post-Gay Collective Identity Construction." *Social Problems* 58 (1): 99–125.

GMCCharlotte. 2011. "Finding Her Here." Uploaded February 6, 2015. YouTube video, 5:07. https://www.youtube.com/watch?v=7ne60lAKsNc

GMCLA.org. 2007. "The Anvil Chorus—GMCLA.org." Uploaded March 14, 2007. YouTube video, 3:06. http://www.youtube.com/watch?v=c3x-pwJGsgU

GMCLA.org. 2009. "Ya Got Me in HD." Uploaded April 6, 2009. YouTube video, 4:53. https://www.youtube.com/watch?v=3eYKTSWzS4I

Gonsiorek, John C. 1995. "Gay Male Identities: Concepts and Issues." In *Lesbian, Gay and Bisexual Identities, Over the Lifespan: Psychological Perspectives*, edited by Anthony R. D'Augelli and Charlotte J. Patterson, 24–47. New York: Oxford University Press.

Gordon, Eric A. 1990. "GALA: The Lesbian and Gay Community of Song." *Choral Journal* 30 (9): 25–32.

Gray, Mary L. 2009. *Out in the Country: Youth, Media, and Queer Visibility in Rural America.* New York: New York University Press.

Green, Adam Isaiah. 2002. "Gay but Not Queer: Toward a Post-Queer Study of Sexuality." *Theory and Society* 31 (4): 521–45.

Green, Adam Isaiah. 2007. "On the Horns of a Dilemma: Institutional Dimensions of the Sexual Career in a Sample of Middle-Class, Urban, Black, Gay Men." *Journal of Black Studies* 37 (5): 753–74.

Green, Adam Isaiah. 2011. "Playing the (Sexual) Field: The Interactional Basis of Systems of Sexual Stratification." *Social Psychology Quarterly* 74 (3): 244–66.

Greene, Solomon, Margery Austin Turner, and Ruth Gourevitch. 2017. *Racial Residential Segregation and Neighborhood Disparities*. US Partnership on Mobility from Poverty. https://www.mobilitypartnership.org/publications/racial-residential-segregation-and-neighborhood-disparities

Grega, Will. 1994. *Will Grega's Gay Music Guide*. New York: Pop Front Press.

Griffin, Horace. 2000. "Their Own Received Them Not: African American Lesbians and Gays in Black Churches." In Constantine-Simms 2000a, 110–21.

Guittar, Nicholas. 2014. *Coming Out: The New Dynamics*. Boulder, CO: FirstForum Press.

Halperin, David M. 2012. *How to Be Gay*. Cambridge, MA: Belknap Press.

Handelman, Don. 1998. *Models and Mirrors: Towards an Anthropology of Public Events*. New York: Berghahn Books.

Harrison, Douglas. 2012. *Then Sings My Soul: The Culture of Southern Gospel Music*. Urbana: University of Illinois Press.

Harrison, Scott D. 2012. "Singing, Men, and Australian Culture." In Harrison, Welch, and Adler 2012b, 65–75.

Harrison, Scott D., Graham F. Welch, and Adam Adler. 2012a. "Men, Boys, and Singing." In Harrison, Welch, and Adler 2012b, 3–12.

Harrison, Scott D., Graham F. Welch, and Adam Adler, eds. 2012b. *Perspectives on Males and Singing*. New York: Springer.

Hauge, Karen. 2012. "Tears and Triumph for 'When I Knew.'" *KCmetropolis.org*, March 27, 2012. http://hmckc.org/tears-and-triumph-for-when-i-knew-2/

Hawkeswood, William G. 1996. *One of the Children: Gay Black Men in Harlem*. Berkeley: University of California Press.

Hayes, Casey J. 2007. "Community Music and the GLBT Chorus." *International Journal of Community Music* 1 (1): 63–67.

Hayes, Casey J. 2016. "Safe Classrooms: A Fundamental Principle of Democratic Practice." In *Giving Voice to Democracy in Music Education: Diversity and Social Justice in the Classroom*, edited by Lisa C. DeLorenzo, n.p. New York: Routledge. Electronic book.

Hayes, Eileen M. 2010. *Songs in Black and Lavender: Race, Sexual Politics, and Women's Music*. Urbana: University of Illinois Press.

Hemmelgarn, Seth. 2010. "SF Gay Men's Chorus Gets New Conductor." *Bay Area Reporter*, November 17, 2010. https://www.ebar.com/news///241153

Herdt, Gilbert. 1992a. "'Coming Out' as a Rite of Passage: A Chicago Study." In Herdt 1992b, 29–67.

Herdt, Gilbert, ed. 1992b. *Gay Culture in America: Essays from the Field*. Boston: Beacon Press.

Herdt, Gilbert, and Andrew Boxer. 1992. "Introduction: Culture, History, and Life Course of Gay Men." In Herdt 1992b, 1–28.

Herek, Gregory M. 1994. "Assessing Heterosexuals' Attitudes Toward Lesbians and Gay Men: A Review of Empirical Research with the ATLG Scale." In *Lesbian and Gay Psychology: Theory, Research, and Clinical Applications*, edited by Beverly Greene and Gregory M. Herek, 206–28. Thousand Oaks, CA: SAGE.

Herek, Gregory M. ed. 1998. *Stigma and Sexual Orientation: Understanding Prejudice against Lesbians, Gay Men, and Bisexuals*. Thousand Oaks, CA: SAGE.

Herrell, Richard K. 1992. "The Symbolic Strategies of Chicago's Gay and Lesbian Pride Day Parade." In Herdt 1992b, 225–50.

Holland, Sharon P. 2005. "Forward: 'Home' Is a Four-Letter Word." In Johnson and Henderson 2005, ix–xiii.

Hollister, John. 1999. "A Highway Rest Area as a Reproducible Site." In *Public Sex/Gay Space*, edited by William Leap, 55–70. New York: Columbia University Press.

Holy See. n.d. "Catechism of the Catholic Church." Accessed October 24, 2019. http://www.vatican.va/archive/ccc_css/archive/catechism/p3s2c2a6.htm

Hubbs, Nadine. 2014. *Rednecks, Queers, and Country Music*. Los Angeles: University of California Press.

Hughes, Holly, and David Román. 1998. "O Solo Homo: An Introductory Conversation." In *O Solo Homo: The New Queer Performance*, edited by Holly Hughes and David Román, 1–15. New York: Grove Press.

Jacobs, Greg. 1996. "Lesbian and Gay Male Language Use: A Critical Review of the Literature." *American Speech* 71 (1): 49–71.

Jagose, Annamarie. 1996. *Queer Theory: An Introduction*. New York: New York University Press.

Janovy, C. J. 2016. "Transgender Singers Harness the (Changing) Power of Voice." National Public Radio, May 21, 2016. https://www.npr.org/sections/deceptivecadence/2016/05/21/478863157/transgender-choruses-harness-the-changing-power-of-voices

Jarman-Ivens, Freya. 2011. *Queer Voices: Technologies, Vocalities and the Musical Flaw*. New York: Palgrave-Macmillan.

Jasper, James M. 1997. *The Art of Moral Protest: Culture, Biography and Creativity in Social Movements*. Chicago: University of Chicago Press.

Johnson, E. Patrick. 2000. "Feeling the Spirit in the Dark: Expanding Notions of the Sacred in the African American Gay Community." In Constantine-Simms 2000a, 88–109.

Johnson, E. Patrick. 2008. *Sweet Tea: Black Gay Men of the South*. Chapel Hill: University of North Carolina Press.

Johnson, E. Patrick. 2009. "Going Home Ain't Always Easy: Ethnography and the Politics of Black Respectability." In Leap and Lewin 2009b, 54–70.

Johnson, E. Patrick, and Mae G. Henderson, eds. 2005. *Black Queer Studies: A Critical Anthology*. Durham, NC: Duke University Press.

Jones, Alisha Lola. 2016. "Are All the Choir Directors Gay? Black Men's Sexuality and Identity in Gospel Performance." In *Issues in African American Music: Power, Gender, Race, Representation*, edited by Portia Maultsby and Mellonee Burnim, 216–36. New York: Routledge.

Kaiser, Charles. 1997. *The Gay Metropolis, 1940–1996*. Boston: Houghton Mifflin.

Kano, Thea. 2017. "Moving the Needle with Love." GALA Choruses Blog, July 1, 2017. https://galachoruses.org/blog/moving-needle-love/

Kansas City Women's Chorus. n.d. "About Us." Accessed October 17, 2019. http://www.kcwomenschorus.org/about/

Kazyak, Emily. 2011. "Disrupting Cultural Selves: Constructing Gay and Lesbian Identities in Rural Locales." *Qualitative Sociology* 34 (4): 561–81.

Kelley, James. 2008. "Song, Story or History: Resisting Claims of a Coded Message in the African American Spiritual 'Follow the Drinking Gourd.'" *Journal of Popular Culture* 41 (2): 262–80.

Kenney, Kirk, and Joseph Serna. 2016. "Major League Baseball Finds San Diego Gay Men's Chorus Mistake Was 'Human Error.'" *Los Angeles Times*, May 26, 2016. https://www.latimes.com/local/lanow/la-me-ln-mlb-gay-chorus-padres-20160526-snap-story.html

Kinney, Janice L. 2010. "'Making Church': The Experience of Spirituality in Women's Choruses." PhD diss., University of Washington.

Kosofsky Sedgwick, Eve. 1990. *Epistemology of the Closet*. Berkeley: University of California Press.

Kulick, Don. 2000. "Gay and Lesbian Language." *Annual Review of Anthropology* 29: 243–85.

Lacour, Michael, and Donald Green. 2014. "When Contact Changes Minds: An Experiment on Transmission of Support for Gay Equality." *Science* 346 (6215): 1366–69.

LaSala, Michael. 2010. *Coming Out, Coming Home: Helping Families Adjust to a Gay or Lesbian Child*. New York: Columbia University Press.

Latimer, Marvin E. 2008. "Our Voices Enlighten, Inspire, Heal and Empower: A Mixed Methods Investigation of Demography, Sociology and Identity Acquisition in a Gay Men's Chorus." *International Journal of Research in Choral Singing* 3 (1): 23–38.

Leap, William L. 1996. *Word's Out: Gay Men's English*. Minneapolis: University of Minnesota Press.

Leap, William L., and Ellen Lewin. 2009a. Introduction to Leap and Lewin 2009b, 1–24.

Leap, William L., and Ellen Lewin, eds. 2009b. *Out in Public: Reinventing Lesbian/Gay Anthropology*. Chichester, West Sussex, UK: Wiley-Blackwell.

Leland, John. 2012. "When Love Conquers All, Even the Loss of Two Jobs." *New York Times,* March 9, 2012.

Lesbian and Gay Band Association. n.d. Accessed November 12, 2019. http://www.lgba.org/about/

Levin, Robert. n.d. "The New Countertenors: Top of the Crop." ClassicsToday.com. Accessed January 14, 2020. https://www.classicstoday.com/review/the-new-countertenors-top-of-the-crop/

Lewin, Ellen. 1996a. Introduction to Lewin 1996b, 1–14.

Lewin, Ellen, ed. 1996b. *Inventing Lesbian Cultures in America*. Boston: Beacon Press.

Lewin, Ellen. 1996c. "'Why in the World Would You Want to Do That?': Claiming Community in Lesbian Commitment Ceremonies." In Lewin 1996b, 105–30.

Lewin, Ellen. 2009. "Who's Gay? What's Gay? Dilemmas of Identity among Gay Fathers." In Leap and Lewin 2009b, 86–103.

Lewin, Ellen, and William L. Leap. 2002. Introduction to *Out in Theory: The Emergence of Lesbian and Gay Anthropology*, edited by Ellen Lewin and William L. Leap, 1–16. Urbana: University of Illinois Press.

Liang, A. C. 1997. "The Creation of Coming Out Stories." In *Queerly Phrased: Language, Gender and Sexuality*, edited by Anna Livia and Kira Hall, 287–309. New York: Oxford University Press.

Link, David. 1996. "I Am Not Queer." In Bawer 1996, 266–78.

Lochhead, Carolyn. 1996. "The Third Way." In Bawer 1996, 50–59.

Long, Scott. 1993. "The Loneliness of Camp." In Bergman 1993, 78–91.

Lortat-Jacob, Bernard. 2006. "Concord and Discord: Singing Together in a Sardinian Brotherhood." Translated and edited by Marc Benamou. In Ahlquist 2006a, 87–110.

Lynch, Frederick R. 1992. "Nonghetto Gays: An Ethnography of Suburban Homosexuals." In Herdt 1992b, 165–201.

MacLachlan, Heather. 2015. "Sincerity and Irony in the 'Gay Music' of GALA Choruses." *Journal of American Culture* 38 (2): 85–101.

Martineau, William. 1972. "A Model of the Social Functions of Humor." In *The Psychology of Humor: Theoretical Perspectives and Empirical Issues*, edited by Jeffrey H. Goldstein and Paul E. McGhee. New York: Academic Press, 101–28.

McQueeny, Krista. 2009. "We Are All God's Children, Y'All: Race, Gender and Sexuality in Lesbian- and Gay-Affirming Congregations." *Social Problems* 56 (1): 151–73.

Mensel, Robert. 2007. "A Music of Their Own: The Impact of Affinity Compositions on the Singers, Composers and Conductors of Selected Gay, Lesbian and Feminist Choruses." PhD diss., University of Oregon.

Meyer, Ilan H., and Laura Dean. 1998. "Internalized Homophobia, Intimacy, and Sexual Behavior among Gay and Bisexual Men." In Herek 1998, 160–86.

Miller, Neil. 2006. *Out of the Past: Gay and Lesbian History from 1869 to the Present*. Revised and updated edition. New York: Alyson Books.

Mook, Richard. 2007. "White Masculinity in Barbershop Quartet Singing." *Journal of the Society for American Music* 1 (4): 453–83.

Moran, Lee. 2016. "Gay Choir 'Humiliated' during National Anthem at San Diego Padres Game." *Huffington Post*, May 23, 2016. https://www.huffpost.com/entry/san-diego-gay-mens-chorus-padres-game_n_5742a298e4b0613b512aa1ec

Mullen, Victoria. 2014. "Do Good: West Michigan's Gay Men's Chorus Creates Change—One Voice at a Time." *Rapid Growth Media*, January 30, 2014. https://www.rapidgrowthmedia.com/features/DG_WMGMC.aspx

Muñoz, José Esteban. 1999. *Disidentifications: Queers of Color and the Performance of Politics*. Minneapolis: University of Minnesota Press.

Murray, Heather. 2010. *Not in This Family: Gays and the Meaning of Kinship in Postwar North America*. Philadelphia: University of Pennsylvania Press.

Nash, Jennifer C. 2008. "Re-Thinking Intersectionality." *Feminist Review* 80:1–15.

National Council of Welfare. 2012. *Poverty Profile: Special Edition—A Snapshot of Racialized Poverty in Canada*. https://www.canada.ca/content/dam/esdc-edsc/migration/documents/eng/communities/reports/poverty_profile/snapshot.pdf

Nero, Charles I. 2005. "Why Are Gay Ghettos White?" In Johnson and Henderson 2005, 228–48.

Newton, Esther. 1972. *Mother Camp: Female Impersonators in America*. Englewood Cliffs, NJ: Prentice-Hall.

Newton, Esther. 1993. "Role Models." In Bergman 1993, 39–53.

New York City Gay Men's Chorus. n.d.a. "Our History." Accessed August 21, 2019. http://www.nycgmc.org/our-history

New York City Gay Men's Chorus. n.d.b. "Staff & Board." Accessed September 5, 2019. http://www.nycgmc.org/staff-board/

North Coast Men's Chorus. n.d. "North Coast Men's Chorus History." Accessed October 18, 2019. https://ncmchorus.org/about-us/history/

One Voice: Minnesota's LGBTA Mixed Chorus. n.d.a. "Home." Accessed October 17, 2019. http://www.onevoicemn.org/

One Voice: Minnesota's LGBTA Mixed Chorus. n.d.b. "Community Impact." Accessed October 24, 2019. http://www.onevoicemn.org/community-impact/

Overby, L. Martin, and Barth, Jay. 2002. "Contact, Community, Context and Public Attitudes toward Gay Men and Lesbians." *Polity* 34 (4): 433–56.

Palkki, Joshua. 2017. "Inclusivity in Action: Transgender Singers in the Choral Classroom." *Choral Journal* 57 (11): 20–35.

Peraino, Judith A. 2006. *Listening to the Sirens: Musical Technologies of Queer Identity from Homer to Hedwig.* Oakland: University of California Press.

Peterson, Zachary. 2017. "4 Rutgers Glee Choirs Were Chosen to Participate in Prestigious National Conference." *Daily Targum,* March 26, 2017. http://www.dailytargum.com/article/2017/03/4-rutgers-glee-clubs-selected-to-participate-in-prestigious-national-conference

Pew Research Center. 2012. "'Nones' on the Rise." October 9, 2012. https://www.pewforum.org/2012/10/09/nones-on-the-rise/

Politico. 2016. "Ohio Presidential Election Results." Accessed October 24, 2019. https://www.politico.com/2016-election/results/map/president/ohio/

Puar, Jasbir K. 2007. *Terrorist Assemblages: Homonationalism in Queer Times.* Durham, NC: Duke University Press.

Putnam, Robert D. 2000. *Bowling Alone: The Collapse and Revival of American Community.* New York: Simon and Schuster.

Putnam, Robert D. 2015. *Our Kids: The American Dream in Crisis.* New York: Simon and Schuster Paperbacks.

Rayside, David. 2008. *Queer Inclusions, Continental Divisions: Public Recognition of Sexual Diversity in Canada and the United States.* Toronto: University of Toronto Press.

Redman, David J. 2016. "Motivation of Adult, Auditioned Community Choirs: Implications toward Lifelong Learning." PhD diss., University of South Florida.

Reinelt, Claire. 1995. "Moving onto the Terrain of the State: The Battered Women's Movement and the Politics of Engagement." In *Feminist Organizations: Harvest of the New Women's Movement,* edited by Myra Marx Ferree and Patricia Yancey Martin, 84–104. Philadelphia, PA: Temple University Press.

Rensink-Hoff, Rachel. 2009. "Adult Community Choirs: Toward a Balance between Leisure Participation and Musical Achievement." PhD diss., University of Western Ontario.

Rimmerman, Craig. 2002. *From Identity to Politics: The Lesbian and Gay Movements in the United States.* Philadelphia, PA: Temple University Press.

Robertson, Carol E. 1989. "Power and Gender in Musical Experiences of Women." In *Women and Music in Cross-Cultural Perspective,* edited by Ellen Koskoff, 225–44. Urbana: University of Illinois Press.

Rosenthal, Rob, and Richard Flacks. 2012. *Playing for Change: Music and Musicians in the Service of Social Movements.* Boulder, CO: Paradigm.

Rupp, Leila J., and Verta Taylor. 2003. *Drag Queens at the 801 Cabaret.* Chicago: University of Chicago Press.

Saitschenko, Marcus. 2014. "Michael's Letter to Momma." Filmed March 17, 2014. YouTube video, 8:39. https://www.youtube.com/watch?v=TQOWubduc2U

San Francisco Gay Men's Chorus. 2011. "SF Gay Men's Chorus—'Gloria.'" Filmed December 17, 2011. YouTube video, 6:58. https://www.youtube.com/watch?v=edqCPS7qwPM

San Francisco Gay Men's Chorus. n.d. "Our Story: Creating Change through Music." Accessed September 3, 2019. https://www.sfgmc.org/about-sfgmc/

Sawyer, Eric. 2002. "An ACT UP Founder 'Acts Up' for Africa's Access to AIDS." In *From ACT UP to the WTO: Urban Protest and Community Building in the Era of Globalization,* edited by Benjamin Shepard and Ronald Hayduk, 88–103. New York: Verso Books.

Seattle Choruses. n.d. "About." Accessed October 17, 2019. https://www.seattlechoruses.org/about/

Shelemay, Kay Kaufman. 2011. "Musical Communities: Rethinking the Collective in Music." *Journal of the American Musicological Society* 64 (2): 349–90.

Simon, Angela. 1998. "The Relationship between Stereotypes of and Attitudes toward Lesbians and Gays." In Herek 1998, 62–80.

Sister Singers Network. n.d. "Home." Accessed November 12, 2019. http://www.sistersingers.net/

Small, Christopher. 1998. *Musicking: The Meanings of Performing and Listening.* Middletown, CT: Wesleyan University Press.

Solomon, Andrew. 2012. *Far from the Tree: Parents, Children, and the Search for Identity.* New York: Scribner.

Sound Circle Sings. n.d. "Mission." Accessed October 17, 2019. http://www.soundcirclesings.org/mission.html

Stein, Arlene. 2001. *The Stranger Next Door: The Story of a Small Community's Battle over Sex, Faith and Civil Rights.* Boston: Beacon Press.

Sullivan, Andrew. 1995. *Virtually Normal: An Argument about Homosexuality.* New York: Alfred A. Knopf.

Tarrow, Sidney G. 1994. *Power in Movement: Social Movements and Contentious Politics.* New York: Cambridge University Press.

Taylor, Jodie. 2012. *Playing It Queer: Popular Music, Identity and Queer World-Making.* Bern, Switzerland: Peter Lang.

Tiemayer, Phil. 2013. *Plane Queer: Labor, Sexuality and AIDS in the History of Male Flight Attendants.* Berkeley: University of California Press.

Tilcsik, Andras. 2011. "Pride and Prejudice: Employment Discrimination against Openly Gay Men in the United States." *American Journal of Sociology* 113 (2): 586–626.

Tims, Dale. 2016. "Out Loud: The Colorado Springs Men's Chorus GALA Set Denver 2016." Uploaded July 31, 2016. YouTube video, 22:16. https://www.youtube.com/watch?v=KT2tP50Q_U0

Trame, Richard H. 1993. "The Male Chorus, Medium of Art and Entertainment: Its History and Literature." In *Choral Essays: A Tribute to Roger Wagner,* edited by William Wells Belan, 19–29. San Carlos, CA: Thomas House.

Triad Pride Performing Arts. n.d. "Home." Accessed October 17, 2019. https://triadprideperformingarts.org/

Triangle Gay Men's Chorus. n.d. "About the Triangle Gay Men's Chorus." Accessed August 21, 2019. https://www.tgmchorus.org/about-us.html#history-and-outreach

Turner, William B. 2000. *A Genealogy of Queer Theory.* Philadelphia, PA: Temple University Press.

Turtle Creek Chorale. n.d. "About Us." Accessed August 21, 2019. https://turtlecreekchorale.com/about-us/

Twin Cities Gay Men's Chorus. 2012. "'Marry Us'—Performed by the Twin Cities Gay Men's Chorus." Filmed March 30, 2012. YouTube video. https://www.youtube.com/watch?v=3fchB_OAi2k

United States Census Bureau. 2019. "Quick Facts—Dayton City Ohio." https://www.census.gov/quickfacts/table/AGE275210/3921000

University of Dayton College of Arts and Sciences, Department of Music Operations

Manual. 2014. "Mission Statement." http://academic.udayton.edu/musichand book/facultybook/mission.html

Vaid, Urvashi. 1995. *Virtual Equality: The Mainstreaming of Gay and Lesbian Liberation.* New York: Anchor Books.

Valentine, David. 2007. *Imagining Transgender: An Ethnography of a Category.* Durham, NC: Duke University Press.

Vermillion, Allecia. 2009. "Jon Sims: Historical Essay." San Francisco Museum and Historical Society. http://www.foundsf.org/index.php?title=Jon_Sims

Vincent, Phyllis. 1997. "A Study of Community Choruses in Kentucky and Implications for Music Education." PhD diss., University of Kentucky.

Vox Femina Los Angeles. n.d. "Home." Accessed August 21, 2019. https://www.voxfemina.org/

Walks, Michelle. 2014. "Raising Queerlings: Parenting with a Queer Art of Failure." *Counterpoints* 437:121–36.

Walters, Suzanna Danuta. 2001. *All the Rage: The Story of Gay Visibility in America.* Chicago: University of Chicago Press.

Warner, Michael. 1993. Introduction to *Fear of a Queer Planet: Queer Politics and Social Theory*, edited by Michael Warner, vii–xxxi. Minneapolis: University of Minnesota Press.

Warner, Michael. 1999. *The Trouble with Normal: Sex, Politics and the Ethics of Queer Life.* New York: Free Press.

Warner, Michael. 2012. "Queer and Then?" *Chronicle of Higher Education*, January 1, 2012. https://www.chronicle.com/article/QueerThen-/130161

Weston, Kath. 1991. *Families We Choose: Lesbians, Gay, Kinship.* New York: Columbia University Press.

White, Edmund. 1991. *States of Desire: Travels in Gay America.* New York: Penguin Books.

Wikipedia. n.d. "Twin Cities Gay Men's Chorus." Accessed August 21, 2019. https://en.wikipedia.org/wiki/Twin_Cities_Gay_Men%27s_Chorus

Wilson, Sarah Ruth Holmes. 2011. "Community Choir: What Motivates People to Join, Stay and Sing—A Mixed Method Research Study." MEd thesis, University of Victoria.

Wilson, Valerie, and William M. Rodgers. 2016. *Black-White Wage Gaps Expand with Rising Wage Inequality.* Washington, DC: Economic Policy Institute. https://www.epi.org/publication/black-white-wage-gaps-expand-with-rising-wage-inequality/

Windy City Sings. n.d.a. "About WCPA." Accessed October 18, 2019. https://windycitysings.org/about/

Windy City Sings. n.d.b. "About: History." Accessed August 21, 2019. http://windycitysings.org/about/history/

Women's Legal Education and Action Fund. n.d. "Little Sisters Book and Art Emporium et al. v. Minister of Justice et al." Accessed October 18, 2019. https://www.leaf.ca/little-sisters-book-art-emporium-et-al-v-minister-of-justice-et-al/

Index